Yours Ayl
Billy Kay.

KNEE DEEP IN CLARET

KNEE DEEP IN CLARET

A Celebration of Wine and Scotland

Billy Kay and Cailean Maclean

Auld Alliance Publishing

Auld Alliance Publishing
60 Aird Bhearnasdail
Isle of Skye IV51 9NU

Revised edition 1994 published by Auld Alliance Publishing
ISBN 0 9523626 00

First published in 1983 by
MAINSTREAM PUBLISHING COMPANY (EDINBURGH) LTD.

Second edition published in 1985

Cover design by Oliver Perritt, Duncan of Jordanstone College of Art, Dundee.

Printed and bound in Great Britain by Adlard Print & Typesetting Services, The Old School, The Green, Ruddington, Nottingham NG11 6HH

CONTENTS

For
Alexander Kay and Alasdair Maclean

FRESH FRAGRANT CLARETS

1

Knee deep in grapes – 15th Century France.

Rich Malmsey from the Peleponnese and ancient Candia lay beside the honeyed nectar called Muscadel from the slopes of Cyprus and the Levant as they were borne West, then North in the holds of Venetian and Genoese trading vessels. The heady vintages of Spain and Portugal - Sherris Sack, Mountain, Canary, Malago, Bastard, Madeira - were brought to the Western Sea by merchants from Alicante, Cadiz and Lisbon. Via the National Staples at Campveere, the Dam, or Middleburg in the Low Countries came the lush white wines of the Rhine or Moselle, and the fruited reds of Beaune in the domains of the Duke of Burgundy. La Rochelle and Nantes gave us the growths of Brittany, the Loire, Anjou and Orléans, while the land of sweet Bordeaux delivered our national favourite, the "fresche fragrant clairettis", lovingly recalled by the court poet, Dunbar. The Stewart Kingdom of the Scots, replete with the finest liquids the vine of Europe could offer.

Wine has been called the Blood Stream of the Auld Alliance and by far the greatest volume of wine to reach our shores came through the Biscay ports of France. Some of it had been transported thither by traders from Catalonia or the

Italian States, but most of it was simply the *vin du pays* brought to Rochelle and Bordeaux for the Scots merchants to pree and buy. The history of Gascony, the region around Bordeaux, and Scotland intertwine greatly in the 13th and 14th centuries due to the intervention of an England determined to hold on to a colony in France and create one in Scotland. Wine, the on-going reason for the considerable links between Bordeaux and Scotland throughout the following centuries, was ironically at the centre of those original far distant conflicts.

The first formal treaty between the Scots and French dates back to 1295 when Philippe le Bel and John Balliol formed a pact against England. The semi-mythical origins of the Alliance, however, go much further back, to the year 777 when Charlemagne of the Franks resisting the Germanic hordes in France heard of the success of a Celtic brother against the Saxons at Athelstaneford in far Caledonia. King Accaius of the Scots received emissaries from Charlemagne suggesting military co-operation of benefit to both peoples ...... and an Alliance was born. Not only that, for the same incident gave us the mythic origins of the banners we still fly today – the white cross of St. Andrew appearing to the Scots as an inspiring cloud formation in the blue sky on the morn of the decisive battle; the Lion Rampant of our Kings from then adorned with Charlemagne's fleurs de lys, "oure Lyone with the Fleure-delyce" as a medieval scribe christened it.

While these stories belong to the realm of myth and legend, there is no denying the truth of frequent early references to names with the suffix L'Escot which appear in the French chronicles of the 8th, 9th and 10th centuries. One, "Gilemers L'Escot", was certainly a military vassal of Charlemagne, while most of his fellow travellers were either scholars or monks, Scots from both sides of the Irish Sea who took the "new knowledge", the teaching of Christianity in the Celtic church to the continent of Europe. The international life-style of these scholars can be gleaned from the tomb of the most famous of them, Duns Scotus, who lies in Cologne:

Scotia me genuit, Anglia suscepit
Gallia edocuit, Germania tenet.

While scholars and soldiers left Scotland for the continent, merchants tended to stay closer to home. In the 12th century they rarely ventured further than the ports of Ireland and England, utilising the latter as entrepôts for the wine transported across the Channel from France and the Low Countries. By the 13th century however, we hear of Scots dealing in wool, fish and hides in Dieppe, Bruges and Lübeck. This formed part of an outward expansion which became vital to the country when towards the end of the century the political turmoil developed which would sever Scotland's friendship with England for centuries to come.

The expansion of Scottish foreign trade was largely paralleled with the rise of the Burghs, with their strict control of sales of goods by burgesses and guild brethren. The merchant guilds were organised for their members' benefit. In the 1280's the records of one of the principal Scots Burghs, Berwick, have frequent references to forfeitures of casks of wine as punishment for infringements of the Guild's laws regulating trade. The fine of a cask of wine or banishment from the Burgh for a year and a day, were the alternatives offered to miscreants. The regularity of the forfeitures suggests that most elected to bide at home and help drink the fine at Guild meetings. The early guilds resembled self-help Friendly Societies and the fine of a cask of wine was levied from anyone selfish enough not to abide by the rules, e.g. when a member sold goods for another member's personal use and made a profit on the deal; similarly if a member took more than he needed for his household at that price, and then tried to sell the surplus, he in turn could be fined the barrel of claret! The wine merchants certainly benefited from this system of punishing wrongdoers.

By the last few decades of the 13th century, Scots merchantmen were sailing directly to Bordeaux, at that time the capital of the English province, Gascony. It was the marriage of Eleanor of Aquitane to Prince Henry Plantagenet in 1152 which heralded three centuries of English rule in this South West part of France, a rule which was broken only by the combined forces of the Auld Alliance in the 1450's. England provided a ready market for Gascon wines and by 1445 the volume of the wine traffic was immense, reaching over 13,000 tuns each year.

The fame of Bordeaux wine probably reached the Scots via their merchant communities in the principal English ports, and soon ships were sailing from the coastal burghs such as Dundee, Dumbarton and Leith to the Gironde. But the extension of trade was not without its problems. In those days maritime disputes regarding seizure of goods, non-payment of debt and acts of piracy did not have recourse to the sophisticated paraphernalia of modern law. If the Burgh authorities or the King himself did not right a wrong committed by one of their burgesses or subjects, the wronged party took it into his own hands to extract goods to the value of those lost, from any poor unfortunate passing by who happened to be flying the wrong flag. The Saltire was frequently the wrong flag, and bad debts the major problem. Both the Justiciar of the Lothians and the King himself suffered the ignominy of having their ships seized at the port of Lynn in Norfolk as security for bad wine debts their countrymen had run up in Bordeaux.

Scots obviously developed a nose for claret at an early date and from the number of charges the Bordelais brought against them, they appear to have loved wine more than sense. The claret madness extended to the noble halls of the Royal Palace itself.

In one year Alexander III pledged all the duties paid in the port of Berwick as security for the repayment of the sum of £2,197 which he owed a Bordeaux negociant for what must have constituted a wine lake deeper than Linlithgow Loch. The merchant in question was probably Raymond Verend of Montauban who was licensed in 1253 to send four hundred hogsheads of wine to the court of Alexander. In the same year a Burgess of Perth, John Fleming, shipped a hundred hogsheads of claret to the old wine quay in the Fair City. If one Bordeaux merchant succeeded in obtaining satisfaction from his trade in the North, another, called Jean Mazun, was long to rue the day he ever shipped claret for the King of Scots.

In the opening lines of his book on Robert the Bruce, Professor Barrow describes the last night of Alexander III. "On the afternoon of Monday, March 18th, 1286, the King sat in Edinburgh Castle, dining late with the Lords of his council and drinking, we may suppose, some of the blood red wine of Gascony for whose payment a Bordeaux wine merchant was to sue for many years in vain". Pulling himself away from the ensnarement of claret, the King set out for Fife, perhaps in hope of yet producing the heir the country desperately needed. He crossed the Forth in a storm, only to fall from his horse over the cliffs at Kinghorn, a short distance from his Palace of Dunfermline and the arms of Iolande, his young French wife. Alexander may have had his faults, but his reign coincided with an all too rare period of plenty for Scotland. The evocative fragment from an unknown poet recorded in Wyntoun's Chronicle, sums up the end of an era and the threat of the one to come;

Quhen Alexander our kynge was dede,
That Scotlande lede in lauche and le, [lauche and le – law and peace;
Away was sons of alle and brede, sons – abundance;
Off wyne and wax, of gamyn and gle. gamyn – mirth;
Our golde was changit in to lede.
Crist, borne in virgynyte,
Succoure Scotlande, and ramede, ramede – remedy, help;
That is stade in perplexite stade – fixed]

"Wyne and wax" – claret and wassail cake – are the symbols chosen by the poet for the reign of Alexander; lead and cold steel were perfect symbols for the Wars of Independence which followed his death. Alexander had no heirs, so Margaret, his three-year-old grand-daughter living across the North Sea was to succeed, but the child died on the journey from Norway. As the disputed feudal overlord of Scotland Edward I of England was asked to arbitrate between the principal claimants to the throne, Robert the Bruce and John Balliol.

The concept of national identity which did not reach some European countries till the forging of the great Nation States in the 19th century, came to Scotland in the Wars of Independence of the 14th century. At this period in the last decade of the 13th century, however, fealty to the local leader was all. The Scots nobles were then a heterogeneous group of Gaels, Normans, French and Flemish. Many of them held lands on both sides of the Border, thus owing allegiance to Edward and supporting his choice of Balliol as King. Not content with oaths of loyalty, however, Edward, fraught with rebellions in Wales and French incursions in Gascony, overplayed his card and sought not so much loyalty as humiliating submission from the Scots. He demanded Scots soldiers for the Gascon campaigns, which were refused, and he insisted that English courts had authority to deal with Scottish cases, which was resented. A predictable complainant at Edward's court was Jean Mazun!

As if Balliol did not have enough on his hands with Bruce straining at the leash, here he was, summoned to London to answer why he hadn't paid Alexander III's outstanding wine bill! Jean Mazun was persistent though, so much so that he procured the arrest of Bishop Fraser of St. Andrews who was travelling through Yorkshire en route for Gascony and an audience with Edward I. As one of the Guardians of Scotland, the unfortunate prelate was fair game as a hostage for an *obsédé* who needed the ready cash to lay out on the Graves Vintage of 1289. Poor Mazun's magnificent obsession got him nowhere, for he died with the bill unpaid in the mid 1290's.

For Balliol, the summons was a test case and he responded to it with the wavering infirmity which gave him the nickname Toom Tabard among his countrymen – now rejecting Edward's summons with resolution, now submitting to the indignity and appearing as the sovereign's liege vassal. The Scots nobility bade Balliol reject Edward's authority, sign the Alliance with Philip le Bel of France and strike out for independence. Edward's army turned northwards, committed terrible massacre at Berwick and garrisoned the country. Balliol escaped to France where his worries were soothed no doubt by tasting fine Burgundy at his residence, the papal Chateau of Gevrey Chambertin, the very heart of the Côte de Nuits. Balliol was among the first in a long line of Scots political exiles who sang the praises of Caledonia, but made little or no effort to return there.

The cause he had been forced to champion was taken up by a better man, William Wallace. While Bruce was biding his time deciding whether Scottish independence would be the best gait for him to gang, the Wicht Wallace fought a guerilla campaign of harassing the occupiers. His chronicler Blin Harry uses wine as a symbol of English conspicuous consumption, as if to beg the question, "Why should a people with such abundance in their own country, want the little we have?"

But Englishmen that riches wantit nane
By carriage brocht there victual full good wayne [wayne – quantity, abundance;
Stuffit houses with wine and good wernage wernage – provisions;
Demande this land as their ain heritage
The kinrik haill they rulit at their will. kinrik – kingdom]

The wine of course was from Bordeaux, indeed during Edward's Scottish campaigns practically all the wine of the region was sent north to provision the army – almost 3,000 tuns per annum. The ordinary people of Bordeaux had to make do with imported Spanish wine to make up for their loss.

On at least one occasion the English forces were to pay dearly for their excess of wine. After a day out in Carrick plundering, pillaging and slaying Wallace's own uncle, a force of 4,000 were stationed in a specially constructed camp of huge barns outside the town of Ayr. Deciding that all local opposition had been crushed, the host sat down to a night's carousing.

Nae watch was set because they had no doubt
Of Scottish men that living … were with-out,
Labourit in mind they had been all that day;
Of ale and wine eneuch chosen have they,
As beastly folk took of them self no keep
In their banes soon slid the slothful sleep,
Through full gluttony, in swarff swappit like swine [in swarff swappit – seized in a stupor]
Their Chieftane then was great Bacchus of wine!

The tone of the piece is that the army of occupation were *Unmensche*, who had it coming. The Scots simply did what they had to do – burned them alive! Barnweill is still there outside that town of "honest men and bonnie lassies", and at least one son of Kyle we know was regaled with the douce paternal words cribbed from Wallace, "Burn ye weill, ye Barns o'Ayr", when passing that way on a Sunday drive! In one 19th century edition of the Wallace, Blin Harry, obviously dissatisfied with mundane stories like the one recounted above, takes his hero off to the vineyards of Guienne where among other things he kills a lion with his bare hands!

If there were no lions in 13th century Gascony, there were plenty of Gascon vassals with Edward I in Scotland in the early 1300's, when with the execution of Wallace, Robert the Bruce entered the fray. Following the massacre of Berwick the town's fortification and anglicisation were undertaken, the former following the model of the *bastides* which had proven so effective against the French in Gascony. Edmond de Caillou of Bordeaux was appointed Governor of Berwick while Guillemin de Fenes, *"chevalier gascon"*, was captain of the garrison at Roxburgh Castle in 1314. Heavily armed Gascon Knights formed part of Edward II's cavalry at the decisive battle for Scottish Independence – Bannockburn on June 24th 1314.

Bruce and the sma' folk won the day and from then on Scotland turned to France as the foreign power most likely to help her preserve her hard-won independence. Bruce ratified Balliol's Treaty with France and while war with England broke out sporadically throughout the 14th century, communication with France was established and consolidated.

In the reign of Robert II, the first of the Stewart line to rule Scotland, the great historian Froissart accompanied 2,000 French knights who came to strengthen the Auld Alliance. While Blin Harry focused on the hedonistic gourmandise of the English, Froissart marvelled at the frugality of the Scots:

> The Scots are a bold, hardy people, very experienced in war. At that time they had little love or respect for the English and the same is true today. When they cross the border they advance sixty to seventy miles in a day and night, which would seem astonishing to anyone ignorant of their customs ... Because they have to pass over the wild hills of Northumberland, they bring no baggage-carts and so carry no supplies of bread or wine. So frugal are they that their practice in war is to subsist for a long time on underdone meat, without bread, and to drink river-water, without wine.

Just under fifty years after that campaign, Froissart, and old man now, was in Bordeaux to describe the wine fleet from the British Isles in 1372. It comprised two hundred ships flying the flags of Scotland, England and Wales. With ships of the period carrying from fifty to seventy tuns of wine, Hugh Johnson in his book *Wine* reckoned that the fleet would have carried three million gallons – "perhaps something in the regions of six bottles of claret per head for every man, woman and child in England, Scotland and Wales."

Just as the wealth, wine and Knights of Gascony had been essential to the English Kings in their ultimately unsuccessful designs to subjugate Scotland, so the formation of a force of Scottish auxiliaries played a decisive role in the French attempt to win back the south west part of their country from the English. An élite group of them formed la Garde Ecossaise du Corps du Roi, the immediate bodyguard of French Kings from these early days of the 15th century through to the 19th century, by which time it was only Scottish in name. When it arrived 6,000 strong in La Rochelle in the 1420's, it represented the flower of Scotland's fighting youth, and was recognised as such by the French King. Charles VIII made its leader, Archibald Douglas, Lieutenant General of the French Army and awarded him the titles Duke of Touraine and Count of Longueville. He did not live long to appreciate the honour. He enjoyed one famous victory over the English at La Baugé, a victory sweetened by the killing of the Duke of Clarence, brother of Henry V of England. However a year later, in 1424, he and at least 4,000 Scots were slain on the field of Verneuil. French historians blamed the Scots' foolish pride and hatred of the English for bringing the carnage upon themselves on that day. The Duke of Bedford had sent an envoy among them to fix the rule of Battle. The Scots replied that they would take no prisoners and give no quarter. They received none at Verneuil. When Joan of Arc and the French ultimately drove the English from Guienne, a campaign culminating in 1453 at the battle of Castillion, the numbers of Scots involved was of less consequence, but the Guard itself grew and prospered. Sir John Stewart of Darnley had survived Verneuil, was granted lands at Aubigny sur Nère, and headed a force of six hundred men. As Comtes d'Aubigny and Dukes of Albany the Stewarts were very much a Franco-Scottish dynasty whose name recurs in prominent events for the next two hundred years.

Just as the Stewarts of Aubigny survived Verneuil, while the Duke of Clarence perished, so the Stewarts of Albany had better luck with a butt of Malmsey later on in the century. In one of the best yarns of English history, the Duke of Clarence is said to have drowned in a vat of that honeyed liquor at the instigation of Richard III. The story of how the brother of James III, the Duke of Albany fared with his butt of Malmsey, is told by Robert Lindesay of Pitscottie in his *Historie and Cronicles:*

> The king of France gat wit of the treasoun be moyen of some that favoured the Duik of Albanie. Thairefter come ane Frinche ship out of France haistelie in to Scotland with secret writingis to the Duik of Albanie quho then was in prison in the castell of Edinburgh, to advertise him that it was concludit with the king and counsal that he sould be justifieit. The ship gaif hir self fourth as ane passinger with wyne, and sent up word to the castell to the Duik of Albanie gif he wald have of the same. Quhen he heard thir nowellis he desyrit the captaneis (of the guard) licence to send for tuo bossis of wyne, quho gaif him leif gladlie and provydit the bossis himself. And then the Duik of Albanie sent his familiear servand to the said frincheman for the wyne and prayit him to send of the best and starkest. The Frincheman sent him the tuo bossis of mavaisie, and in the one of the bossis he pat ane role of wax quhairin was clossit ane secreit writing quhilk schew the Duik of Albanie sic tydings as he was content with, bot in the other boss thair was ane certaine fadame of cordis to support him in his need at that tyme. The bossis was of the quantatie of tuo gallouns the peace, quhairfoir they war the les to be knawin that thair was ought in them bot the wyne.
>
> [be moyen – by means; advertise – warn; justifieit – sentenced to death; nowellis – news; boss – leather container; starkest – strongest; mavaisie – malmsey; clossit – enclosed; sic – such; fadame – length]

With his four gallons of the best and strongest Malmsey, his length of rope to throw over the castle wall and help him scramble to safety, and his secret instructions of how to win to the ship awaiting him in Leith, the Duke was well prepared for his getaway. There remained only the small obstacle of the captain and his three guardsmen. No problem, they would be plied with the Malmsey while the Duke and his chamberchyld remained sober and ready for action. The guards found the wine irresistible:

> The fyre was hott and the wyne was stark and the captane and his men became merie quhill at last the Duik of Albanie persaueit his tyme and saw them merrie and maid ane signe to his chamber chyld to be redy as he had instructit him befoir.
>
> [quhill – until; persaueit – perceived, realised]

Albany and his servant burst into action and slew their befuddled captors with their own knives. Thus by keeping a clear head on the night, Albany avoided a beheading on the morrow. But as is often the case in Medieval Scots history, there is an added cruel, black twist to the tale. For, not content with murdering the guards and making off, Albany and his lad took time to drag their bodies from where they fell and "cast them in the fyre". The Duke then fled to Leith and from there, France, and by the time the alarm was raised in the morning, all that remained of the party for the King to see were the left-overs from the roast – "the captain and two others in the fire, burning, which was very dollourous and fearful to them." Nevertheless, Albany escaped and married a French woman, and James III was protected from the conspirators because they feared the Duke's return – a happy ending for all but the poor captain and guards, marinated and basted in Malmsey over a roaring *feu de bois*. As we Scots have composed songs about the pleasures of drowning in alcohol, the conclusion must be that once again the English, in the shape of the Duke of Clarence, got it easy!

One thing is certain, even wine used for cooking in Scotland was of the purest kind. Throughout the 15th century several laws appear safeguarding the quality and price of wine sold, and citing severe penalties against anyone mixing or corrupting it. In 1436 the Parliament forbade anyone buying claret from Flemish merchant ships come from Bordeaux to Leith. The Flemish, who normally shipped Rhenish and Burgundy to Scotland were suspected of adulterating the claret and sent packing. They were perhaps fortunate for native traders found cutting wine could be given the death penalty. Merchants in wine-growing countries today, frustrated in bad years by the restrictions of Appellation Contrôlée laws which forbid the blending of wines of different origins, might ponder on the ringing phrase "on pane of dede" and feel if not satisfied, at least safe, with their lot. The esteem in which wine was held is also revealed in an Act of Parliament of 1431 which ordained that those who dealt in salmon, the country's most precious export, should only exchange it for English silver or gold, for half of the price, and Gascon wine "or siclyk gude pennyworthis" for the other half.

The purity of the wine guaranteed, the Scots not only drank claret, they revered it. In Sir Gilbert Hay's "Buke of the Governance of Princes" the author waxes lyrical on the wine's beneficial properties. His advice against excessive indulgence is just as relevant five hundred years on.

> Claret wyn is helesum til all complexiouns, nocht ower poignant or ower sweit, bot delytable of hew and gust, chosin be the odour colour and savour, grund and nature ... Sik wynis confortis the stomak and helpis to the natural heit and the guid digestion ... and convertis the meitis suner in substance and blod and flesche na other wyn dois, and garris it serve better to the necessiteis of the dispositioun of the harnis with a temperat heit, and amendis the wit and the mind of the man, and makis a man mair wys and sure in his wit with discretioun and reasoun, and blithis the hert and makis guid hew vermilioun and ... garris a man speik cleirlie and redilie, and puttis vain thochtis fra a man, makis man hardy and givis him guid appetyt ... and mony uther profitable thingis dois. Bot quhasa ower meikle takis of the wyn, quhilk is lyf and heil to mankynd, yit sal it be til his nature as poysoun til undo him.
>
> [gust – taste; garris – makes; harnis – brains]

One of the country's other major exports in the reign of the Poet King James I was Princesses; Eleanor to the Duke of Austria, Mary to the Count of Grandpré in Holland, Annabella (returned, unsuitable) to the Count of Geneva, Isabella to the Duke of Brittany and Margaret to the Dauphin who became Louis XI. When the last named voyaged to France she was accompanied by a retinue of noblemen and women and escorted by a thousand soldiers distributed in three Hulks and six Barques. When their spies passed on word of the fleet's departure, the English prepared a force of 80 ships to intercept and capture this ransomer's dream.

The Clyde at Dumbarton

However, while they lay in wait in the coves of Brittany further spoils presented themselves in the shape of a convoy of Flemish merchantmen, low in the sea with the weight of barriques of Charentais wine. The English attacked, seized the cargo and were about to round on the Scots, when they in turn were attacked and robbed of their spoils by a force of Spanish adventurers. The Scots meanwhile sped to La Rochelle and the Dauphine arrived, somewhat shaken but safe and sound.

It was the marriage of James II to Mary of Gueldres, a niece of the Duke of Burgundy, which helped develop a taste for the produce of that other great wine area of France. There are numerous mentions in the Royal Exchequer Rolls of the 1450's "Pro vino de Beoun (Beaune) empto ad usum regine" – rich red wine from the Côte de Nuits – for the Queen's use, a taste of her homeland. The Duke of Burgundy sent James II a present of a pipe of Beaune wine at the same time, while the accounts mention a white Burgundy called Osey – Auxois – also popular at Court. This wine could however have been of Portuguese origin – an ancestor of Moscatel de Setubal, one of the world's great dessert wines. Ships certainly plied between the Tagus and the Clyde in the reign of James IV. Osey was probably a sweet wine, rather than the delicate, fresh, fruited growths from Auxey-Duresses which we know today.

In the retinue of Mary of Guelders was one Matthieu de Coussy who was horrified by the lack of style in the fashions worn in Edinburgh: "Several of them appear to be quite savage, rather resembling barbarians." A colleague, Godefrey, in his *History of Charles VII* describes the pious way the Scots clergy celebrated this most Holy and Royal of Matrimonies – "a Cardinal, three Bishops, an Abbot and several other churchmen (were) all drinking profusely from an enormous wooden bowl, wine flowing as freely as the water of the sea."

The wine of Beaune also ran freely at the great jousting tournament held at Stirling Castle in 1449 when Jacques de Lalain the Burgundian champion met John of the proud Douglas line, a family then challenging Stewart supremacy in Scotland. Neither man could overcome the other, so James II as arbiter called a halt to the contest. Shortly afterwards the Earl of Douglas, the Knight's brother and head of the clan, was slain at Stirling on the orders of James, and for sport, his body was thrown out of the castle window into the garden below. If the Stewart Kings were brutal to their rivals, they were nevertheless kind to animals and foreign Knights whose European tournament circuit brought them to town. Among the accounts of the Lord High Treasurer in 1506 we read: "Item to Robert Galloway for wyne to bais the Frenche knychts hors feit – 4 shillings". To these enthusiastic *amateurs de vin* who can hardly afford to splash their gums with fine Burgundy, the image of a medieval cuddie up to his haunches in Romanée Conti is somewhat galling and the knowledge that it was used as an antiseptic does little to assuage the pain.

James IV

James IV's reign lasted from the death of his father at the battle of Sauchieburn in 1488, till his own equally tragic demise at the bloody climax of his invasion of England on France's behalf in 1513. A popular King, he combined an impetuous love of the martial arts with the interests of the typical Renaissance Prince in architecture, music, literature, languages and the fine things in life. His was an international court which the Spanish Ambassador Pedro de Ayala compared favourably with the glittering palaces of Europe. His reign coincided with a period of peace and plenty for the people and a flowering of the Arts, particularly poetry, at the Court. William Dunbar, possibly the finest poetic craftsman alive in Europe at the dawn of the 16th century, reflects the King's tastes, in his court poetry. In the *Dregy of Dunbar* he addresses the King in a mock religious tone, entreating him to leave his life of "penance" in provincial Stirling, to join the brilliant set in his capital.

We that are heir in hevins glory,
To yow that ar in purgatory,
Commendis us on our hartly wyis;
I mene we folk in parradys,
In Edinburgh with all mirrines,
To yow of Strivilling in distres,
Quhair nowdir plesance nor delyt is,
For pety this epistell wrytis,.
O! ye heremeitis and handkersaidilis, [handkersaidilis – anchorites.]
That takis your pennance at your tablis,
And etis nocht meit restorative,
Nor drynkis no wyn confortative...

The rise from the "Hell" of Stirling to the "Heaven" of the Court is rendered all the more irresistible when the King is reminded of the sensual pleasures of cellar and table which await him there:

To eit swan, cran, pertrik, and plever, [pertrik – partridge; plever – plover]
And every fische that swymis in rever;
To drynk with us the new fresche wyne,
That grew upoun the rever of Ryne,
Fresche fragrant clairettis out of France,
of Angers and of Orliance,
With mony ane course of grit dyntie:
Say ye amen for cheritie.

The poem follows a Church rite for the dead, and the final "responses" are in a holy Latin which has echoes of the Paternoster and other religious offices:

A porta tristitie de Strivilling
Erue, Domine, animas et corpora eorum.
Credo gustare statim vinum Edinburgi,
In villa viventium.
Requiescant Edinburgi. Amen.

From the gate of dolour of Stirling
deliver, Lord, their souls and bodies,
I believe that they will yet
taste the wine of Edinburgh
in the land of the living. Amen.

Dunbar had a guid conceit of his talents and was not always the most gracious of men when he felt his artistic services were not being adequately rewarded. Prime targets for his vitriolic satire were James' foreign favourites, Irish, Italian and French...

"Soukaris, groukaris, gledaris, gunnaris; [soukaris – suckers; gledaris – hawks;
Monsouris of France, gud clarat-cunnaris;
Inopportoun askaris of Yrland kynd;
And meit revaris, lyk out of mynd." revaris – thieves]

Every Scots burgh had its official "aill cunnar" or ale taster. Dunbar's mention of the office in connection with claret is probably a poetic device to describe the dilettante, pretentious, wine connoisseurs of the Court compared to the useful, honest Scots ale tasters. Claret cunnars are high on his list of useless Royal expenditure. Much of Dunbar's best poetry is set away from the Court and in *The Friars of Berwick,* claret, the Church and sensual pleasures all combine in an hilarious burlesque. Here a good lady whose husband is from home, has her fun with a Grey Friar, watched by two Friars of the Jacobean Order from the loft. When Friar John, the lover, arrives at her house, he brings not only his lust, but the wherewithal to satisfy all the lady's appetites.

"my awin luve deir,
Haif thair ane pair of bossis, gud and fyne, [bossis – containers;
Thay hald ane gallone full of Gascone wyne;
And als ane pair of pertrikis richt new slane, pertrikis – partridges;
And eik ane creill full of breid of mane; eik – also; breid of mane – finest bread;
This I haif brocht to yow, my awin luve deir,
Thairfoir, I pray you, be blyth, and mak gud cheir;
Sen it is so that Semon is fra hame, Semon – the Husband;]

Those who wish to be titillated by more than the reference to the two ... full ... luscious ... barrels of Gascon wine, will have to buy their copy of Dunbar to find out what happens when the husband comes back.

In the more prosaic text of the *Accounts* of the Lord High Treasurer of Scotland we are given vivid vignettes relating to the role wine played in society, the King's liking for it, and occasionally the political events of the time. Thus an entry for 1504 reminds us of James' frequent naval expeditions to the Hebrides to break the power of the MacDonald Lords of the Isles: "Item the 18th day of Aprile in Dunbertane, to Martin the Frenchman, for 10 tun of wyne to the schippes vitalling in the Isles – £70."

James' fascination with his navy took him often to Dumbarton, his main port on the West Coast: "1497 – item the 14th day of March, in Dunbertane, giffin to the gudwife quhair the King luggit. Item to ane bote, to fech wyne, frae the ship twyis, quhen she lay at the New Werk – 4/8d." Whether the gudwif's wine did not meet the King's standards and whether he sent to his own ship or that of one of the foreign wine merchants in port to try their wares, we do not know. We do know that there were also payments to a piper and clarsacher, so all the ingredients were on hand for a good night's carousing. James also used his visits there to buy unusual wines for himself and his friends, presents of wine being a common way to indicate Royal approval. I wonder if the Grey Friar mentioned is the protagonist in Dunbar's farce: "May 1498. Item, payit be me to the Portingale merchant, for 1 tun of wyne the King gaif the Early of Lennox, 1 pipe he gave the Grey Freris, 1 pipe he gaif to Alexander Stewart, for ilk tun £12; summa £24."

The Portuguese merchant would ship Sack, Tent or Alicante from Spain or perhaps the rich Muscatel from Setubal or the then delicate white from Carcavelos near his home port of Lisbon. Whatever it was, it pleased James for he went back for more: "Item Payet to John Farnhae, the merchand of Portingale, for 4 tun of wyne to the King yet liand in Dunbertane. £48."

On a hunting trip to the borders, political politesse comes into play when he buys wine from a Dumfries merchant called Cunninghame, to send a present of it to Lord Dacre, the English Warden of the West March. The niceties are observed on both sides when Dacre sends a gift of a stag – venison to be roasted over an open fire at the Royal camp in Eskdale and washed down with the Malmsey sent to James' party by the "Priour of Carlile". On a pre-nuptial tour at the other end of his Kingdom James avails himself of the opportunity of buying some good Hock, newly landed at Aberdeen. He conveys a present of a hogshead of it to his hostess [and probable mistress] of a few nights before at Darnaway Castle, and sends the rest on its southward journey to his cellars at Leith and Holyrood. In peacetime, even the great naval commander Sir Andrew Wood of Largo could be relied upon to ship a little wine: "1502. Item the 23rd day of Januar, payet to Schir Andrew wood for 2 rubbouris to put the Rins wyne in and for carriage of the samyn to Edinburgh from Perth. 14/-."

The other great seadog of James' reign was Robert Barton of Leith who with Wood supervised the construction of the *"Great Michael"* and the other vessels of the King's powerful navy. When James eventually joined in battle against Henry VIII in support of his auld allies, tragically it was on land that the decisive engagement took place. All the power and skill of the Scots were deployed uselessly at sea, unused by the French. In peacetime however naval commanders practised their seacraft as merchants and adventurers. The effort to build new ships therefore was done in the realisation that Scotland's independence relied as much on a thriving foreign trade as a strong navy. Thus in 1507 the Accounts contains a payment to one of the Barton boys, Andrew: "be the Kingis command, to mak hering to send in France for wyne, and fournis the schip biggit in Dumbertane to Burdeaus."

In an age when French craftsmen were employed beautifying the palaces and churches at Linlithgow, Stirling, Falkland and Edinburgh, it is perhaps not surprising, though somewhat amusing today, to note the delightful expenses incurred at Stirling Castle in 1501. With so much of his exports paying for wine, James was advised to try his luck: "Items … giffin to the French gardiner passand to Irewin for wyne treis, and to gar carry the samyn. … giffin to the man that brocht the wyne grapes fra Air to Strivelin … be the Kingis command to the Frenchman that set the wyne treis at Strivelin…"

We have combed the records and can find no further payments for pickers or trampers at the time of the *vendange!* The vines, like the flouers o the forest at Flodden, were gey suin aw wede awaw.

LITTLE FRANCE 2

Flodden was a tragedy which bit deeply into Scottish consciousness, so many thousands of families felt its effect personally. One has only to hear the lament played at Selkirk at the end of the Common Riding, and see the Saltire lowered to feel the echoes that remain from that day. Flodden also exposed the weakness of a small nation fighting for its survival by trying to play two mightier nations off against one another. Scotland invaded England at the request of the French. The French stayed at home and the Scots were massacred. In the Auld Alliance with France as with the Act of Union with England, the larger partner held sway while the smaller … endured.

In the same year as Flodden, the larger partner made a nice gesture to the smaller. Louis XII passed a law, which has never since been revoked, naturalizing Scots living in France as French citizens.

> *General Edict authorising naturalisation for the Scottish nation from King Louis XII in 1513.*
> Louis, by the Grace of God, King of France, would remind, make known to all living and all eternity (to come) that since most ancient times there has been between the kings of France and Scotland and the princes and subjects of our kingdomes, the closest of friendship, confederation and perpetual alliance … and that in more recent times, during the reign of our great Lord and relative Charles VII, several princes of that said kingdom of Scotland accompanied by large numbers of people from that said nation did come to our assistance to help us eject and expel from our kingdom the English who were detaining and occupying the greater part of the said kingdom: in the course of which action the Scots did conduct their persons with such virtuous boldness against the English that the latter were driven out … and because of the great loyalty and boldness which they manifested, Charles took 200 of their number to be his personal bodyguard. All of this being taken into account we have resolved, with due regard to the great loyalty and fidelity which has always and without any alteration been found in that people, to declare and ordain that all those from the Kingdom of Scotland who may live and die from now on in our said kingdom, whatever their degree, shall be permitted to acquire in our land any goods, titles and belongings that they may legitimately acquire as if they were true natives of our said kingdom.

The privileges of Scots merchants in France and the growth of French cultural influences in Scotland reached their height from the death of James IV until the Reformation. Then, the country was controlled by the Regent Albany, James V, Marie de Guise and Marie Stewart, all of whom were formed by their experience of

Lettres de Naturalité Générale pour toute la Nation d'Escosse par le Roi Louis XII en 1513

LOUIS PAR LA GRACE DE DIEU ROI DE FRANCE

Sçavoir faisons à tous presens et avenir, que, comme de tous temps et ancienneté, entre les rois de France et d'Escosse, & les princes et subjects des royaumes, y ait eu très estroite amitié, confederation & alliance perpetuelle ... et dernièrement du temps du vivant de feu nostre très cher seigneur et cousin Charles VII, pleusieurs princes du dict royaume d'Escosse, avec grand nombre de gens de la dicte nation, vinrent par deça pour aider a jetter et expulser hors du royaume les Anglois, qui detenoient & occupoient la plus part du royaume; lesquels exposerent leurs personnes si vertueusement contre les dicts Anglois, qu'ils furent chassés ... et pour la grande loyaulté & vertu qu'il trouva en eux, il en prit deux cents à la garde de sa personne ... PARQUOI NOUS ... ayant regard ... à la grande loyaulté et fidelité que toujours et sans avoir jamais varié a esté trouvé en eux AVONS RESOLU DECLARER ET ORDONNER tous ceux du dict royaume d'Escosse qui demeureront et decederont ci-après dans nos dicts royaumes ... de quelque etat qu'ils soient ... pourront acquerrir en icelui tous biens, seigneuries et possessions qu'ils y pouront licitement acquerir comme s'ils etoient natifs de nostre dict royaume.

Naturalisation of Frenchmen

MARIE, QUEEN DOWAGER AND REGENT,

Cap. 65. 29th November 1558.

"Because the maist Christian King of France has granted ane letter of naturalitie for him and his successors to all and sundrie Scotsmen – registered in the Chalmer of Compts – therefore the Queen's Grace, Dowager and Regent of this Realme and the Three Estaites of the samin, thinks it guid and agreeable that the like Letter of naturalitie be given and granted by the King and Queen of Scotland ... to all and sundrie the said maist Xtaine King of France subjects being or sall happen to be here in the Realme of Scotland in onie time to come with siklike privileges."

The Auld Alliance confirmed with dual nationality for Scots and French.

the French court. Writing in 1537, Bishop Leslie detailed the effect of French extravagance on the more frugal Scots:

> There wes mony new ingynis and devysis, alsweill of bigging of palaces, abilyementis and of banquating, as of men's behaviour, first begun and used in Scotland at this tyme, eftir the fassione quhilk they had sene in France. Albeit it semit to be very comlie and beautifull, yit it was moir superfluous and voluptuous nor the substance of the realme of Scotland mycht beir furth or sustaine; notheles, the same fassionis and custom of coistlie abyliements indifferentlie used by all estatis, excessive banquating and sic lik, remains yit to thir dayis, to the greit hinder and povertie of the hole ralme.
>
> [alsweill of bigging – as well as building; abilyementis – dress]

With James V in his infancy, Albany was brought over from his castle Chatelhérault in France to rule, in broken Scots, over the unruly Lowland barons. In 1518 he took pains to improve the privileges of the Scots wine merchants plying to Bordeaux, aided by the French Ambassador in Edinburgh "Francis de Bordeaux". The Scots certainly enjoyed privileged status in France, paying less duty on goods than merchants from other countries. The English, still smarting from the loss of their wine colony, were obviously peeved at the advantages their neighbours now enjoyed. An Englishman writing of the Scots in France in this period stated "because he hath always been an useful confederate to France against England ... he hath right of pre-emption or first choice of wines in Bordeaux; he is also permitted to carry his ornance to the very walls of the town." While the Merchantmen of Bristol and London heaved to at the Citadel at Blaye, gave up their "ornance", their arms, were subjected to humiliating curfews, and had to apply for passports before being allowed up river, those of Leith, Dundee and Dumbarton were already in Bordeaux and Libourne loading the pick of the new wine.

Any advantage that accrued to the Scots as we have seen, was dearly bought. Despite this, the Scots had constantly to send envoys to France to make sure the individual ports, Dieppe, La Rochelle and Bordeaux were in fact following the laws agreed by their King. In 1483 the Three Estates sent Walter Bertram to negotiate with the French authorities the confirmation of the privileges the French were currently enjoying in Scotland but which had lapsed vis-à-vis the Scots in Paris. Royal Warrants were fine but it was difficult to convince local authorities sometimes to adhere to them. To 16th century traders a wrong against them committed by members of even a friendly nation could be righted by extorting the value of the wrong from any innocent who happened to belong to the same nation. Thus in the same year that Albany was re-negotiating Scots privileges in France we notice among the Calendar of Royal Letters, the following paraphrased extracts.

James V, the Regents, Chancellor and Council to the President and Lords of Parliament and Senate of Bordeaux, Edinburgh, Dec. 30, 1518.

George Wallace sailed to bring wine from Bordeaux in 'Le Volant', a merchant vessel purchased bona fide and owned for more than three years. A man of Bordeaux, on the allegation that Robert Gardiner and Duncan Campbell in that ship had, some years before, despoiled him of certain casks of wine, caused arrest the ship when she was almost laden, and brought Wallace before a subordinate of the admiral delegate of France. From his sentence Wallace appealed to the Bordeaux authorities, urging that the ship was his purchased property, no longer in the hands of the delinquents. It seems absurd that an

Marie de Guise

innocent man should lose his ship and gear, and thereby four thousand francs. There is said to be a custom with them according to which a ship touching at a French port, though in question at law, should not be arrested for that turn when she has begun lading. That, however, must be left to their judgment. This letter is in response to Wallace's solicitation. The Scottish government is well aware of their impartiality, and hopes that a speedy decision will obviate the necessity for an appeal to the French king or more serious measures.

James V, the Regents, Chancellor and Council of Francis I, Edinburgh, Dec. 30, 1518.
The Scottish government tells George Wallace's story, adding that he was compelled by the arrest of the ship to hire another and transfer the cargo at a heavy loss. Francis is asked to write to Bordeaux for speedy justice, and by letters patent to restore Wallace in integrum should distance prevent him from keeping any term of appeal.

As the line between merchant and pirate was a fine one, crossed at will as we shall see when we discuss the great mercantile families in Leith, there is no place here for moral indignation. However, in their favour, the Scots tended to obtain restitution of goods by force from enemy shipping only, preferring to go through legal and less arbitrary channels in a dispute with their Auld Ally. The Divergences between the Letter of the Law and the practice of the local authorities in France are revealed in all the documents relating to the Scots Privileges throughout the 16th century. The following is a Grant by Charles IX ordering no more custom to be taken from the Scots nation for Wine than that due by existing treaties.

Grant, or Letters Patent, by Charles IX, King of France, under his Great Seal, and directed to the Treasurer of France, established at Ageri; Bearing, That it was humbly meant and shown his Majesty, by the Merchants of Scotland trading to France, that the Receiver-General at Bourdeaux had for two or three years past compelled them, and intended as yet to compell them, to pay ten souls for ilk Tun of Wine that they should load or take in at the Port and Harbour of Bourdeaux, for exportation to Scotland, over and above the twenty-one shillings four pennies which they had been in use to pay conform to the old composition agreed upon in the treaty made betwixt the said nations of France and Scotland; And seeing that this was contrary to the said old Treaty, and that his Majesty had no intention to alter or innovate anything therein contained: Therefore his Majesty, willing to relieve the said Scots Merchants of this burden and charge, and honestly to treat them as old Allies and Friends of his Crown, His Majesty expressly commanded his said Collector at Bourdeaux, to allow the said Scots Merchants who should load and take away wine from the said Port of Bourdeaux and to import into Scotland without fraud, and from that time forth his Majesty quitted and discharged the foresaid ten souls for the tun, and all other new taxation, except the twenty-one shillings four deniers which they had been in use to pay, and should not be bound to pay any other thing, or that they should be any ways troubled or molested thereanent.

> These Letters Patent are granted by the King in his council, and bear date at Bourdeaux the 20th of April, 1565, and of the King's Reign, the 5th year.

Only five years after the King's Grant we find the Convention of Burghs raising the sum of 1000 marks to send their representative Nicholas Uddart to France "for doun getting of the 10 sous of the tun of wyne in Bordeaux raissit afore the merchants of this realm thair". Similarly in 1514, the Scots were trying to remove a custom of 12 deniers in the franc. If they succeeded temporarily, it could not have made much difference in the long run for, in 1541, James lent £2,000 to the Convention who tried via the diplomacy of Cardinal Beaton to have the same duty removed. The frustration of Scotland's expanding merchant class is expressed in the instructions given to their envoy to the French King in 1524; they state that:

> Since war with the English began, our merchants are debarred from trade communications with England, Flanders, Spain and other realms. These realms were formerly allied with us or friendly; now owing to our friendship, alliance and punctilious good faith with the French, we are suffering heavily. These many years past a very few of our merchant men have succeeded in eluding the enemy ships and reaching France, the only country which professes to be friendly to us. Those who most recently braved the dangers of the sea and got through to France are being detained there an unusually long time. Our forbearance in the matter is too well known to make oral or written presentations necessary: we have clearly before our minds how much we have endured for our friendship and alliance with France.

If the commercial value of Scotland's special relationship with France was questionable, the French cultural legacy was brilliant. In architecture, the Renaissance palaces of Falkland, Stirling, Holyrood and Linlithgow were built on models found on the Loire – Chenonceaux, Blois and Amboise; Sir David Lyndsay's favourite was Linlithgow:

> *Lithgow, whose palyce of plesance*
> *Micht be ane pattern in Portugal and France.*

The masons who wrought these magnificent buildings were mostly French, working under their own countrymen, Merlioun, Roy, or Franche, or alongside French-trained Scots master masons Cochrane, Mylne, Jackson or Hamilton. In printing, the pioneers Chapman and Myllar learned their craft at Rouen, returning home to publish the classic texts of Scots literature and ensure that literature's survival into our own day. The poetry of the Mediaeval Makars itself, drawing inspiration from Villon in France or Ariosto in Italy was thoroughly European compared to the insularity of the English poets of the age excepting Chaucer. Scotland's intimacy with France in this period gave it access to the mainstream of European thought; its intellectuals were part of a wider European culture. That English literary critics should classify Henryson, Douglas, Lyndsay, Montgomerie and Dunbar as "Scottish Chaucerians" reveals both their chauvinism and cultural imperialism. Wine writers in England occasionally reveal the same symptoms when they suggest that, like the rest of the Empire, the Gascons really wanted to be an English colony till the end of time. The same writers are characterised by their frequent use of the adjective "English" when they really should know better and use the much more precise "British". In *Decanter* magazine, July 1981, Michael D. Symington of Oporto drew attention to the practice in a reply to a normally accurate scribe: "I wonder what the unfortunate British Port Wine Shippers (British please, not English as the majority of the families and firms here in Oporto are of Scottish rather than English descent) have done to incur such an acid attack from the pen of Mr. Edmund Penning-Rowsell."

The very language both the Makars and the masses used was spairged (fr. asperger, eng. to sprinkle) with words newly coined from France. As one might expect the greatest borrowings from French into Scots were terms associated with gastronomy and wine. Many of the words are still in current use.

FOOD

Scots	*French*	*English*
ashet	assiette	a deep dish
aumrie	armoire	cupboard
gigot	gigot	leg of mutton
grosset	groseille	gooseberry
petticoat tails	petites gatelles	thin shortbread
sybo	cibo	spring onion

DRINK

Scots	*French*	*English*
bonnally	bon aller	stirrup cup
boss	boisson	a leather bottle, a small cup
broach	broc	pitcher, flaggon
chopin	chopine	a quart
tappit hen	topynett	flaggon holding a chopin
gardyveen	garde-vin	wine case, cellarette
tassie	tasse	cup
verry	verre	tumbler
symler	sommelier	wine taster, cellarman.

So in late Mediaeval Scotland the vessel you drank it from, the place you kept it and the measures you sold it by were as French as the wine itself.

It was James V's taste for French women which created this thoroughly Francophile Scotland. Taste is inaccurate, as dynastical ambitions played a more important role than personal attraction. However when the feeble Dauphine, Madeleine de Valois died six months after their sumptuous wedding at Notre Dame in 1537, surviving Edinburgh haars for only a few weeks, James immediately sent to France for the hand of Marie de Guise. In the retinue of the first queen was Pierre de Ronsard, one of the most famous French poets of the Middle Ages. He composed a beautiful poem *"le Tombeau de Madeleine de France"*, which mourns her death. In its beginning though, Ronsard describes the meeting of James with the French King Francis I, the latter so impressed by the regal bearing of James that he is happy to give his daughter to his charge:

Ce roy d'Escosse estoit en la fleur de ses ans,
Ses cheveux non tondus, comme fin or luisans,
Cordonnez et crespez, flotans desus sa face
Et sur son col de lait, luy donnoient bonne grace.

Son port estoit royal, son regard vigoureux,
De vertus et d'honneur et de guerre amoureux;
La douceur et la force illustroient son visage,
Si que Venus et Mars en avoient fait partage.

Ce grand prince Francois admirant l'estranger
Qui roy chez un grand roy s'estoit venu loger,
Son sceptre abandonnant, sa couronne et son isle,
Pour recompenser luy accorda sa fille,
La belle Magdeleine, honneur de chastete,
Une grace en beatue, Junon en majeste.

Madeleine's dowry of gold, arms, jewels, velvets, satins and tapestries were carefully negotiated as were the two ships which accompanied them back to Leith. One of them, the *"Salamander"*, is today a street name in the port near which Madeleine first kissed the soil of her new Realm. The fates were on the side of the wife in the second marriage, for Marie de Guise lived long after James' demise at a Border skirmish against the English. James was also associated with poetry and *"Christ's Kirk on the Green"* was almost certainly written by him. In the persona of a poor man "The Gudman of Ballengeich" he loved to wander around Scotland finding out how the ordinary folk lived, and by all accounts how Scottish girls compared with French Queens. His poetry is far from the Court, and reveals his delight in simple country matters:

Off all thir maidens myld as mead,
Was nane sa gymp as Gillie,
As ony rose hir rude was reid,
Her lyre was lyk the lillie;
But yallow yallow was hir heid,
And sche of luif so sillie
Thocht all hir kin suld have bein deid
Sche wald have bot sweit Willie
Allane,
At Chrystis Kirk on the grein.

With the luxury of his Palace and the pleasures of the common folk James could still find enthusiasm for the unusual alfresco hospitality afforded him when he went hunting in Atholl.

> ...a fair palace of green timber, wind with green birks, that were green both under and above which was fashioned in four quarters, and in every quarter and nuik thereof a great round, as it had been a block-house, which was lofted and gested the space of three house height; the floors laid with green scarets spreats, medwarts and flowers, that no man knew whereon he geid, but as he had been in a garden ... Further, this Earl gard make such provision for the King, and his Mother, and the Embassador, that they had all manner of meats, drinks, and delicates that were to be gotten, at that time, in all Scotland, either in burgh or land; that is to say, all kind of drink, as ale, beer, wine, both white and claret, malvesy muskadel, Hippocras aquavitae.

Throughout James' reign and during the Regency of Marie de Guise there was a constant coming and going of ships and soldiers from France to Scotland. In 1524 there were reckoned to be 5,000 French soldiers here, while in the 1540's when Henry VIII attempted to exploit the confusion after James' death, Marie de Guise brought Jacques de Montgomery, the Captain of the Garde Ecossaise to Edinburgh to help her organise her defences. He was shipped a force of 1,200 Provençal and Gascon soldiers from Bordeaux and we are told that he used the opportunity to obtain some fine claret for the Queen Regent, to make sure their relationship got off to a good start. Perhaps this was the consignment the Royal coopers were busy racking in 1544. In the Treasurer's Account for that year we read of an expense incurred "for dressing and girthing of certaine wyne within the castell". A French ecclesiast, Estienne Perlin, visited Edinburgh in 1551 and wrote:

> It should be noted that nothing is scarce but money. Wine is brought them from Bordeaux and Rochelle and it must be understood that the Scots do not pay for the wine they buy from the people of Bordeaux, but in lieu thereof give them other merchandise.

It is interesting that despite the abundance of wine available Perlin saw little sign of excess. In an age when every nation delighted in accusing their neighbours of drunkenness, Perlin retained this stigma for the English whom he depicted as "villainous drunkard and reprobate". If Perlin had visited Edinburgh a decade later when Mary attempted not unsuccessfully to transplant the glittering court of France to dreich Auld Reekie, he may have witnessed degrees of abandon unkent, at least in public, in these airts. When Mary married the Dauphin in 1558, the douce citizens of Edinburgh, as if determined to have a final fling before the Reformation, constructed a fountain which spouted wine throughout the festivities. In the Burgh Records we read of expenses for "ane wyne puntioun till put wyne in, till be run upon the Croce" and to pay the man responsible for the working of the fountain: "Item gevin to Johnne Weire, puderar for making of pypis to the out passage of the wyne and awaiting upon the samin ... with the recompense of his laubores. 30/-"

In the same year Mary's mother reciprocated the French decree of 1513, giving Scottish citizenship to Frenchmen living in Scotland. With the number of French soldiers, builders, chefs and musicians in Edinburgh, it was a wise political move.

Naturalisation of Frenchmen
Marie, Queen Dowager and Regent, 29th November 1558
Because the maist Christian King of France has granted ane letter of naturalitie for him and his successors to all and sundrie Scotsmen – registered in the Chalmer of Compts – therefore the Queen's Grace, Dowager and Regent of this Realme and the Three Estaites of the samin, thinks it guid and agreeable that the like letter of naturalitie be given and granted by the King and Queen of Scotland ... to all and sundrie the said maist Xtaine King of France subjects being or sall happen to be here in the realme of Scotland in onie time to come with siklike privileges.

The retinue which accompanied Mary from Paris was so numerous that the overspill from Craigmillar Castle settled a new village near Edinburgh which is still called "Little France". Local tradition has it that another part of the city, Burdiehouse, takes its name from Burdeous – one of the countless spellings for Bordeaux in Middle Scots. Philologically it is quite feasible but the suggestion that it was the place Bordeous wine was stored when it arrived in Edinburgh is unlikely given its distance from the Forth.

Installed eventually in Holyrood, looking ravishing in the white mourning she still wore for the Dauphin, Mary presided over a sumptuous Court. Monsieur Pinguillon, the Comptroller of the Royal Household provided feasts with a choice of beef, mutton, chicken, pigeon, hare and rabbit, washed down with liberal quantities of claret and Hock – a quart of each per person was the usual measure, drunk out of the ubiquitous Topynett or Tappit Hen. Wine also played its part in the Franco-Scottish cuisine of the Court. One recipe which survives from Holyrood calls for a haunch of venison to be stuffed with spices then marinated for six hours in claret before roasting.

The increasing extravagance of the Court throughout the century had its parallel among the people too. The old asceticism which poverty had produced in the Scots made many react against the French influence with its stress on pleasure for pleasure's sake. In the early 1500's, Hector Boece wrote of the change in manners:

> No fish in the sea nor fowl in the air, nor beast in the wood may have rest but is sought here and there to satisfy the hungry appetite of gluttons. Not only are wines sought in France, but in Spain, Italy and Greece, and sometime, both Africa and Asia sought for new delicious meats and wines to the same effect ... through immoderate gluttony our wit and reason are so blunted within the prison of the body, that it may have no knowledge of heavenly things.

Such criticisms were voiced with growing conviction in the next fifty years, till by Mary's time they had reached a crescendo. The Reformer, John Knox, who had spent years on bread and water as a galley slave in the ships of Catholic France, was one who did not look upon the self-indulgence of the Court with favour: "The affaires of the kitchen were so gripping, that the ministers stipendis could nocht be payit."

Tending a vineyard – Mediaeval France.

THE WYNE-YEARD OF THE LORD

3

> And finalie, they haiff cast down the dyk, cutted the hedge, demolished the toure, broken the wyne-pres, banished the watchmen and laborars, the sneddars and delvars of the wyne-yeard of the Lord.

The ringing confident tones belong to a Presbyterian reformer conjuring the image of the spiritual vineyard whose perfection the corruption of the Catholic church had destroyed. In our own day the Reformation has been reduced to clichés – Calvinism equals gloom and doom. Unfortunately, the clichés stem more from long boring Sundays this century and the claustrophobic creative stuntedness of the Victorian Age, rather than the vision of the Reformers. The Reformers, it is true, were more concerned with eternal glory rather than temporal *joie de vivre* and could pass laws such as that of 1588 which put an end to "superfluous banqueting". They also made Scotland the most advanced nation in Europe with Knox's idea of universal education, a legacy which from that time on gave the ordinary Scot the basis for the pride he still has in the people he stems from. For most European nations the education of the masses was not even contemplated for another three hundred years. For that fact alone the Reformers deserve a better press.

The easiest cliché levelled is that they stopped people enjoying themselves. James Marshall, former Associate Minister of South Leith Kirk, chuckled when he discovered the amount of wine drunk at the first Presbyterian Communion held after the Covenanting period. In a radio interview he said:

> The wine for the communion cost £23. 2/- and in addition to the wine they bought a barrel to put the wine in. It doesn't say what the size of the barrel was but there was a considerable number of gallons in it. And in addition to that a special order was put in for £8 worth of Sack for the visiting preachers all through the communion season. Going back over the history of our own congregation, I've been struck by the huge amount of wine that was consumed at communion times. This was due to the fact that people didn't take a little sip of wine in the olden days, they took a big mouthful, and refreshed themselves, as it were, ye see.

It was not only those taking communion who were getting their share of the prevailing "gloom", the whole population seems to have been at it. Grant, in his *Economic History of Scotland* states:

> In Edinburgh, at least, by the end of the sixteenth century, even the common artisans and the rascal multitude drank a good deal of wine, and the people chose to indulge this taste even when prices rose considerably. The price of wine increased by nearly eight times its original cost between 1556 and 1599 and yet the demand for it continued.

The Reformation then gave man a different framework to order his existence, but his nature remained constant … and wine drinking was second nature to him. Even his spiritual nature could not be reformed or transformed. The Scots have always maintained an obsessively curious interest in a Universe which the official Church, Protestant or Catholic, could not wholly explain. In the *Complaynt of Scotland* published in 1549, amidst the folklore of astrology we find the following passage relating to the effect of the dog star on men, dogs … and wine.

> Siklyk there is ane sterne callit canis, the evilll constellation of it begynnis at the sext daye of iulye, and endis at the XX daye of august. The natur of it is contrar tyl everie thing that is procreat on the eird. The tyme of the operation of it in our hemisphere is callit be the vulgaris the caniculair days. The evil natur of it enflammis the sun with an unnatural vehement heat the quhilk oft tymis trublis and altris the wyne in ane pipe in the deep cave ande alse it generis pestilens, feuyrs and mony ither contagius seiknes quhen it rings in our hemisphere – then dogs ar in dangeir to ryn wud, rather nor in ony uther time of the year.
>
> [canicular days – dog days; rings – reigns; ryn wud – run wild]

Similarly, the Scots fascination for the shades of good and evil, light and dark, God and the Devil, existed before the Reformation. Dunbar's Devil in the poem *"In My Sleip"* could be the fiend of a Presbyterian fire and brimstone preacher, yet the work was written half a century before such preachers existed. The Deil goes through the trades of the town, indicates all the petty swindles going on, and invites these mild sinners to join him in hell for their false claims in regards to their product.

The fleschour sweirs be godis woundis
come never sic beif unto yir boundis
na fattar muttoune can nocht be –
"fals" quod the fiend and till him roundis
Renunce thy god and cum to me.

Be goddis blud quod the tavernneir
Thair is sic wyne in my selleir
hes never come in this cuntree
Yet quod the deuill, "thou sellis ower dear
With they fals met cum doune to me."

To be a Taverner in Mediaeval Scotland had its perils – you could be put to death for mixing the wine, fined heavily for selling it above the fixed price, closed for buying it from anyone but a guild brother … and committed to eternal damnation for boasting about the quality of your Malaga Sack and trying to get a good price on it!

The persecution of women in the late 16th century, burned as witches and devil worshippers, was common to Catholic Spain as well as Protestant Scotland. However, in James VI we had a witch hunting *obsédé* who wrote books on the subject. In his *Newes from Scotland* he recounts a contemporary devilish and detestable practice, that of a poor merchant who in his sleep is transported by witch power to a wine cellar in … yes, Bordeaux. Most Scots then and now would put such an eventuality down to divine providence, but not James. What is interesting is that Bordeaux is cited in so many 16th century texts as an exotic place with which everyone is familiar. In the woodcut which accompanies the story, the look on our compatriot's face is hardly horror struck … more the quiet satisfaction of one who had (a) made love to a beautiful Bordelaise, (b) smoked a hand-rolled Havana or (c) drunk a magnum of old Pape Clement 1561.

The story of being whisked off to claret country obviously appealed to the average Scot, for it became part of our store of legend. Two centuries later, Burns, writing to Captain Francis Grose about the Witch Stories relating to Alloway Kirk he drew from in composing *"Tam O' Shanter"*, recounts the following:

James VI's witch book – the merchant's fate in woodcut.

On a summer's evening, about the time that Nature puts on her sables to mourn the expiry of the cheerful day, a shepherd boy belonging to a farmer in the immediate neighbourhood of Alloway Kirk had just folded his charge, and was returning home. As he passed the Kirk, in the adjoining field, he fell in with a crew of men and women who were busy pulling the stems of the plant ragwort. He observed that as each person pulled a ragwort he or she got astride of it, and called out, "Up Horsie!" on which the ragwort flew off like Pegasus, through the air with its rider. The foolish boy likewise pulled his ragwort and cried, with the rest, "Up Horsie!" and, strange to tell, away he flew with the company. The first stage at which the cavalcade stopped, was a merchant's wine cellar in Bordeaux, where without saying 'by your leave', they quaffed away at the best the cellar could afford, until the morning, foe to the imps and works of darkness, threatened to throw light on the matter and frightened them from their carousals.

The poor shepherd lad, being equally a stranger to the scene and the liquor, heedlessly got himself drunk, and when the rest took horse, he fell asleep and was found so next day by some of the people belonging to the merchant. Somebody that understood Scotch, asking him what he was, he said he was such-a-one's herd in Alloway, and by some means or other getting home again, he lived long to tell the world the wondrous tale.

I am, Dr Sir
Robt. Burns

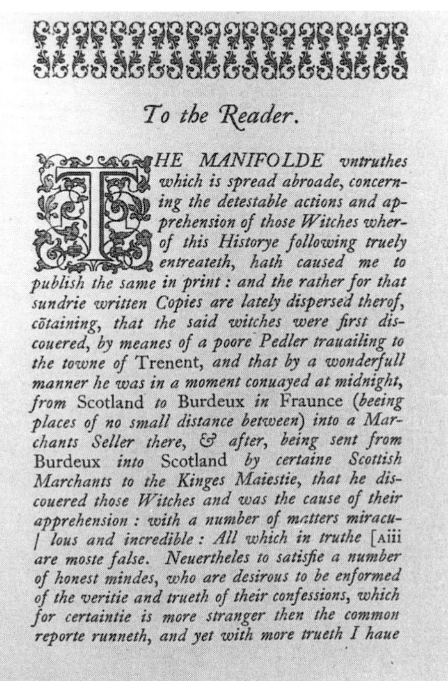

To the Reader.

THE MANIFOLDE vntruthes which is spread abroade, concerning the detestable actions and apprehension of those Witches wherof this Historye following truely entreateth, hath caused me to publish the same in print: and the rather for that sundrie written Copies are lately dispersed therof, cötaining, that the said witches were first discouered, by meanes of a poore Pedler trauailing to the towne of Trenent, *and that by a wonderfull manner he was in a moment conuayed at midnight, from* Scotland *to* Burdeux *in* Fraunce *(beeing places of no small distance between) into a Marchants Seller there, & after, being sent from* Burdeux *into* Scotland *by certaine Scottish Marchants to the Kinges Maiestie, that he discouered those Witches and was the cause of their apprehension: with a number of matters miraculous and incredible: All which in truthe* [Aiii *are moste false. Neuertheles to satisfie a number of honest mindes, who are desirous to be enformed of the veritie and trueth of their confessions, which for certaintie is more stranger then the common reporte runneth, and yet with more trueth I haue*

James VI's witch book.

Of course there was an element among the Reformers of the 16th century who tried to close down the world so that God's Kingdom on Earth would not be tainted. To these men, the merchant in the witch story was in deadly danger simply by being in a Catholic country, never mind the Inquisition. In 1592 the Edinburgh Presbytery, a powerful law making body at that time, alleged that "the merchands could not mak voyage in Spayne, without danger of their saulis". The merchants won their battle to continue the Spanish trade, asserting that otherwise they could never recover the debts owing them there. The ministers accepted this sound reasoning. A principle is a principle but money is money – thus has the Protestant ethic walked hand in hand with Capitalism for four hundred years; the passage in the Records concludes "for thir respectis, the ministers had patience for that time". Besides, Malaga, Mountain, Tent and Sack were probably the cheapest communion wines on the market!

To the narrow-minded zealots on the Protestant side, Maister Burne addressed his *"Disputation"* from the safety of Paris in 1581. In this Tract, written in the form of a dialogue between a Protestant and a Catholic, Burne allows the Protestant to voice his criticisms of the old Church, before contradicting them. In this extract he cites the commonplace criticism of idolatry in the Catholic Church as one in which the Protestant confuses the abuses made in relation to the images, with the existence of the images themselves.

Protestor: The images quhilk war usit in the Kirk war the caus of horribil idolatrie.

Catholic: This is ane commone place, quhairfra ye collect sophistical arguments from the abuse of a good thing to destroy it alluterlie and the richt use thairof.
Be the sam argument ye may collect that the sun and the moon should have been tane out of the firmament, because thay were worshippit be the gentils as gods: and ye may collect that your merchandis sould nocht pas to Burdeouse to bring home wyne, because it makis monie of your headdis dissie."

Burne obviously chose the last image as the one that would drive home his point in the debate – the clergy loved their wine but few would admit they ever abused it enough to let it go to their heads.

If the Reformation put an end to Scotland's political alliance with France, it did little to effect trade or the intellectual exchange which existed from the days of the founding of the Collège des Ecossais in 1325 until well after the creation of the Scots Universities themselves. Between 1494 and 1500, over 160 Scots graduated from the Sorbonne, forming "La Nation d'Ecosse" within the University. It was now the turn of the French Huguenots to look to the Scots for teaching, and we find scores of Teachers and Regents at Saumur, Montaubon, and the Collège de Guienne in Bordeaux, with names like Boyd, Primrose, Cameron, Hegate Johnston, Melvin and Balfour. Hundreds of French Huguenots settled in Scotland, bringing their vital weaving skills from Lyons and Flanders. It was persecution by the Catholic potentate, Archbishop Beaton, that forced Scotland's great Humanist poet and intellectual, George Buchanan, to travel to the Collège of Guienne. A Protestant who despised the fanatics on both sides, he straddled the reigns of James V, Mary, Queen of Scots, and her son James. Buchanan's genius ranged over Europe, influencing the University of Coimbra in Portugal, the teaching of the philosopher Montaigne in Bordeaux, and the formation of the young prince James VI in Edinburgh. He wrote the finest Latin poetry and drama of his day. In poetry he could soar from the lofty to the erotic and to the light. While in Bordeaux he composed a few verses in the latter vein, including one telling the youth of Bordeaux to scorn temporary pleasures ... and concentrate on learning Latin literature! The poem begins:

Vasconis tellus, genitrix virorum
fortium, blandi genitrix Lyaei

Aquitaine, mother of brave heroes
Mother of delightful Bacchus.

The reference to Bacchus would certainly have got home to the youth of Bordeaux and they may just have smiled at Buchanan's irony, given his reputation as a votary of the wine god himself. In the city archives there is a story that one night Buchanan staggered out of his lodgings on the Chartrons, roaring fu', wearing nothing but his dressing goonie and baffies. He was last seen hovering near a British ship loading claret. When he woke up he was somewhere off Ailsa Craig! After the Reformation it was safe for Buchanan to return to Scotland, and be trusted with the education of James. James appears to have been a clever enough scholar but where he most resembles his great tutor is his interest in poetry and music, and his love of the grape.

If the Reformers tried to ban from Edinburgh, "all menstrallis, piperis, fidleris, common sangsters and specially of badrie and filthy sangs, and siclike all vagabonds and maisterless persouns quha hes na service nor honest industrie to leif by", James made the Court a haven for his Castalian band of poets, led by Alexander Montgomerie, a Catholic newly returned from France with one of the Aubigny Stewarts. Already planning to take the English throne when Elizabeth, the murderess of his mother, finally died, James made the last Scottish Court one in which the native muse and the conviviality associated with it flourished. When he moved to London in 1603, both the language and its poetry ceased to have royal patronage, and the Court poets from then on wrote in English. Sir Robert Ayton went south with James, leaving his Scots behind as he crossed the Tweed:

Faire famous flood which some time did devyde
But now conjoynes two Diadems in one.

In James' Edinburgh period, wine played its part both in and out of court. With so many poets and minstrels to support, and no Arts Council to subsidise them, James, like every politician since, decided to tax the people's pleasure. In the diary of Robert Birrell, an Edinburgh Burgess we read these extracts from the year 1600:

> The 15 of Januarii there wes ane proclamation that the King sould have 12d (pennies) Scottish one everie pynt of wyne sold in taverns; the lyk of which imposte had not be heard tell of before.

The Vintners were obviously none too pleased, and most disobeyed the law … to their own peril. Before acting, James denounced the Vintners as rebels, putting them "to the horn" as the diarist says, i.e. he declared them rebels by sounding three blasts on a horn:

> 10 days of Marche, the Vintenars of wyne put to the horn for non payments to the King of 12d of the pynt of their wyne sauld.

James orders them to sell the wine at a higher price and the threat of punishment as rebels galvanises them:

> The 19 day of Marche, ane proclamation that nae Vintenars sould sell wyne better chepe nor 6/- the pynt under the paine of confiscatioune of the wyne; notwithstanding the Vintenaris willinglie sold the wyne for 5/- the pynt, and payit the impost.

James obviously was aware of the size of the Vintners' profit margin, given the fact they could make more money and pay the tax by selling a lot of wine at 5/- rather than raise the price to 6/-. He obviously felt justified in raising the impost because in 1600 we read that claret, the common drink was taxed at the same level as in 1578: "Burdeous wyne gave V schilling the pynt and wyne sek VII schillings." The continuing popularity of claret and the close trading links that survived between Scotland and France after the Reformation are confirmed by both a Frenchman and an Englishman. In 1568 Jean Bodin wrote, "The English, Scots and Scandinavians buy our wines, saffron and plums, but above all our salt." The salt from La Rochelle was essential to the West of Scotland fish curing industry; the East coast with its numerous salt pans, e.g. Prestonpans, came to rely on its own supply. The wine of the Charente, "Scherand" in Scots, was also popular in these days before it went into the production of cognac. The Englishman, Fynes Moryson, travelled Scotland in 1590, giving invaluable impressions of life and work.

> The cheefe trafficke of the Scots is in four places, namely at Camphire (Campveere, the Scots staple port) in Zeland, where they carry salt, the skins of weathers, otters, badgers and martens and bring thence corne. And at Burdeaux in France where they carry cloathes and the same skinnes and bring thence wine, prunes, walnuts and chessenuts. Thirdly within the Balticke Sea, and lastly in England. They drink pure wines, not with sugar as the English, yet at feasts they put comfits in the wine, after the French manner.

Is there perhaps a hint of James already drifting south in his taste for wine? In the Treasurer's accounts there is an entry dated "January 31st 1597. Item allowet to John Dougall for 42 pund succour to mixt his majesties wyne seck ye said monethe."

Despite what Moryson says, in those days before the cork gave wine the longevity which can make good wine great, people naturally flavoured the wine with spices and sugar to preserve it and make the oxidised taste of old wine more palatable. Sack became popular in Scotland during James' reign, along with other Peninsular wines. Wyne Sack is simply the Scotticization of the French *Vin Sec* or the Spanish *Vino Seco,* meaning Dry Wine. It is the progenitor of the great Sherris Sack. A Scots versifier of the period describes an argument breaking out among some friends, unsure whether the blame lies with the personalities involved or the strength of the peninsular wine:

> *"Whidder his malison tuike effect*
> *Or gif it was the gude wyne sect."*

Tent, from the Spanish *tinto* meaning red and associated with the port of Alicante, also grew in popularity then, as did "Hullock" – Aloque, Malaga, Canary and a sweet-honeyed wine called Bastard which was especially popular in Dundee!

James certainly has his eye on the English throne and the good favour of Elizabeth, when he passes on some spying information gathered by one of the Scottish merchants dealing in Canary, a strong fortified wine which many of the mainland Iberian wine-makers tried to copy. The letter to Elizabeth reads:

> January 1602 ... in the mean time I have thought good to inform you of such things as one of our wine merchants newly arrived out of Spain reported to me (as I shall never fail to acquaint you of anything that shall ever come to my ears which may concern your state). His news are these, that he was in the Canaries buying wine: it was written to him by friends of his out of Spain that 12,000 are prepared for Ireland against the beginning of April next, under the conduct of one Don Juan de Cordova.

However the only successful Spanish invasion at the time was that of her wine.

The wealth of wines, Spanish and others, available in Edinburgh is revealed in an anonymous poem, probably written by one of the Court circle and published in 1603, *"Ane verie excellent and delectabill Treatise intitulat Philotus."* It concerns a young girl who is offered a life of luxury if she will consent to be an old sick man's wife. The bawd, who acts as go-between, paints the delights she will enjoy, including fine clothes, servants, haute cuisine and fine wines.

Than tak to stanche the morning drouth,
Ane cup of Mavesie for your mouth,
For fume cast sucker in at fouth,
Togidder with a Toist:...

...Ane pair of plevaris pypping hait,
Ane Pertrick and ane Quailyie get,
Ane cup of Sack, sweit and weill set,
May for ane breckfast gaine...

... And now quhen all thir warks is done,
For your refresching efternone,
Gar bring unto your chalmer sone,
Sum daintie dische of meate:
Ane cup or twa with Muscadell...

...for your Collation tak and taist,
Sum lytill licht thing till disgest,
At nicht use Rense wyne ay almaist
For it is cauld and clene.

[Mavesie – Malmsey; fume – fragrance;
sucker – sugar; in at fouth – in abundance;
plevaris – plovers; chalmer – bedroom;
Rense – Rhenish]

Malmsey to quench the thirst first thing in the morning, a pair of plovers, a partridge, a quail and a glass of sack for breakfast, a tassie or twa of Muscadell instead of 4 o'clock tea and every evening a nice chilled bottle of Rhenish Beerenauslese to end the day on a honeyed note. However, it would take more than a Hogshead of Hullock to make this virtuous quean anybody's. The lass has her priorities right when she replies:

I grant all day to be weill tret,
Honours anew and hicht upset,
Bot quhat intreatment sall I get,
I pray you in my bed?
Bot with ane lairbair for to ly,
Ane auld deid stock, baith cauld and dry,
And all my dayes heir I deny,
That he my schankes sched.

[hicht upset – set up high;
lairbair – impotent weakling;
deny – rue, regret; schankes sched – legs parted;
lyre – skin; happing heit – covering warmth;
rumisching – erupting]

His eine half sunkin in his heid
His Lyre far caulder than the leid,
His frostie flesche as he war deid,
Will for na happing heit;
Unhealthsum hosting ever mair,
His filthsum flewme is nathing fair,
Ay rumisching with rift and rair,
Now, wow gif that be sweit."

All the sweet wines of the Levant will not perfume the breath of this old bag of phlegm, says the lass, rejecting his suit in future expectation of the lover her youth and beauty deserves. It was an Irishman who wrote that a queer was a man who preferred women to alcohol. Chateau d'Yquem is a beautiful liquid but pity those who have taken all their earthly pleasure from the glycerol *cuisses* in a wine glass!

When he was not enjoying the poetry of the Court, James VI loved to leave that sophisticated milieu and enjoy the pleasures of tavern life. He shared his Stewart ancestor Robert II's penchant for that most basic of old Scots delicacies – sheep's heid. The inn at Duddingston, known today as Ye Sheep's Heid Tavern was where he sampled it. On the site of one of the oldest taverns on the shore of Leith today, The King's Wark, stood an earlier building of the same name, gifted by James to one Bernard Lyndsay. Lyndsay was James' loyal Groom of the Royal Chamber – Chalmer Chield in the vernacular – and his lease of this huge building was on the proviso that one of the four cellars underneath would be retained as the King's personal wine cellar. Like the Vaults, a few hundred yards away, the cellars provided perfect conditions for laying down the King's vintages. Bernard, who gave his name to one of Leith's main streets, provided four-star accommodation with a tennis court – "for the recreation of His Majesty, and of foreigners of rank resorting to the Kingdom, to whom it afforded great satisfaction and delight."

The hospitality was such that John Taylor the Water Poet from England who included a visit to the King's Wark in his "Pennyless Pilgrimage" could write of Bernard,

> Hee knew my estate was not guilty, because I brought guilt with me (more than my sins, and they would not pass for current there), hee therefore did replenish the vaustity of my empty purse, and discharged a piece at mee with two bullets of gold, each being in value, worth eleven shillings, white money.

Taylor seems to have been treated similarly everywhere he went. If the Scots were poor, they were always hospitable! It may be Bernard's cellar that is referred to in the Treasury Account books for 1598 when both Scots and Dutch had a good carousal!

"8th June. His Majestie causit certane Duchemen be tane to the wyne sellar to drink."

No portraits of James' Chalmer Chield survive, but in the portrait of Viscount Stormont, Cup Bearer to the King, we see a fine symbol of the royal court. In the original painting, the liquid is the colour of "the blood red wine" the Ballad says the King quaffed in the time of Sir Patrick Spens and the Auld Alliance. After 1603, and the removal of the Court to London, few Kings would return North to toast the country or its people.

Viscount Stormont, cup-bearer to James VI.

THE PIER O' LEITH

4

When Agricola attempted to extend his Empire north of the Forth and Clyde in 83 A.D., it is likely that his main supply depot for arms, food and wine, was somewhere near the shore of what is now the town of Leith. Wine and Leith then have an intimate relationship going back to Agricola, and Quintus Lollius Urbicus, the man who built the Antonine Wall. Wine was the everyday beverage of the legions and containers for its storage have been found in the Lothians dating from the Roman Occupation.

If the tunnage of wine imported from Gaul to Leith at the end of the 1st century is pure conjecture, eleven hundred years later we enter the period where documents exist to substantiate Leith's claim as an ancient wine port. The Vaults, those dank, gloomy caverns hanging with a fungus known only in ancient wine cellars on the continent, have stored claret from the time they are first mentioned in the records of the 12th and 13th centuries, through to the present day. From the reign of Alexander III we saw how Leith exported dried fish to France, its shippers supplying food for the Catholic faithful on the numerous fast days imposed by the Church, when no meat was allowed. In return for the fish, the shippers brought home Gascon wine. The Church engaged in commerce itself and we know that the Abbot of Holyrood, an Abbey long before it was a Palace, had several fishing vessels at North Leith. It also had an ample cellar, for there's reference to the King storing his wine there.

That Religious Orders did not merely use wine for communion is evident in the close links between the Vaults and the Monks of St. Anthony after the foundation of their preceptory in 1430. It was the local laird, Robert Logan of Restalrig who brought over Canons of the Order of St. Anthony from Vienne in France, and helped establish them with income from rents of land around Edinburgh. 13th century documents relating to the Vaults suggest the Abbey of Holyrood held lands there and it is likely that it was Holyrood which originally received benefices from the wine landed at the Wine Quay a few hundred yards away. It was certainly the wine trade which built the preceptory, garden, orchard and hospital of St. Anthony after 1430.

Coming from Vienne on the Rhône, the brothers would be connoisseurs of their excellent local Côte Rôtie wine, so would have a good initial grounding in the wine trade. The Canons had the right to a chopin (quart) of wine out of every tun landed at Leith. Undoubtedly they kept a few choice chopins to themselves, but such was

their allowance that good profits must have accrued on what they sold. An underground passage, part of which can still be traced under the Kirkgate, linked the preceptory with the Vaults, so the Canons could keep a close eye on their *caisse d'épargne.* They also controlled the auction of the wine to the Edinburgh Vintners, who in turn formed themselves into a Guild called the Fraternity of St. Anthony, the good Saint becoming the patron of Auld Reekie's wine merchants. The monks, then, held a lucrative as well as privileged position. At that time only Burgesses of the Royal Burgh, Edinburgh, had the right to deal in foreign produce, so while Leithers could keep ale houses, the more expensive commodity, wine, was the monopoly of the Edinburgh merchant Burgesses. The French Leithers were the only citizens of the port allowed to touch the precious liquid. The monks were free from the taint of resentment Leithers reserved for their monopolist overlords, as their profits endowed a hospital for the poor, and probably a school for the children of the port as well.

Roman wine jug with Bacchus, found in Scotland.

The number of restrictive laws passed by the Royal Burgh against the growing band of Leith merchant adventurers in the 16th century, shows how desperate the Vintners were to hold on to what they had, and how important was the faith they had in the monks' honesty. It was an incident when the latter was brought into question that gave rise to a piece of Leith folklore, recounted in *Tales of Old Leith* by James Marshall. Legend has it that on dark, quiet nights the sound of a cooper's

◄ *The Pier of Leith.*

tapping can be heard from the warehouses at the head of the Kirkgate. The old cooper, on the few occasions he has been sighted, works wearily at his barrel, but just when it looks as if one final tap will knock the final stave in place … crash, the wine cask falls apart and he has to start again.

The legend stems from the 15th century when the Abbot, to his horror, found out that someone was stealing wine from the Vaults. As the monks were well aware of the privileges they enjoyed and would be foolish to hurt them, suspicion fell on the cooper Henry Douglas who did not belong to the order. Douglas denied any knowledge of the theft, but he was eventually caught out by a wily hermit who dwelt at St. Anthony's chapel on the slopes of Arthur's Seat. He decided to investigate the problem for himself:

> So off he went to the vaults, and there he found Henry Douglas busy making a cask. The hermit began talking to the cooper about the missing wine and the cunning man said he hoped the thief would soon be discovered, and punished as he should be. At this, the hermit looked at Douglas, and said 'I think you know more about this than you have admitted.' Henry Douglas looked scandalised. 'Me?' he said, 'I don't know a thing about it. I swear I know nothing. And if I'm telling a lie, may I never head this cask!'
>
> The hermit looked at him for a moment in silence, and then said, 'Amen! And may it please holy St. Anthony to grant your prayer'.
>
> The words were hardly out of his mouth, when the cask Henry Douglas was working on

The Vintner's Room, the Vaults.

fell apart into staves at his feet. Stricken by conscience, the wicked cooper ran away in a panic. He ran into the furthest parts of the great vaults, and was never seen in daylight again, although the sound of his hammer was often heard by the monks when they had to visit the vaults.

Many years later the Preceptory was cleared away, and the ghostly cooper carried on his endless work in the Tobacco Warehouse in Quality Street. He spent all his time trying to put a cask together, only to see it collapse just before it was finished. The old Tobacco Warehouse has gone now, and no one has heard the ghostly cooper at work for a long time past, but maybe he is still at work in some other building in Old Leith. Who knows??

If Mr. Douglas had confined his stealing to the property of the haughty Burgesses of Edinburgh he would have been applauded by the majority of the citizens of Leith. The lack of love between the sister burghs, which many attribute to the class divisions of the 20th century, have their origins in the struggle between two groups of the Scottish middle class over a period of three hundred years. Nowhere is the struggle seen more clearly than in the wine trade.

Leith's subservience to Edinburgh stems from the end of the 14th century when Logan of Restalrig granted Edinburgh the privilege of extending the Port of Leith, renouncing at the same time and for all time the right to deal in retail goods, including wine. The early Stewart Kings who levied tax from the Royal Burghs, granted more and more privileges to the Edinburgh burgesses, giving them the right to tax every ship coming into port, charging "Strangers", and that included Leithers, a higher rate of duty than citizens of the capital. In the reign of James III the Edinburgh council were allowed to reduce the Leithers to an intolerable level of second-class citizenship, "it is statute and ordainit that gif ony merchand of this toun takes ony man of Leyth in company with him in his merchandice making, he sall pay an unlaw (fine) of 11/- to the Kirk werk, and tyne fredome for year and a day." The "fredome" referred to is the freedom to trade; Leithers as unfreemen were to serve the freemen. In the Wine Act of 1520 it is stated that representatives of the "confraternitie of Sanct Anthone" should evenly divide any parcel of wine arriving in Leith and fix its price "within this toun of Edinburgh and nocht in Leith, and that nane of the tavernars wyffis, nor wemen servandis, pas to Leith in time to cum till waill (choose), see or buy ony wynis under the pane of the unlaw contenit in the auld actis." The difficulty in enforcing such a restrictive law is revealed in the constant processes brought against Leithers in the Royal burgh:

21 Dec. 1514. "My Lord Principale Provest President, baillies and counsall ordanis the officers to warn and charge all men of Leyth that tappis or sellis wyne or other merchandise stuf within the said toun of Leyth, in hourting of the privilege of this toun of Edinburgh, to compeir befoir thame."

> 26th October, 1525. The provost, bailies, and counsall statutis and ordanis that na manner of persoun, tavernour, and other nycht-bour of this burgh sell nor tape wyne in thair taverne or houssis darrer nor for 12d the pynt, under the pane of escheiting and deling of thair wyne but favoris; and als ordanis ane officer to pas to Leith and dischairg all maner of personis in Leith fra ony buying, tapping of wyne in thair houssis with certificatioun, and thai do in contrare heirof, that the toun will putt the Kingis lettres and proces of hornying till execution upoun thame without favouris.

> On 9th August 1520 – The Provest, Baillies and Counsall decernis and ordanis William Forsyth to content and pay to the Dene of Gild, for reparation of the kirk, the soume of £5 for the selling of his wyne openlie in the taveroun in Leith.

The bourgeois of Edinburgh huffed and puffed and jealously guarded their ill-deserved monopoly. Meanwhile, the reign of James IV saw the rise of a class of merchant adventurers in Leith, men such as William Brownhill, David Falconer, the Bartons, who were equally useful to the expanding maritime nation as naval commanders, foreign traders or pirates. Judicious marriages and alliances had given Scots favourable access to the Baltic and the Low Countries, and it was to the Scots staple port at Bruges, then Middleburg and Veere that the merchants repaired, making profit on, among other goods, wine from the Rhineland and Burgundy.

The status of the shippers and the importance of the Scots trade to the Netherlands is revealed in 1509 when, after the Scots had moved their community to Veere, the Burgesses of Middleburg, anxious to win back the Scots, entertained Robert Barton, "One of the principal merchants of Scotland", and presented him with three flagons of Hock.

To give an indication of the expansion of Scottish trade in James' reign, one can examine the toll figures of ships traversing the Oresund between 1497 and 1503 and discover that Scots vessels doubled from 21 to 43. James, trying to build Scottish political influence in Europe, favoured his skippers and allowed them to flaunt Edinburgh's petty controls. He also gave them licence, through issuing letters of marque, to attack any ship of a nation that had previously attacked a Scottish ship, a licence to plunder and rob recognised by all the men who undertook the "wyld aventoures" as foreign trade was aptly called. The status of families like the Bartons is described by Patrick Tyteler:

> The family of the Bartons which for two generations had been prolific of naval commanders, were entrusted by this monarch (James IV) with the principal authority in all maritime and commercial matters: they purchased vessels for him on the continent, they invited into his kingdom the most skilful ship-wrights; they sold some of their own ships to the King, and vindicated the honour of their flag whenever it was insulted with a readiness and severity of retaliation which inspired respect and terror.

The Portuguese pirates who had robbed John Barton's ship the *"Juliana"* at Sluis in 1473 certainly brought terror on any of their countrymen who came across a Barton vessel. James IV, having tried unsuccessfully to have his favourite's goods restored through the intercession of the King of Portugal, allowed the Bartons free rein. John's sons Robert and Andrew restored family and national honour and wealth with interest. In one gruesome incident in 1506, Andrew, carrying herring to Bordeaux for claret, not only attacked a Portuguese vessel and appropriated its cargo, but also decapitated the sailors, packed the heads like soused herring in an empty barrel and sent the cargo of "potted heid" back to Leith in triumph.

In 1509 John Barton was still getting his own back on the Portuguese, attacking two ships laden with sugar off Madeira. The fact that both were carrying cargo for English and Flemish owners made no difference, John told the Englishmen that he could not read the bill of lading, threw it away and took everything he fancied. James IV, building up his navy for its abortive intervention for France in 1513, turned a blind eye to his mariners' hobby, as it gave them good practice for war. Bishop Leslie wrote of the adeptness of the Bartons in destruction and robbery; "Nather culd the King of Portugal be counsel, nather his subjects of Portugal be strength or force ever hinder the Bartons fra spoilzie and reife".

With the death of James IV after Flodden, Edinburgh again tried to curb the freedom of the skippers, but Robert Barton held onto his political influence. As Royal Comptroller, he was able to pay off the Royal Burgh authorities against the superior Crown Authority to the benefit of himself and his fellow burgesses of Leith. The Bartons grew in wealth and influence and it is against their story that we must balance the constant law suits of the Edinburgh burgesses – for every prosecution, there must have been ten Leithers who built their trade surreptitiously and successfully, if somewhat dishonestly. The letters of marque, which were the foundation of the Barton family's wealth were finally revoked in the Reformation parliament of 1563. Piracy and privateering were not going to be part of God's Kingdom on Earth.

Neither was the confraternity of St. Anthony. With the vigorous self-assuredness which characterises the Provost's and Burgesses' dealings with the unfree men of Leith before the Reformation, they now turned on the Canons of St. Anthony and their privileges. The Edinburgh Records for 1561 state:

> The provest, baillie and counsale understanding that in the time of blindness and myscknawledge of the treuth, there wes be the consent of the nychtbouris of this burgh ane confrarie and bruderheid of ventares of wyne, quhilk payet of every puntioun wyne ane choppin to Sanct Anthonis altar for systenying of idolatrie and wikitnes. And sen at this present it hes plesit the Almychtie to open the eyes of all people, sae that it is knowin

that all sic confrareis, bandis, and promisses, inventit by the ungodlie sort of papists for filling of thair bellies, ar contrair to the will and glorye of God, thairfore ordainis proclamatioun to be made at all pairtes of this burgh neidfull, discharging the confrarie of Sanct Anthonis, the Hally Blude, and all uther confrareis quatsumever quhilk hes bene heirtofore in tyme of ignorance. And all sic duties as was gevin thairto according to the statutis maid heir-anent, to be uptaikin and applyit to the puir, under all heist pane that to the offender may be input at the will and plesour of the juges present and to cum.

[puntioun – barrel; choppin – quart]

The Presbyterians' bark was a lot worse than their bite and no harm was done to the Canons who passed away the rest of their days in Leith. Actually, the use of the impost was little changed pre- or post-Reformation. Another extract from the Records is more specific, "that now of the tun of wyne there be uplift … 12d allanerlie to be put in a box and disponit for sustenying of the puir and falit brethren merchants and craftsmen of this burgh." The rents of the land and other properties belonging to St. Anthony were bestowed by James VI on the Kirk Session of South Leith, the local Parish church. The stone of the old hospital run by the Canons, and destroyed during the English siege in 1560, was probably used in the construction of the new King James Hospital, which was opened in 1620 and maintained from the wine fund. The new hospital continued to be supported by the wine trade and lasted through the great days of Leith-bottled claret and port, eventually closing in 1822. Astonishingly, the King James Fund is still in existence in 1994 and pays out small pensions to the needy in the Port of Leith.

The sense of unbroken continuation from pre-Reformation to the present day is also provided by the Vaults. After the demise of the Confraternity of St. Anthony,

The Porters' Stone.

the control of the wine trade was continued by the Vintners Guild, a division of the Merchant Guild of Edinburgh. In the Vintners room, whose 17th century stucco relief represents babes frolicking among vines, the auctioneer, normally the President of the Guild, stood in his alcove and sold off the wine to the guild brothers. The wine had already been tasted and its price fixed so the auction was simply concerned with its distribution. When that was agreed upon, the merchants were faced with the task of transporting the casks to Edinburgh. Prior to the construction of Leith Walk by General Leslie in 1650, the dirt tracks between the Port and the City were muddy and dangerous, and quite apart from the bumping the wine would have suffered, there was the added peril of casks falling off the cart and breaking. It appears that an inferior branch of the Dock Porters Corporation of Leith, the Rollers, were entrusted with the task of transporting the wine to the city. As their name implies, they operated in a line spaced ten yards from one another, rolling the barrels along, with the last one to roll the barrel looping round to place himself in front of the first person in the line. The rollers were not Freemen porters and did not have the right to vote in the Porters Corporation. They did however have controlled entry and they still existed as a trade as late as 1763: "We likewise ordain that no man shall be admitted as a roller unless he pay the sum of 10 shillings to the box and one shilling for a rent and one shilling yearly."

One hopes that by that time the farthest they had to roll the barrels was from the Wine Quay to the Vaults. At the same period the Porters were divided into four companies, one of which, Telfers, was also known as the Wine Company. This suggests a closed shop of Porters who handled only the wine landed in Leith. A sculptured stone which used to be seen in Tolbooth Wynd, dating from the 17th century, illustrates the work of the Wine Porters. It depicts a ship arriving at the shore, a winch to wind the hogsheads out of its hold, the Porters, or Stingmen as they were also known, carrying the casks slung on a pole balanced on their shoulder, and finally a building which could represent the Vaults as they were in 1673 or the King's Wark on the shore which was used as a customs house for storing wine. The Wine Porters appear to have enjoyed a privileged position among the incorporated trades in Leith.

If the wine trade in Leith was becoming more and more organised, it still had to contend with Edinburgh's futile attempts to control it. Realising the high taxes he drew from the wine merchants in the Royal Burgh, but aware of the enterprise of the inhabitants of the Burgh of Barony in procuring the wine, James VI endeavoured to please both sides, but above all he procured for himself as much wine and wine impost as he could legally obtain.

During James' minority, the Regent Morton in 1576 insisted that he be "first servit" with the choice of wines landed, appropriating them to his residence at Dalkeith, rather than Stirling where they could do the Prince harm. James appointed as "symleir" or sampler, a wine baillie who made sure that the Royal household got its cut of any wine imported:

> Stirling 3rd May 1578 – The Kings Majestie and Lordis of Secreit Counsale being informit that thair is divers schippis with wynes laitlie arrivit and to arrive at the portis of Leyth, Dundee and utheris pairtis of this realme of the first and best thairof it is convenient that his majestie be servit for the use of furnissing of His Heines hous … Thairfour ordanis letters to be direct to officiars of the Kings sherreffis in that part, chargeing them to pas, command and charge all and sindry persons alreaddy arryvit or that sal happin to arryve with ony wynes … that they reteine and keep the same wynis within the ship burde unlossit, quhill the same be taistit, waillit and ane tun of every ten tunnes of the saidis wynes markit and laid in sellar to oure Soverane Lordis use be his Hienes sumleir or Thomas Lindsay, Snawdoun herauld in Leth.
>
> [Unlossit – untouched; quhill – until; waillit – chosen]

The civic dignitaries of Edinburgh were most perturbed that a Leither, Thomas Lyndsay, should have the privilege of supplying the King's wines and remained "greitlie hurt" until the King agreed to see them and cancel Lyndsay's commission as Symleir – "this toun to tak upon handis to cause the King be furnist of wynis". James ignored the appeal but made sure that he kept in with the Burgesses. If they could be overbearing with their insistence on the form "Lord-superioures of the toun of Leyth" after their title, and boring with their petty jealousies and prosaic language, their strict trade controls were extremely useful to a sovereign who valued their revenue earning power. Besides, as James proved when he taxed the taverners on the wine sold by the pint, the taverners in Leith selling wine illegally could well afford at least the first and second fine imposed on them: "fyve pundis for the first falt, and ten pundis for the second falt, and ane puntioun of wyne for the thrid falt, so oft as they failye."

In 1591 James "as becomes a provident Prince" delighted the capital's merchants by waiving the impost on wine they sold outwith Scotland, which had previously been taxed on the same level as the wine they landed at home. The wine landed at Leith raised £8 for James on every tun. His letter to the Royal Burgh's convention of April 21st 1591 concludes that he will always be a "loving prince … so lang as the said impost is liftit and that the saidis merchants behafis themeselfis dewtifullie and thankfullie towards his majestie and defraudis him nocht in payment thereof!" Yet, while he sweet-talked the Royal Burghs he set about loosening their restrictive monopoly in the selling of wine. Perhaps as a prelude to taxing the wines sold in taverns, his ordination in 1596 allowed Leithers to sell wines there where previously

Hogsheads of wine being landed at Leith circa 1800.

they could only sell ale:

> ... the kingis majestie ... gevis license and libertie to the haill ventaris of wyne within the toun of Leith to vent and sell their wynis notwithstanding ony discharge gevin be the saidis provest and baillie of Edinburgh on the contrair.

The true mark of a politician, James gives the Leithers what they want, and has a joke with them at Edinburgh's expense, but what he is actually doing is opening up more premises which can be legally taxed in the near future. S.G.E. Lythe and J. Butt have estimated that in the early years of the 17th century, Leith was importing something in the region of 250,000 gallons per annum. With the impost for wine settling at around £32.8/- per tun in 1612, one sees why James looked after his wine trade – in Leith alone it brought him an annual income of over £32,000.

THE LAND OF SWEET BORDEAUX

5

One of the earliest references to claret in Scotland was in 1253 when Alexander III took delivery of 100 tons of Gascon wines thanks to the efforts of a citizen of Perth, John Fleming. This was probably not the first time Scots were able to enjoy claret – it was not to be the last. Claret, or as it has been variously given in Scots – Clarette, clarrett, clarit, and so on – became a staple beverage throughout Scotland, a position it shared with locally produced beer and ale.

Early in our acquaintance with this wine, claret was a thinnish, light-coloured liquor which was shipped almost immediately after the *vendanges* and fermentation had been completed, and drunk with almost indecent haste for fear of it turning sour. By the following summer the wine was exhausted, and attempts to rectify the sourness through sugaring would serve to disguise the wine's taste rather than improve. But the wine-drinker was consoled in the fact that his cellar would be restocked with claret before the year's end. John Nicoll, the 17th century Edinburgh diarist, records one astonishingly early delivery:

> Upone the 21 of October 1659, thair come to the raid of Leith, ane schip full of Frensche Burdeaux wyne, quhich was thocht to be vary airlie, and by the accustumat tyme of bringing in Frensche wyne so airlie.

Nicoll's observations suggest that there is little "new" in the concept of Beaujolais Nouveau. The "miracles" of modern wine production technology which will allow drinkable wines from that part of France to be ready by mid-November have, it appears, some way to go before the achievements in 17th century Bordeaux can be matched.

Despite the urgency with which Scots then disposed of their wine, it was only a matter of decades later that they were differentiating their clarets into "old" and "new". "New" claret was wine produced within the previous year, while "old" ones were wines which had been around longer. The latter were neither pricked nor turned – in fact in many instances they were preferable to the "new" wines, and wine merchants anxious that clients would drink claret at its best often gave instructions to ensure that it was not inadvertently drunk too soon. The Earl of Marchmont in taking delivery of claret in 1767 from his supplier, Oliphant of Ayr, is advised:

> As the wine is new ... it will be very unfit to drink for some time, we would recommend that your Lordship would order it into a good cellar and let it lye ... by giving [it] a little more time it will prove a very high flavoured excellent wine.

About this time Bishop Forbes of Ross and Caithness while on an episcopal visit to one of his flock – Munro of Culcairn, was happily drinking a 13-year-old claret. Had he attempted this less than a century before, poisoning would have been the least of the consequences.

The rapid transformation of claret's nature was dependent on one simple invention – the cork. Before this the means available to stopper wine were ineffective. Air would leak around and through bungs on hogsheads, and within days the wine would spoil. Storing wine in hogsheads was in any case unsatisfactory. As each successive pint was drawn off, a corresponding amount of air would occupy the space vacated, thereby accelerating the wine's oxidation. Unless the hogshead was to be consumed at one sitting the only alternative was to have its contents bottled. But rags stuffed in the necks of bottles were only marginally better a means of preventing the wine's contact with air. The cork was a crucial invention which precipitated a fundamental departure in the history of wine. When forced into the bottle's orifice, the cork's elastic qualities moulded it perfectly to the shape of the neck, and as long as it was not allowed to dry out, it formed an effective barrier between wine and air. Once sealed with wax the wine within was safe. Doubtless the security this combination of cork and wax afforded inspired the simile in the Gaelic song *"An Earbag"* in which the impermeability of the eponymous ship's hull was compared with a *"botul fion 's ceir oirr' "* – a waxed wine bottle.

The cork made its appearance towards the end of the 17th century and was to pave the way for a range of innovations in wine production technology during the following century. The introduction of these innovations has incidentally created what is probably the most notable misnomer in the business. "Clairette", the Gascon word from which claret is derived, implies a freshness and lightness of colour, resulting from the practice of mixing red and white grapes in the wine's making. In contrast, today the word claret is evocative of a deep red and full-bodied wine, capable of ageing many years before its optimum quality is attained. Curiously, despite the changing nature of the wine, the provenance of claret has always remained strictly defined – true clarets are invariably red wines produced in the vicinity of Bordeaux – in other words, within that area of Gascony and Guienne which is roughly coincident with the Department of the Gironde in modern day administrative terms.

Warner Allen once said:

> A great claret is the queen of all natural wines and ... the highest perfection of all wines that have ever been made. It is delicate and harmonious beyond all others; the manifold sensations that it produces are of the most exquisite subtlety, and their intensity is so

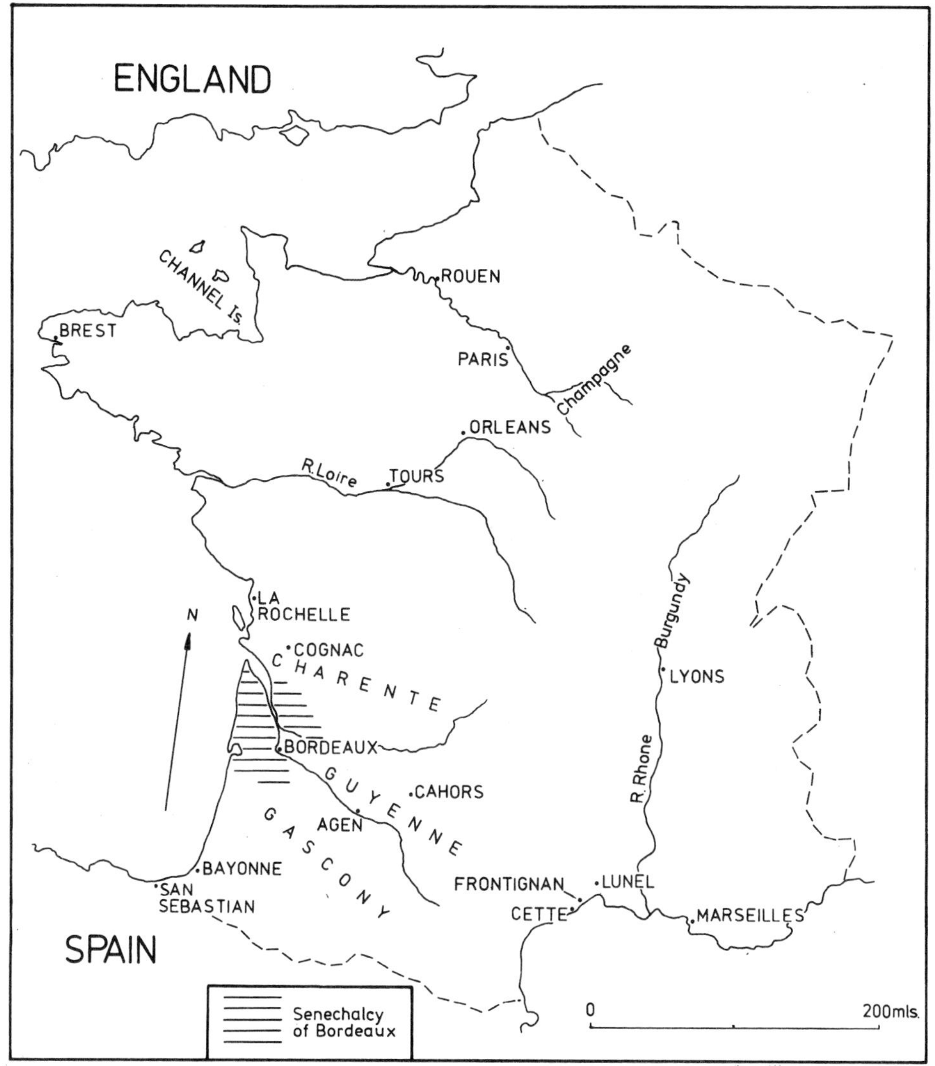

The Vineyards of France.

> perfectly balanced and their quality so admirably harmonised that there is no clash or predominance, but bouquets, aroma, velvet, body and all blended into an ideal whole.

Given such eloquent praise from such an esteemed connoisseur, it may seem contradictory to suggest that if French vignerons were given the equivalent of 200,000 acres of vines, to plant anywhere in France strictly on the basis of climatic and soil suitability, their choice would probably exclude the homeland of these great clarets – the Bordeaux region. Eminent French geographers, meteorologists and wine scientists have in recent years tended to question the area's suitability for viticulture, pointing to its characteristically wet Springs, early Autumn frosts, variability in Summer temperatures from year to year, and so on. But the fact of the matter is that there are 200,000 acres of vineyard in the Bordeaux region, producing somewhere in the region of 4 to 5 million hectolitres of wine annually, one-third of which is white and the remainder claret. No fewer than 30,000 vignerons pamper these vineyards assiduously, lavishing care and attention on the wines produced, and despite what learned scientists say, 30,000 Bordelais cannot be wrong!

This paradox is explained in the fact that the Bordeaux vineyards' existence relates more to historical factors than geographical ones. A fortunate blend of social and political circumstances in the past initiated and fuelled the development of wine production in the area. The vineyard itself must be more than 1500 years old since already by 300 AD the wines of the region were being highly recommended. Ausonius, the Gallo-Roman poet whose links with the area are maintained through the name of the celebrated St. Emilion growth, Chateau Ausone, wrote nostalgically about his Bordelais homeland, its vine-carpeted slopes resembling waves; its creditable wines. Fortunately for Ausonius, and certainly for us, the edict of the Emperor Domitien a couple of centuries before, ordering the uprooting of all vineyards in the Empire outside Rome, had been effectively ignored. An *amateur* of wine like Ausonius would have been grateful that the vineyards of the region survived that particular attempt to stifle them virtually at birth.

The development of Bordeaux's vineyard over the seven or eight centuries after Ausonius was hardly remarkable since similar progress had been made almost universally throughout continental Europe. Every town of any size supported vineyards to cater for local demand – the possibilities of satisfying thirst through trade being somewhat limited. Even unlikely places such as England could at the time of the Domesday Book boast some vineyards, most of which were sporadically distributed in the south of the country. The English need hardly have bothered, at least according to Peter de Blois, a French camp follower of Henry II, who claimed that English wines could only be drunk with closed eyes and clenched teeth. We have no record of the success of Scottish attempts to produce wine at the time and to be fair to our southern neighbours whose wine produced such physical reactions, the facial contortions and grimaces resulting from a slug of "Chateau Kirk o' Shotts 1195" would probably have been much worse. Very wisely, buying in wine from coastal vineyards on the continent was generally considered a better option by the Scots.

Foreign trade in wine was well advanced by an early date. Alexander III's household expenditure in 1267 included the payment of £439 Scots on 178 hogsheads of imported wine. Scottish ships visited Bordeaux in search of Gascony wine, the best growths of which came from the upper reaches of the Garonne and

The Vendange at Lafite

Dordogne rivers, where the climate proved more suitable to wine production than in the moister coastlands in the Bordeaux area. Haut Pays (High Country) wines, as they were to be called in later centuries, were produced in the general vicinity of the towns of Cahors, Gaillac and Bergerac, but for their exportation were obliged to go through the port of Bordeaux. Other ports on the French west coast were also frequented for consignments of wine. The contemporary epic *"La Bataille des Vins"* records Scots among the nationalities making regular visits to La Rochelle for wine.

Lors dist le vins de Li Rocele...
Je repais trestoute Engleterre
Bretons, Normans, Flamens, Galois
Et les Escos et les Irois
Norois et cels de Danemarcke

Though now totally eclipsed by Bordeaux as a wine port, La Rochelle, in the 12th century when this epic was written, seemed a very attractive proposition for foreign traders since shipments of both salt and wine could be uplifted. Lack of variety in exportable produce operated against Bordeaux.

The Middle Ages swept aside any early commercial disadvantages besetting wine production in the Bordeaux region, and also created circumstances which made irrelevant its climatic drawbacks. This upturn in fortune had its origins in one event

– the marriage in 1152 of Henry Plantagenet to Eleanor of Aquitaine. Eleanor was considered one of the most eligible women in French history, indeed anyone with a dowry which included a massive chunk of western France – Poitou, Brittany, Gascony, the Auvergne and Limousin – would be hard to upstage. The English were delighted for they could now open their eyes and unclench their teeth, in the sure knowledge that their "home brew" could be replaced with wine from that part of France which Henry secured for the English kingdom through ensnaring Eleanor.

Not that the French were ecstatic about the loss of the greater part of their western seaboard. Over the ensuing couple of centuries their armies pared away at these English possessions and by the end of the 14th century only a relatively small area focusing on Guienne, Gascony and Bordeaux remained. Simultaneously the vineyard which catered for the high English demand was increasingly concentrated around the confluence of the Garonne and Dordogne rivers, and the wines were shipped through the city itself.

Theoretically the Scots merchants who visited Bordeaux at this time were negotiating with the "Auld Enemy", but it seems that they were rather more interested in the practical considerations of supplying themselves with wines, than avoiding patronising the foe. On the other hand the Bordelais had no compunction about dispatching vast quantities of wine to encourage the English army while on one of its many bellicose excursions into Scotland. In 1317 the Mayor and Magistrates of Bordeaux granted a gift of 500 hogsheads for one such venture and some 15 years later another 50 hogsheads arrived at Perth for the English army encamped there.

Fearful of the inexorable diminution of their territory in France, successive English monarchs tried to shore up their remaining toehold in Guienne and Gascony by sweetening the local population with certain privileges concerning their wine. It was decreed that only wines produced in the Seneschalcy of Bordeaux, the "vins de ville" as they were called, could be brought to the city, sold there and exported without restriction. On the other hand, wine from beyond the Seneschalcy, the Haut Pays wine, was subject to an array of measures designed to impede movement and deny access to markets. The eventual return of Bordeaux to French rule did not remove these privileges for locally produced wine. Instead they were reinforced as a means of ensuring that any residual pro-English sentiments were submerged by such a magnanimous gesture by the new authority. One significant difference was introduced – only the wines produced by burgesses of the city were privileged. Non-burgess wine from within the Seneschalcy were deprived of any rights they might have had.

Despite continuing objections from the wine-producing areas in the high country against the *"Privilèges"* which threatened their vineyards' lifeblood, legislation in favour of the local burgess population developed. At their apogee just before the French Revolution when they were ultimately abolished, the privileges were blatant, crude and unsubtle measures. They were simply designed to protect the interests of the Bordelais burgesses against competition from vineyards which had the misfortune of having to export their produce through Bordeaux. The Haut Pays wines were not allowed to enter Bordeaux before the 11th of November in any year. By that date the Seneschalcy wines had been sold to foreign traders at premium prices. Few traders would have remained in the city as late as the middle of November since returning North before winter began with a vengeance, or in the case of the Baltic ships, before ports iced up, was a major consideration. The Haut Pays wine could be sold when the fleet returned in the Spring, but then prices would be lower, the wine was beginning to turn and commercial possibilities were at a pretty low ebb. Were there Haut Pays wines remaining unsold in their special cellars in Chartrons, then on the outskirts of the city, they were returned upriver to their place of origin or distilled into brandy. All this had to be achieved by the 8th September to ensure that the new vintage of "vins de ville" once again had the market to themselves. To distinguish high country wines from privileged ones the *Parlement de Bordeaux* specified hogsheads of different gauges in which they were to be stored. Fair enough one might imagine, but the reality was anything but fair. The Haut Pays hogshead was smaller and much less robust than that of the privileged wines and consequently more prone to damage and spoilage. As if to rub salt in an already gaping wound, the taxes to be paid on hogsheads brought to the city for sale was by the container irrespective of its volume. With their larger hogsheads the Burgesses could bring about 1/7th more wine for the same tax than producers in the high country. It was little wonder that there was a concentration of vineyards in the Seneschalcy of Bordeaux while those in districts beyond stagnated and contracted. These regulations were strictly enforced and there was no quarter for anyone found guilty of their contravention. In 1556 for example some Scottish merchants who attempted to steal a march on others by having Haut Pays wines brought to the city before the permitted time were punished with a hefty fine.

Claret shipments were organised at the Bordeaux end by local négociants (dealers) and the masters of the vessels involved in the trade formed the main contact between the Scottish client and his supplier. Towards the end of the 16th century, it became increasingly possible for buyers to deal with compatriots in Bordeaux as Scots emigrés joined the growing colony of foreign businessmen established in the city. As his by-name "L'Escot" suggests, one of the earliest among these was an Alexander Bezet (Bissett?) who was already established in Bordeaux by 1540. The wine trade was his major preoccupation, but in his spare time he arranged for members of his family to be found apprenticeships in Bordeaux. His brother William was set up with a local surgeon, Guilhem Beguey, while a relation, his namesake, was apprenticed to Jeannot de Saulx to learn the wine business. In a reciprocal agreement de Saulx's son Jean was apprenticed to a business in Edinburgh. A little more about Bezet is discovered when in 1552 he was required by the Bordeaux lawyer Douzeau to vouch for three Perth merchants – John Forrester, Adam Wallace and William Valentine, whose ship had been hijacked by Spaniards on her way to La Rochelle with a cargo of herring, cloth and leather. The minute of Bezet's testimony reads,

> Le sire Alixandre Bezet, bourgeois et natif d'Abredin, aussi en Écosse, a, comme dessus, certiffié et attesté cognoistre lesdicts Forester, Valloyos et Vallantin, dix-huict ans ou envyron, et les avoir logés en la maison qu'il tenoit pour lors en la present ville et cyté de Bordeaux ... scituée en la parroisse Sainct Remy.

> [Alexander Bissett, burgess, and native of Aberdeen, also in Scotland, has confirmed that he had known the said Forrester. Wallace and Valentine for about 28 years, and has accommodated them in his house in the city of Bordeaux ... situated in the St. Remy parish...]

As for the Perth men little more is known other than the fact that Valentine was active in the wine trade in later years. There is a report of him and several other Scots negotiating the purchase of wine in the Bergerac area some years afterwards.

The infiltration of the Bordeaux end of the wine trade had begun and over the ensuing couple of centuries continued apace. Scots along with Dutch, Flemish, German and other northern dealers who established businesses within the city were now contributing significantly to a development which the English had initiated some four hundred years before. Whether Scots had any role to play in the transformation of claret from its original form as light, short-lived wine to the strong deep-coloured liquid we associate the name with today, is unclear. What is certain is that Scotsmen appreciated the benefits of the changes and demonstrated their approval by drinking vast quantities of the wine.

Claret up until the first years of the 17th century was little more than an ordinary beverage which was differentiated from the many other types of wine imported into Scotland mainly on the basis of colour. For example, it could be easily distinguished from the *vins noirs* of Cahors – so called because of their depth of colour. The wine drinker of the period may also have been able to recognise a qualitative difference between the two. The more favourable climatic circumstances of Cahors and the Haut Pays in general produced wines which were better, more robust and stable than claret. Were it not for the "Privilèges" they would have made a greater impact in wine-drinking circles than was allowed by the Bordeaux burgesses. By 1750, however, claret was a much more competitive commodity and probably would have been capable of retaining its share of the market purely on the basis of its excellence, without the artificial support of the privileges.

Claret was becoming increasingly differentiated according to district of production. There is evidence of this trend in the papers relating to a shipment of wine in 1675 from Henry Lavie of Bordeaux aboard the *"Amitye"* of Glasgow for John Cauldwell of that city. The accompanying invoice refers specifically to 47 tuns of "Graves Clarrets", as if to imply they were somehow different from and better than the normal ones. In other correspondence between Lavie and Glasgow merchants about the same time the wines of "Medocq" and "Bloy" (Blaye) are identified. Scarcely 40 years later clarets were being differentiated not only by district but also by growth. Between 1714 and 1719 the letter book of Shairp of Houston, the Edinburgh wine merchant, mentions several famous growths including "Obrian" (Haut-Brion) and "Margeaux". If it can be accepted that the greater the degree of differentiation according to district and growth the better the overall quality of the wine, then the vintage reports sent by Bordeaux-based Scottish négociant Walter Pringle, suggest that the concept of quality in relation to claret was well advanced. Take, for example, his assessment of the 1736 vintage forwarded to Edward Burd, the Leith wine merchant.

> The quality of the Clarets in Graves and Medoc I think is generally good. Before I tasted them I was informed that they were much better than those of vintage 1734, but in my opinion that was a very kindly year and I believe that you may depend that the present wines are much on a par with them in goodness which is giving them a very good charracter, and I believe such as they deserve ... There are a great many wines already bought and pryces have hitherto gone higher than 1734, though generally somewhat lower than in 1733 ... The Graves white wines are partly good and some indifferent. The white wines of Prignac, Barsac and thereabouts are generally good but the quantity is very defficient of what is usual ... I think they have in Graves and Medoc much about the same quantity as last year ... My advices bear that Cotte Rottie, Hermitage and Frontignan are good but the quantitys small, I don't yet know anything of their pryces.

The circumstances which produced the transformation have been investigated by M. René Pijassou of Bordeaux University. His findings suggest that the changing nature of the English market at the turn of the 18th century was largely responsible. Up until that period this market had been of tremendous importance to Bordeaux but the animosity which characterised relations between France and England during the 17th century and the scraps with which it was punctuated had taken a toll on

The work of the estate, circa 1723.

the amount of claret being traded. English purchases of wine were a valuable source of revenue for the city, England being one of the few nations which paid cash for wine, most others exchanging merchandise. Poor relations between her and France and England's continuing concern to curry favour with her allies in Iberia, culminated in the Methuen Treaty of 1703 between England and Portugal which raised the duties paid on French wine being imported to half as much again as those applying to Iberian wines entering England. Fearful of the complete loss of the English market, Pijassou argues, the reaction of the Bordeaux vignerons was to experiment with new techniques in order to produce specialist wines of high quality whose value would serve to overcome the various "barriers" set up by the English Government. Poorer vines were gradually eradicated from the vineyards; better viticultural practices were employed; greater care was taken in vinification and in the subsequent care of the wine, the end product being a general improvement in the quality of clarets, for sale to discriminating Englishmen of wealth. With corks generally available by this time, there was now the possibility of allowing the inherent qualities of these clarets to develop over time.

Producing wine of higher quality was not cheap – the extra care and attention being lavished on the vineyards and in "bringing-up" the wine proved a tremendous drain on resources. Happily for the wine-grower who could afford high initial outlays the value of his claret rose as its quality increased, and access to the top end of the English market was assured. But not all the producers of claret were in a position to produce high quality wine. The burgesses of Bordeaux with vineyards in the Seneschalcy, somewhat protected by the "vins de Ville" privileges, reaped benefits. They were able to sell their wine at prime prices and the wealth they had amassed over the years could then be re-invested in quality wine production. Other wine-growing classes were in a less favoured position, their production being considered as "foreign" wine on the Bordeaux market and subject to every inconvenience the authorities in Bordeaux could possibly imagine and get away with. They remained at a subsistence level of viticulture and in such circumstances the quality of their wine was hardly the highest priority. So potent were the privileges as a force that not only did they constitute, in Marcel Marion's words, "la cause permanente de la ruine pour la viticulture du Haut-Pays", but also effectively ensured that only the burgesses of the city were able to produce wines of quality. Travellers such as Arthur Young and Thomas Jefferson were intrigued to find adjacent plots of vines producing vastly different qualities. The accepted explanation was that subtle changes in the microclimate or soil characteristics produced such variable quality over short distances. In fact the disparity in quality was simply a reflection of the social class of the producer; where burgess and peasant had contiguous vineyards the character of the wines produced could be vastly different.

Some of the qualitative differences were due to environmental factors since the more wealthy wine producers were able to seek out and buy land which better suited their production needs. The Magistrates of the Parliament of Bordeaux, the institution which endorsed and maintained the privileges applying to the "vins de ville", were amongst the wealthiest people in the city and illustrate the link between social standing and quality of production very well. The councillor of Brane owned Château Mouton, the President de Cazeaux had his vineyard in Margaux, the councillor of Laroze in St. Julien and so on. The Magistrates derived three quarters of their income from the land by selling top quality wine at high profit. Locating vineyards sensibly and applying appropriate production techniques the Magistrates gave rise to some of today's most celebrated growths – Latour, Haut Brion, Margaux and so on.

In the early 18th century, the *London Gazette's* columns are punctuated by advertisements announcing the sale of many of these growths in various coffee-houses in the city. The Marine Coffee-house was the venue for one such sale in 1705. Buyers were invited to come along to sample and bid for "120 hghds new red French wines, viz Pontack, Margoose, Obrian etc" (Pontac, Margaux, Haut-Brion). At Garraways some time later nearly 100 hogsheads of various clarets "Le Fit, La Tour, Margaux, Obrion and other of the best growth of France" were auctioned, and in 1707, 200 hogsheads of "Obrian Clarets" were on offer. Clearly the Methuen Treaty had little effect on the market for the high-value, high-quality growths.

The cracking pace set by the "grands crus" percolated downwards through all levels of the social and quality hierarchy. While the peasant wine producer could hardly take advantage of the innovations being introduced, the ranks further up the social scale were in a position to do so. Clarets in general were rapidly improving in quality. A side-effect of the process was a tremendous expansion in the vineyard area at the beginning of the 18th century as vignerons tried to cash in on the success of the wine in the market place. The whole of the Seneschalcy was gripped by a fever of vine planting – the notorious *fureur de planter.* Vineyards burgeoned everywhere within the area, creating a virtual monoculture. Areas once under meadow became vineyards, wheat lands were now under vines, woods were removed to make way for more. When it dawned on the authorities that the Seneschalcy was no longer self-sufficient in corn and increasingly reliant on imported wheat from northern countries including Scotland whose merchants were adding "Lothian Wheat" to traditional cargoes, drastic solutions were proposed. Serious attempts were made in 1725 to arrest further plantings and to uproot the offending vines. These, however, were hardly more successful than that of the Emperor Domitien 1500 years before. Those proposing a brake on vineyard development were vigorously opposed and their pleas for restraint simply ignored. Perhaps we should be thankful that the Bordelais vignerons displayed such a healthy contempt for any attempts to curb their activities. If they had not the Medoc today might have been just another cornfield.

IMPOST TO BE PAYED FOR WYNES BROUGHT IN SCOTLAND BY SCOTTISMEN OR STRANGEARIS. **Fol. 22.**

Wynes	Gascoigne and French wynes and all vther wynes of the Frenche Kingis Dominionis in Impost for euery tun thairof Threttie sex pundis quhairof thair is to be rebatted to the marchand for his lekkage the tenth penny extending to thrie pundis tuelf shillingis sua restis to be ressauit frie to the Kingis Majesteis vse of euery tun . .	xxxii li. viii s.
	Muscadels Maluaseis and all vther wynes of the grouth of the Levant seas in Impoist for euery tun thairof Thretty sex pundis quhairof thair is to be rebaitted to the merchand for his lekkage the tenth penny extending to thrie pundis tuelf shillingis sua restis frie to be ressauit to the Kingis Maiesteis vse of euery tun . .	xxxii li. viii s.
Wynes	Sackes Canareis Malagas Maderais Romneyis Hullokis Bastards Teynts and Allacants in Impoist for euery tun or tuo pypes or butts thairof threttie sex pundis wherof thair is to be rebaitted to the merchand for lekkage the tenth penny extending to thrie pundis tuelf shillingis sua restis frie to be ressaued to His maiesteis vse of euerie tun . . .	**xxxii li. viii s.**
Rhenish wyne the awme in Impoist		**vi li**

Wines imported to Scotland in 1612.

THEIR NATURAL ELEMENT 6

In 1679 Thomas Kirke of London wrote *A Modern Account of Scotland by an English Gentleman.* The travelogue included the following observation: "Wine is the great drink with the gentry, which they pour in like dishes, as if it were their natural element. The glasses they drink out of are considerably large, and they always fill them to the brim and away with it..." Not only the gentry, for as we shall see the Scots middle class and in times of plenty, the masses, continued to drink claret throughout the 17th and 18th centuries.

If the Scottish wine trade lamented the departure of James VI's court for London in 1603, it was only because of the special cachet of serving the King. With James gone the merchants and burgesses could carry on their profitable business without fear of immediate and direct intervention by a King in need of instant cash. It was now the lot of the English wine trade to cope with James' avarice. They already had their problems. With the Thirty Years War raging across the vineyards of the Rhineland after 1618, Rhenish became so scarce that the taste of the nation veered towards beer and Hollands. James, anxious to play a role in this grand European theatre of war, intervened on the side of his son-in-law the Elector Palatine, and duly raised impost on all wines to 40/- a tun to pay for the campaign. Four years after that blow, the merchants of Bristol and London were banned from dealing in French produce, when England's Francophobia erupted into war in 1624. James, with the Scots' liking of the French, did not see why war should get in the way of raising taxes, so he sold exemptions to those willing and able to pay. Besides the ban did not affect the King's favourite tipple in his later years, which appears to have been Frontignan, a sweet white muscat style of wine. From the sun-baked South of France, Frontignan was all shipped through Leghorn and could be passed off as Italian!

While England's war with France cleared away the last vestiges of English privileges in Bordeaux, the Scots jealously guarded their trading rights in that city, Dieppe, La Rochelle and Nantes. The Scots wine trade, still mainly in the control of the Convention of Burghs, frequently sent agents to Paris to remind the French Kings of *la Vieille Alliance.* Given that the latter was now reduced to a sentimental attachment, hurt by both the Reformation and the Union of the Crowns it is not surprising that by the 1680's, the French were beginning to see through the nostalgia and demand the same duty from the Scots as from other nations. However, until 1663 they were still exempt from the duty of 50 sous per tun which

Colbert had imposed on all foreign vessels trading with France in 1659. The knowledge that Colbert's family were Franco-Scottish, incidentally, made no difference to the pragmatic economist. His family tomb in Champagne reads:

En Ecosse j'eus de berceau
Et Rheims m'donne le tombeau

The value of the privileges to the Convention, and indeed, the feeling of rightness by which they held them are revealed in the attempts to have the new impost removed and altered to the old "privileged" level in the 1670's and 1680's. Both the courts of Charles II and Louis XIV were harangued by the Convention, and in 1676 the sum of £4,500 was used to sustain the appeal while £1,500 was also set aside as payment to the Scots nobleman Lauderdale, should he be successful in the "doun getting" of the customs.

While the Convention was unable to convince the French, it does not appear to have hurt the trade. Wine drinking was so ingrained in the Scots character, that to refrain from drinking it then would be the equivalent of the British breaking the tea habit today. The Aberdeen Burgh records of 1662 list wine as one of "such necessarie foreign commodities". In 1620 Aberdeen had imported 20,000 gallons of wine per year, Dundee 50,000 gallons and Leith 250,000 gallons. The importance of the latter figure to the Burgh of Edinburgh is brought into perspective when one examines the city's revenues. In 1692, £37,000, over one-third of the Burgh's income, came from the duty on the wine landed at Leith. Wine, then, was essential to the Scottish economy and played a much more important role in the economic and social life of the country than in England throughout the 17th and 18th centuries, until wine legislation for both countries gradually became inseparable towards the 1780's.

The Scottish trade was also important to the French economy. While the heyday of the 1600's had gone, when the English Secretary of State, Cecil, advised his merchants to pass themselves off as Scots so as to have safe conduct in France, there was still enough money in the Scottish trade for the French to remark upon it. As in Scotland, the late 17th century saw the sons of the landed gentry enter the world of commerce for the first time. One Parisian courtier expressed his disdain for this in verse, citing Spain and Scotland as the places where his fellow aristocrat was making a fast buck, in preference to the amorous intrigues of Versailles.

Tury vous quittez donce la cour
Pour vous jeter dans le négoce
Ce n'est plus celuy de l'amour
Mais celuy d'Espagne ou d'Escosse.

A revealing insight into the importance with which bourgeois Scots revered their wine is provided by the texts of the various Edinburgh Testaments stored in the Scottish Records Office. If they had to leave this world, the Burghers of Auld Reekie were determined to leave in their last will and testament the wherewithal for their family to remember them kindly. Here are a few examples:

"I leive to my said dochter … the wyne cave or sellar" (1653)

"… ane littel cave for wyn, without glasis" (1643)

"… in his wyne taverne … 4 tunes burdeaux wyne" (1594)

"… twa littell wyne selleris coverit with selch skynes … " (seal skins)

"ane punscheon of Boyane wyne in ane Burdeaux trie." [Bayonne wine in a mini barrique bordelaise] (1596).

"ane litell barrell malligo (Malaga) wyne" (1624)

"aucht gallons auld Tent" (1620)

Whereas there is some dubiety re the quantity left to the in-laws of the deceased in most of the testaments, the confident exact statement of the last would be just about the right amount for a good going family wake.

The everyday nature of possessing good wine was such that when anything happened to upset the regularity of the wine shipments or even worse, the purity of the wine, it was worthy of note. John Nicoll, Edinburgh Writer to the Signet, not the last of that august body to express an interest in the grape, has left us his diary of the years 1650-1667. His advocate's love of an ordered universe is shocked one Autumn day when a claret ship arrives in Leith on October 21st, "quhich was thocht to be very airlie, and by the accustomat tyme of bringing in Frensche wyne, so airlie!" The vendange must have been unnaturally early that year for a Scots merchant to be back in Leith with wine by October 21st. Nicoll goes on to say, "The owner of the wyne is Walter Cheisly, now present baillie of Leith". Was the Leither trying to steal a march on the Edinburgh Vintners with the new wine or was his ship full of last year's Bordeaux?

Whatever it was, Nicoll would have been concerned with its quality and purity. Scots law had traditionally been hard on adulteration of wine, and in an entry for December 1656, he rails against magistrates who do not bring their power to bear on offenders in order to protect the ordinary citizen. Through the magistrates' leniency "much wynes sauld in Edinburgh wer corruptit and mixt drawn over and kirned with milk, brimstone and uther ingredients". Even at that the wine drinker was drinking pure nectar compared to the beer lover whose beverage was "maid strong and heidie with hempseid, coriander seid, Turkie peppir, sute and salt." A potent compound no doubt and as Nicoll says, definitely "heidie". While both ale and claret drinkers were guilty of excess in the following century, the ale drinkers were definitely used to "heidie" mixtures. Scotch broom, a well known, hallucinogenic, was one of the ingredients used in the beer brewed at Maggie Johnstoun's howff at Bruntsfield Links. It was a popular haunt of young blades including the poet Allan Ramsay, who gave the secret away of the brew's strength. "Some said it was the pith o' brŏom, that she stow'd in her maskin-loom, Which in our heids raised sic a foum, Or some wild seed ..."

Life went on however and one trusts that pure wine returned to the tables of the capital. Not only that, as quantities imported became greater, the price decreased:

> 26th January 1663. Great quantities of wyne come in this yeir to Scotland, and quhairas this former sex or sevin yeiris the pryce of every pynt of Frensche wyne sold at 24 schillings Scottis the pynt, it fell first to 20 schillings, thaireftir to 16 schillings Scottis, thairefter in sum partes of Edinburgh it was sold at twelff pence the pynt.

If the Scots of the following century were "Knee Deep in Claret", the Edinburgh mob of the late 17th century were swimming in it, at least on the occasion of Charles II's birthday.

> 29th May 1663.
> And eftir denner, all taking of joy and thankisgeving was gevin by the Toun in buskine of their croce with greyne bransches rynning of wyne fra thair spouttes. The magistrates being upone the croce, they drank mirrelie, and brak their glasses, threw them and their sweetmeatis and confeittis upone the Hie Streit: erectit ane lairge skaffold upone the eist syde of the croce, quhairin thair was placed sex [sic, six] daunceris. All the tyme the violes playing, the drums beating, the bellis ringing, and the trumpetits sounding and cannounes roaring, with numberis of pepill threw all the streitis dauncing about the fyre, both men and women.

For scenes of such mass celebration on the streets today, one would have to travel to Rio de Janeiro at Carnaval time. The comparison is not so far fetched when another witness describes the central figure in the parade, "A meikle blak fellow ryding upone a meikle punschioun (cask) presenting Bacchus... the fountain all this time was running with wyn of several collors and Spanish wine, and continued so two or three hours."

Sandwiched between the Puritanism of Cromwell's Commonwealth and the triumph of the fervently Calvinist Covenanters, it is no surprise that Restoration Scotland allowed its citizens an opportunity to celebrate the sensual as opposed to the spiritual in life. At the celebration which followed Charles' coronation, the spouts of the Cross again ran with claret and the High Street was littered with the fragments of three hundred dozen glasses, used to hansel the young King's reign.

By the sound of things, the revellers at the King's birthday celebration would not have been sober enough to know whether the wine was mixed or unmixed. However, Nicoll's abhorrence of cut wine had its echoes in other chroniclers of the mid-17th century. John Lauder of Fountainhall visited Orléans and Poitiers in the 1660's, one of many young aristocratic Scots who studied law and the good French of the Loire Valley at the same time. His journal continually refers to the French "brimstoning" the wine, a practice legislated against in his native land. Lauder is obviously proud of this and ends one entry with the words, "I have heard the English confess that they wished they had the like".

An Englishman who supports Lauder's claim is one James Howell, who in 1639 wrote to Lord Clifford in London from an Edinburgh tavern:

> I had sent for a shoemaker to make me a pair of boots and my landlord, who is a pert, smart man, brought up a chopin of white wine; And for this particular, there are better French wines here than in England and cheaper, for they are but a groat a quart, and it is a crime of a high nature to mingle or sophisticate any wine here. Over this chopin of white wine my vintner and shoemaker fell into a hot dispute about bishops.

What else? Wine and religion were the staple fare of the age, the former helping men and women balance their tendency for excessive zeal in the latter.

Lauder's journal of his travels abroad contain many references to wine, the young man obviously fascinated by seeing the source of one of the common comforts of home, there, in the field so to speak. The abundance of the harvest in the Loire in 1666 leaves him wide-eyed in wonder, remarking the fact that if you bring two casks to the vineyard and pay for one to be filled with grapes, "they'll let you carry as many grapes with you as the other will hold". Coming from a country where there was rarely a surplus to give away, the fruitful bounty of the South obviously impressed the lad. By the winter he had travelled East to the steep terraces of the Rhineland where again he is bemused by the versatility of the vine. From the sun-kissed fecundity of France, he is now confronted with the Germanic phenomenon of Eiswein:

> In many places of Germany there grow very good wines, in some none at all. The Rhenish wine which grows on the renowned Rhein, on which stands so many brave tounes, is weill enough knowen. They sometimes sell their wine by the weight as the livre or pound, etc. which may seem as strange as the cherries two tymes a yeir in France. This they are necessitate to do in the winter when it freizes so that they must break it with great mattocks and axes and sell it in the faschion we have named.

Lauder's taste for Rhenish lasted all his life, for among his accounts for 1670 we see payments: "Spent on Rhenish wine at Haddington 30/-; for Rhenish at Kirkcaldy 55/-." Rhenish was more expensive than the other wines which satisfied his sweet tooth, Sack and Malaga. Most of these expenses were incurred in business hours, for among the legal fraternity especially, the parting cup of wine concluded most bargains. In hours of relaxation too, wine played its part and there are several expenses for wine, incurred "at Leith, on the race day".

From the few account books and household books which survive, a detailed picture of the social life of the late 17th century in the great houses in Scotland can be constructed. Nowhere is this done with more skill than in Rosalind K. Marshall's book *The Days of Duchess Anne,* which vividly describes life in the household of the Duchess of Hamilton from 1656 to 1716. Powerful in politics, Protestant and anti-Union, the Hamiltons were at the centre of the life of the high aristocracy of the period. Their lifestyle demanded a residence in Edinburgh for Parliament, one in London for entertaining while at Court, and of course, their opulent Palace at Hamilton itself with its huge retinue of well-paid Scots, French and English servants. One of the latter was a butler hired in London, called Nathaniel Jennings. His sole responsibility was to look after the ale and wine which lay in adjacent cellars beneath the Palace. Not content with possibly the least taxing job in the Palace, he ran off South with 50 dozen of the Duke's choice vintages, possibly as revenge for having to suffice with ale while the family drank of the best. Dr. Marshall describes the drinking customs of the Hamiltons:

> On the whole, though, tea remained very much a novelty and other beverages predominated. There was always milk to drink, and ale was taken in large quantities by the servants, but the family themselves, including the children, always drank wine at meal-times and the Palace cellar was kept well stocked. In the 1690's over five hundred bottles of claret, about two hundred bottles of canary, and several dozen of Rhenish and Madeira wine were consumed by the household each year. The Marchioness of Hamilton had actually sent abroad for wine. Her accounts for 1638 include an entry of £133.7/- "To Spain for wine", but her successors were content to deal with Scottish merchants. Usually the Duke supervised the buying of the wine himself, making an enjoyable expedition to Glasgow to see William Anderson the Provost or John Spreull so that he could select the hogsheads he wanted. These were then removed to the Palace cellars, where the contents were bottled. After the Duke's death this personal supervision was not always possible, but there were other methods of ensuring that the wine ordered was to the liking of the buyer. On at least one occasion the Hamilton postmaster took over to the Palace three pints of canary "for a taste" before the Duchess committed herself to buying the entire consignment. Normally, two or three hogsheads were bought at one time, costing in the

region of £60 each for French wine, although the Duke paid only £12 for a hogshead in 1673 and another cost his wife as much as £120 in 1711. From time to time a small quantity was purchased for a special purpose, as in 1702 when eight pints of Rhenish wine were sent from Glasgow for Lord Basil's wife "when lying in childbed".

In 1693 when the Duke of Hamilton was in residence at Holyrood as the King's Commissioner to Parliament, he presided over several sumptuous banquets where different glasses were available for the various wines on offer to complement "such delicacies as lobster and oysters, and as the season advanced, they enjoyed oranges, gooseberries and strawberries with cream, accompanied by a choice of canary, claret, sherry, brandy and white wine".

The Duke was very fond of sweetmeats and wine and in both his preference was distinctly French. Through the recommendations of a French wine merchant in London, he hired a French confectioner called Daniel Gazeau, who delighted his master by creating "counterfeit cherry things". Most of the wine came from his Glasgow merchant friend, Provost Anderson, but if he came across anything interesting in London, he would have it shipped up to his home port of Bo'ness. On one occasion the Duke was not there to supervise the latest addition to the cellar, so he forwarded detailed instructions to his wife, advising her to "cause ding [knock] out the head of the barrell with the 2 dozen bottles of Loupain wine and cause set it in the best cellar, and taste it how you like it; and if it be beginning to spoil, dispose of it to friends".

The Duchess combined the Duke's taste for wine and sweets in the delicious syllabubs which were such a feature of traditional Scots cuisine. The Duke succumbed too to the fashion for growing exotic fruits and plants on his estates. James IV was not alone in attempting to cultivate his own vineyard in Scotland. On a visit to Hamilton in 1668 Lord Fountainhall reported seeing: "Great abundance of as good vines, peaches, apricots, figs, walnuts, chestnuts, filberts … excellent boncrestian pears in it as in any part of France". As the pears, nuts and wine were the staple export to Scotland from Bordeaux, the growers and merchants there should have had cause for concern. But two centuries later their market was still intact – we Scots sometimes blow our own trumpet a wee bit too hard.

Yet regarding vines, in Nicholl's diary too there is an entry for 1652 which states, "This yeir producit rype wyneberris and grapis". Whether they were for eating or drinking, he does not say! Apart from an 11th century reference to a vineyard near Edinburgh, the giant Kippen Vine near Stirling, James IV's abortive attempt to create Chateau Striveling, and these eccentric 17th century references, vineyards in Scotland are as rare as a cheap Burgundy today, and no proof exists of any vineyards yielding wine. Even Müller-Thurgau has it hard this far north. However, with wine ships setting out from ports ranging from Inverness and Leith in the East and Port Glasgow and Wigtown in the West, and from there plying the sea routes to the Biscay ports, every great house and small hamlet in the country was supplied with its wine, and increasingly in the later 17th century, its brandy. Thomas Kirke, the English gentleman whose writing introduces this chapter had like many of his countrymen begun to lose familiarity and therefore appreciation of claret. From the following passage we can deduce that he "stuck" to claret only because he could not keep up with his hosts if they turned to cognac, his preferred tipple:

> The nobility show themselves very great before strangers who are conducted into the house by a good many servants where the lord and his troop of shadows receives them with the grand law, then enter into some discourse of their country till you are presented with a great queigh of syrup of beer, after that a glass of white wine, then a rummer of claret, and some time after that a glass of sherry sack, and then you begin the round with ale again, and ply you briskly: for it's their way of showing you're welcome by making you drunk. If you have a longer time to stay, you stick close to the claret, till Bacchus wins the field, and leaves the conquer'd victims on the place where they receive their overthrow...
>
> Some of them have arrived at the perfection to take brandy at the same rate. Sure these are a bowl above Bacchus and of right ought to have a nobler throne than a hogshead.

Kirke's use of military terminology to describe a night's carousing in Scotland is repeated by a contemporary French visitor, Jorevin de Rocheford, who resided with a chef from his own country during his sojourn in Auld Reekie in 1661. Following a day's hunting in Restalrig he writes:

> I was very much fatigued, yet nevertheless lent my hand as heartily to the business, as any present in getting the supper ready in order to have it the sooner done. When in the combat that ensued, everyone did wonders – where the glasses served for muskets, the wine for powder and the bottles for bandoliers: when we returned from the field all conquerors and "unwounded".

The implication in both passages is that one needed the stamina of an infantryman and the strategy of a general to survive the season in the Scottish capital. De Rocheford also mentions the survival of the Auld Alliance influence in the kitchen, a century after the ties are broken: "In the best houses here they dress their victuals after the French method..." But having admitted equality in cuisine, he cannot resist the prevalent criticism of Edinburgh from strangers and adds "... but not so cleanly".

Although Scotland and England shared the same king after 1603, it was to be another century before the Parliaments were united and a long time after that before the ancient mutual animosity was tempered. From national disasters such as the Darien Scheme to constant personal squabbles whenever Scot met Englishman, the intensity of the distrust that existed in the relationship between the two Kingdoms in the 17th century is revealed. Throughout the period Scots maintained close cultural and trading links with France, and as the century wore on, Scots Jacobites saw France as their natural political and military ally in their attempt to overthrow the Protestant Ascendancy and re-establish the old Stewart Catholic dynasty. The Garde Écossaise du Corps du Roi still existed though its native Scots content had been diluted. Other mercenaries, adventurers, political refugees, and also young men of good families getting experience of foreign life, continued to live and travel in France. Naturally, there were congregations of Scots at the principal ports dealing with their homeland. In Bordeaux in 1614 a quarrel broke out between a group of young Englishmen and Scots. During the fracas, William Kerr shot and killed one of the English, and both he and young Robert Lyndesay, brother of the Earl of Balcarres in Fife, were arrested and put in jail. The letter from Robert to the Earl survives and it confirms the strength of the Scots presence in the port, for he begs his brother to intercede on his behalf with Maister Balfour, then Principal of the College of Guienne in the city. The combined influence of Balcarres and Balfour appears to have been enough to save Lyndesay, as it is almost certainly the same man who appears as a soldier in Flanders in the 1650's.

Towards the end of the 1600's, as England moved closer to Portugal and its wines, the Scots continued to drink claret but also to supply the diminishing English demand for the wine, whether legally imported or smuggled. In 1682 over 200 ships left Bordeaux with wine bound for Britain, but most of them flew the flag of St. Andrew or the tricolour of the Dutch states. An administrator of the province of Guienne wrote in 1699: "Les Anglais viennent peu à Bordeaux; on y voit quelques Ecossais". The Dutch and Scots were not rivals in trade, rather trading partners through their long historical association with the Scots staple port situated at Veere.

The English claret drinkers, an increasingly embattled minority, with their wine prohibited from 1679 to 1685, and again during yet another Anglo-French conflict from 1690 to 1696, turned to the smugglers for their supplies. Apart from a brief Golden Age between these periods of drought when the claret was cheap and plentiful, the Whigs who took control in England succeeded in pushing the country's drinkers towards the heavy fortified wines of the Douro. In the early days there was some marked resistance, particularly among Tories, loyal to the Stewarts, but as Port improved and claret became a memory for most, the potent growths of the Douro became the Englishman's national drink. Richard Ames' famous broadsheets, *In Search of Claret* (1691) and his admission that his search had been futile, *A Farewell to Wine* (1693), can be read as the final lament for and the severance of England's ancient link with Gascony. In place of the healthful elixir of the wines of the Médoc, just coming into prominence then, he was confronted with a bottle which elicited the following reaction:

Mark how it smells, methinks a real pain
Is by its odour thrown upon the brain
I've tasted it, tis spiritless and flat,
And has as many different tastes
As can be found in compound pastes.

Offered alternatives from all over Iberia, he resigns himself to his fate:

Hold, you prating whelp no more,
  But fetch a pint of any sort,
Navarre, Galicia, or anything but port.

From then on, claret in England would be the preserve of a small wealthy minority who paid large amounts for small quantities of the finest growths. The same minority existed north of the Border, but for almost another century claret remained also the drink of the people, from the Lowland masses to the Highland chiefs. For in a period when Scotland endured bitter religious conflict, the crippling economic disaster of the colonial venture in Darien, two bloody rebellions and above all the ignominy of the loss of her Parliament, claret emerged as a symbol of that most potent and fundamental of Scottish feelings – her sense of national identity.

THE WANCHANCIE COVENANT

7

"Here's tae the Cassin o' the Wanchancie Covenant"
(Old Anti-Union Toast – Here's to the repeal of the unlucky Union)

One of the most ancient, Scotland was almost unique among the nations of Europe in peacefully giving up the foundation of her sovereignty, her Parliament. The reckless abandon which characterised the drinking habits of all sections of society in the country following the Union, could be interpreted as national escapism, a people drinking to oblivion in order to forget the shame of giving up its responsibilities. The equally excessive brilliance of Scotland's intellectual achievement throughout the century can however also be interpreted as a reaction to the Union; the north Briton proving his superiority over the teeming populace of the south. The fact that both forms of excess mingled without apparent incompatibility in the same individuals, is a cultural phenomenon worthy of examination.

The conditions that led to the Union of the Auld Enemies have their origins in the religious wars and economic movements of the later 17th century. With Colbert's protectionist policy in France depriving the Scots of their privileged trading there, and England banning the Scots from trading with her colonies, the Scots increasingly looked to England itself as an outlet for their produce. In 1669-70 Charles II and his Scottish henchman Lauderdale had tried to push through a Parliamentary Union, but economic facility or necessity was still governed by historical antipathy. Rosalind Mitchison sums up the situation in *A History of Scotland:* "Lauderdale's group saw the inevitability of adherence to England; as Tweeddale put it, gloomily, 'all we doe or can is bot fending over to put off ane evil time that must com unless that be doun.'"

When the famines of the 1690's were compounded by the failure of Scotland to establish itself as a colonial power in Central America and Africa, the economic necessity to link itself with England became even more pressing. Yet England's deliberate blocking of the Darien scheme, and scorn for Scottish interests, made the idea of Union all the more repugnant to ordinary Scots. Several unfortunate English seamen were hanged at Leith in 1705, accused of piracy against the Scots colonists, but in reality symbols of the frustrating impotence of a people forced to do something alien to its history and self-respect. While England waged war with France the Scots Parliament passed legislation designed more to annoy her sister

Kingdom than to acquire profit for herself. The Wine Act authorised Scots to ignore England's war and trade with France in wine, the English knowing full well that the enemy wines would then be smuggled across the border by the Scots. England turned the economic screw tighter, threatening Scots with the Aliens Act which would prohibit their trading in linen and cattle south of the Border. The one advantageous card the Scots had to play in any settlement was that of succession – her power to choose between a Stewart or Hanoverian King to follow the reign of Queen Anne. The English who had settled their succession on the Protestant House of Hanover were anxious that the Stewarts should never return by the back door of Scotland, and wanted to bring the Scots into an incorporating Union in which they could be manipulated.

Daniel Defoe was one of many English Government agents in the foreign capital of Edinburgh, with money and power to sway the wavering pro-Union faction in Parliament. He published a propagandist tract entitled *The Advantages of Scotland by an Incorporate Union with England,* in which he mentions the Scots wine trade in a disparaging manner, as one which would be replaced in the future by trade with England and her colonies: "[the Scots live by] the sending of lead, wool and skins to France, Stockholm and other places, by which they make 80, 90 and cent per cent and return wines, a commodity piss'd against our walls once a year, by which also they have their profit". The latter remark is a comment on the seasonal nature of wine consumption at a time when the invention of the cork was only gradually allowing longevity, rather than a recommendation of wine's diuretic properties. In Scotland, the wine fleet would arrive home in time for Hogmanay, and it was certainly best drunk before oxidisation took place. Another possible interpretation of the remark is that coming from claret-starved and port-fed England, the standard of wine being drunk there was only fit for watering back street walls.

In the years before Union the Scots were already filling the gap in the English trade caused by the ban on French wine. Edinburgh Burgh records contain fierce arguments between merchants and the city collectors concerning the impost on wine which was landed at Leith but immediately transported to England. Despite the loss of revenue to the city, the practice had become so prevalent that the Council had to allow it. October 26th, 1705: "It is declared it shall be lawfull to the merchant burgesses of Edinburgh ... to send all sorts of wine from Leith to the south country ... free of impost providing the said wines be carried straight from Leith Wynd up the same and down St. Mary's Wynd without stopping, or lodging in any other place except the waiter's lodge". The merchants in turn were alert for others trying to invade this latest lucrative branch of their business. Several unauthorised groups of non vintners were not contributing to "the good tounes impost upon wynes", especially guilty being "coatchmen, cairters, sledders, coallmen and burdine bearers, for imbazalling the said impost by importing the wynes in sinistrous and clandestine wayes under the collour of other goods". One of the "clandestine ways" mentioned was to make an already clarty city even filthier, so that wine could be secreted and moved when the Town Guard was not watching. The city tacksman protested against "the rubbish of buildings at the head of Leith Wynd, which were still to be seen [and] gave opportunities to great imbazalments".

The tacksman had every right to feel desperate. Only wine sold in the city was taxed and with the merchants turning more and more to the English market, the income drawn from a tack of £50 Scots the tun, was reduced from 33,000 merks in 1706 to 20,000 merks in 1716. The reduction was also the result of higher duties temporarily affecting local consumption of wine. If the tacksman was observing a revolution in the Edinburgh wine trade, there was at least one constant which had existed for hundreds of years. In 1713 he complained that he had not received "ane farthing of the impost from Leith tho't be expressly comprehended in the tack".

Anxious perhaps to emulate their Glasgow colleagues with their success in taking over control of the tobacco trade, in the pre-Union years the wine shippers were already building up their credentials illegally for a similar development in the wine trade, should the Union take place. If it did not, well the illegal trade would be just as rewarding. A month before the Union was ratified the *London Gazette* contained the advertisement: "On Friday the 19th of March 1707 will be exposed to sale at Lloyds coffee house, in Lombard Street about 30 hogshead of Graus (Graves) clarets and 40 punschions Bourdeaux Brandy, lately imported from Scotland." The wine merchants would have it good either way and adopted a business as usual posture while the great patriotic debate went on in Edinburgh. Among the money circulating in Edinburgh at the time, and who knows, perhaps one of the sources of the bribes reputed to have been given to those who voted for Union, was that of English wine merchants trying to exploit the customs anomaly between the two countries. From the passing of the Union in February 1707 and its formal ratification in May, English and Scottish merchants had imported large quantities of goods into Scotland to take advantage of the custom differential. So great was the traffic between Scotland and England in re-exported goods that in June 1707 some 40 vessels, low in the water with claret and brandy were temporarily impounded by English customs officials pending a decision by Parliament on the legality or otherwise of this exercise. The Commons eventually dismissed prosecutions against the Scots, but even the reduced customs differential following Union was still large enough to make shipments of wine from Leith to the London Market an attractive proposition.

Leith's reputation as a wine port, which was to reach its zenith at the turn of the next century when Leith claret and port bottled by its established firms enjoyed a world-wide acclaim, originated in the decades before the Union. Scotland's reputation for good wine had been long publicised by every English writer who visited the country between 1500 and 1707. The Scots merchants were to draw on both sources of their reputation after the Union, to establish themselves in every branch of the expanding colonial wine trade. While London and Bristol merchants "re-captured" the diminishing English claret trade in the south, the Scots merchants appear to have held the north of England as a wine colony until late in the 18th century. Writing to *The Times* on December 2nd, 1807, William Ballantyne, now of London, but a descendant of one of the many Scots negociants in Boulogne, wrote, "As late as 1770 when at York, Newcastle and Durham on the East; and Manchester on the West, I found all the five Northern counties supplied from Edinburgh and Leith from 1767 to 1774."

While the merchants used legal and illegal methods to supply the new English market in the 18th century, wine could not be counted as one of the many commodities which benefited from the Act of Union, for by far the greater demand for it was within Scotland itself. The Methuen Treaty which gave preferential treatment to Portuguese wines at the expense of claret, took a long time to affect the Scottish market. If the Act of Union was eventually passed, it was met with riots among the populace in all the major cities and by seething disgust among groups as disparate as Kirk ministers who feared the Episcopalians' domination of England, Catholic Highlanders who wanted the succession to fall on the Stewarts, and not a few Nationalist Scots Episcopalians who resented the Presbyterian hegemony in Scotland sanctioned by the Union. All the groups who valued the Scots independent tradition eventually came to be classed under the umbrella title "Jacobite", but as time passed many sentimental Jacobites had little desire for the return of James (Jacob), Prince Charles, or any of the Stewarts they took their name from. Jacobitism was a focus for Scottish nationalism at a time when the Scottish identity was under threat following Union. Now, if to be a patriotic Englishman was to support the Methuen Treaty and leave French wine for port, then Scots patriotism could be evinced by continuing with the Bloodstream of the Auld Alliance. Both standpoints were expressed in rhyme. The English:

Be sometimes to your country true
Have once the public good in view;
Bravely despise champagne at court
and choose to dine at home on port.

The Scottish:

Firm and erect the Caledonian stood
Old was his mutton and his claret good.
Let them drink port, the English statesman cried.
He drank the poison and his spirit died.

That epigram written long past Union reveals how claret was identified with Scottishness, be it Whig, Tory or Jacobite. Its author, John Home, was a Whig along with other great claret lovers such as Henry MacKenzie.

Robert Fergusson.

Another barometer of Scottish patriotism in this North British era was the interest in old Scots poetry and the re-assertion of Scots as a literary medium. Allan Ramsay, Hamilton of Gilbertfield, Hamilton of Bangour, Robert Fergusson, all described life in Scotland using the racy vernacular of the streets blended with the language of the Makars of the 16th century. These poets were Jacobite, active and passive, Episcopalian, nationalist and … claret drinkers. These verses date from just after the Union till the 1770's, but the tavern and club life in Auld Reekie was part of a remarkably homogeneous culture which thrived until the move to the New Town broke it up at the turn of the 19th century:

The dull-draff drink maks me sae dowff
A' I can do's but bark and yowff;
Yet set me in a claret howff
Wi folk that's chancy,
My muse may len me then a gowff
To clear my fancy.

Then Bacchus-like I'd bawl and bluster
And a' the Muses 'bout me muster
Sae merrily I'd squeeze the cluster
And drink the grape
'T wad gie my verse a brighter lustre,
And better shape.

(William Hamilton of Gilbertfield. 1665-1751)

The grace is said; – it's nae ower lang; –
the claret reams in bells; –
Quo' Deacon, "Let the toasts round gang:
Come, here's our noble sel's,
Weel met the day".

(Robert Fergusson, 1750-1774)

Then fling on coals and ripe the ribs
And beik the house baith but and ben:
That mutchkin stoup it hauds but dribs,
Then let's get in the tappit-hen.

Gude claret best keeps out the cauld,
And drives away the winter soon;
It maks a man baith gash and bauld
And heaves his saul beyond the moon.

Let neist day come as it thinks fit,
The present minute's only ours:
On pleasure let's employ our wit,
And laugh at Fortune's feckless powers.

(Allan Ramsay c.1685-1758)

The last stanza of Ramsay's poem sums up the whole spirit of sensual recklessness which marks the age. By Fergusson's and Burns' time in the last quarter of the century, the poets' adherence to the Scottish cause was not paralleled with support for what Burns called the "wrong headed house of Stewart", rather theirs was a sentimental attachment to a movement which twice that century had asserted Scottish pride in open rebellion. If few Lowlanders took up arms for the Stewarts, even fewer took up arms to defend the status quo. All Scots in England too were grouped together as rebels and taunted as traitors, whether they were Whig loyalists or not. One of the great autobiographers of the century, Alexander Carlyle of Inveresk was in London with the novelist Smollett in 1746, when news of Culloden arrived. Neither man was Jacobite:

> The mob were so riotous, and the squibs so numerous and incessant that we were glad to get into a narrow entry to put our wigs in our pockets, and to take our swords from our belts and walk with them in our hands, as everybody then wore swords; and, after cautioning me against speaking a word, lest the mob should discover my country and become insolent, "for John Bull", says he, "is as haughty and valiant tonight as he was abject and cowardly on the Black Wednesday when the Highlanders were at Derby…"

Such experiences, the fact that the Jacobites were all harshly tried in England after the Rebellion, and the shame of the suppression of the Scots militia all galvanised Scottish opinion and gave the most fanatical Whig sympathy for the Jacobite cause, or at least enough tolerance of it to give his toasts in claret. If the Jacobitism of many Scots was questionable, their anti-Union sentiment was continually inflamed, and of course remains a political issue which is very much alive today. Fergusson was unequivocal:

> *Black be the day that e'er tae England's ground*
> *Scotland was eikit by the Union's bond.*

Curiously, for many there was no dichotomy in being a patriotic Scot and a patriotic Briton. Others, self-styled "North Britons" or for a time even "Englishmen", despised their native culture and wanted to unScotch themselves completely. They too thought they could best serve Scotland by being the best kind of Briton. Post-Union Scotland was then a confusing *mélange* of disparate identities pulling in different directions, often within the individual, often among families and friends. The tensions in the society gave it its intellectual launching pad which produced the Enlightenment and the literary revival concentrated on vernacular poetry, song, and romantic novels. It also resulted in a glittering social life which floated on a lake of claret.

London, with its exclusive gentleman's clubs and strict caste system, was the antithesis of the Scottish capital. There, like New York today, lack of space meant that houses were built high, with every human type living literally on top of one another and sharing the same close and stair. The lack of space also resulted in eating out, cheaply, in the hundreds of howffs which served man and woman, aristocrat and artisan, individual and club. The day's work culminated in supper with your cronies in a howff:

Nou mony a club jocose and free
gies a' tae merriment and glee.

(Fergusson)

Now although meeting places such as the Poker Club were more up-market than the Cape, and Fortunes Tavern posher than John Dowies, exclusivity was unknown. James Cumming, a painter and antiquarian, was an active member of the Cape, the Jolly Society, the Canongate Catch Club, the Royal Company of Archers, the Society of Fair Anglers, the Masonic Thistle Lodge, the Gormondising Club, the Royal Order, the Royal Oak, the Society of Teachers, and Mrs. Hamilton's Club.

The Clubbists, By Sir David Wilkie.

The Cape Club whose Knights included the song collector David Herd, the painter Raeburn, the poet Fergusson, the musician Arrigoni, the printer Wotherspoon, the composer Schetky and numerous other figures, kenspeckle and otherwise, gathered for nights of music, conversation and boisterous good humour. Most of the clubs included forfeits of claret as part of their rules, should any of their members fail to appear. The Cape had no problem in rallying its clan, and on occasions the boyish high jinks got too wild. In their records we hear of one night when

> Sir Boot, Sir Brown Stout and Sir Watch remained there till seven in the said Sunday morning committing all manner outrage and noise by tossing about the chairs in the room by way of beating time to the songs or rather vociferation of his (Sir Boot's) only beloved and trusty friend Sir Brown Stout … A Riot roused in another house that evening by Sir Boot was attributed to the Knight of the Cape and the report in consequence goes that they are never otherwise.

In contrast to that detailed account, it is amusing to read a Knight's recollections of the heyday of the Club: "The strictest decorum is observed". The conviviality of the Cape spread as its renown travelled with its members, and Cape Clubs were founded in places as far apart as London and Charleston, South Carolina.

The Tappit Hen dwarfs the Chopin and Mutchkin.

While the Cape had also cultural aspirations, other club names reveal their chief *raison d'être:* The Mutchkin Club, the Claret Club, the Aye Fou, the Topers, the Two Bottle, the Dirty Sark Club, the Pie Club, the Boar Club. The Wig Club initiated its members' "powers of Bibulation" by insisting they empty the club's "thimble-full" – a huge horn measure holding a quart of claret – "without pulling bit". A quart seems to have been the standard measure, and thousands of pewter tappit hens full of wine must have been consumed in the some 600 licensed premises existing in Edinburgh in the 1750's.

Some of the clubs combined Bacchus worship with Phallus worship, indeed one or two had quart measures specially shaped in the form of a Pintle, one of the numerous Scots words for the male member. In a modest reference to the practice one chronicler of the Wig Club remarks "...the first Monday of every February was to be known as St. P . . . .'s day, but it is impossible to denominate this saint more frankly here." A 19th century writer in the Illustrated Edinburgh News lists the "Hell Fire Club", "The Damnation Club", "The Swearing Club", "The Sweating Club", "The Dirty Club" as among those "founded to afford an opportunity for indulging in riot and licence of every kind, or were attended to encourage habits as disgusting as they were brutal".

While outrageous behaviour frequently erupted at even the most serious-minded of clubs, it is fair to say that in the opening decades of the century scores of clubs existed principally as a focus for political action. As early as 1702, when negotiations for Union were beginning to concern Scottish patriots, a spate of political clubs grew up and over 200 anti-Union societies were formed. In Edinburgh between 1702 and 1710 over seventy clubs flourished with such names as "The National", "The Anti Union", the "Auld Scots", the "No Surrender", "Scotia's pride", the "Never Give In", the "Anti English" and the "Auld Reekie". The latter had as its first toast of the evening "The Confusion of the Union". As many of these grew up in the wake of the musical clubs from the end of the 17th century, we find that nationalism and music were fused together, and the outpouring of Jacobite songs the result. Many of the Musical Clubs which had rejoiced in names such as "the Toon Cross Minstrels", "The Nor' Loch Sangsters", and "The Lawnmarket Warblers", simply became political clubs at the turn of the century, so stirringly brilliant accompaniment was heard emanating from the closes to songs like *"The Loyal Health", "The Plot is Rent and Torn", "Donald Couper",* and later on *"The Wee German Lairdie", "Donald McGillivray"* and the *"White Cockade".* In the early years, it is said Scots songs were sung "from end to end of Edinburgh, even staunch Hanoverians chanting a Jacobite stave provided it had a rap at England in it".

Besides political and military songs there were those that expressed the sadness of exile. When James VII fled to France in 1688 and established his court at St. Germain, hundreds of Jacobite political exiles went with him. *"The Sun Rises Bright in France"* is a simple song, written long after the event, but it is one which has tremendous emotive power:

The Sun rises bright in France
and so sets he
But he has tint the blink he had
In my ain countree.

Chorus:

So drink with me a glass of wine
And sing with me some Scottish rhyme
That I may think on Auld Lang Syne
And my ain countree.

The bud comes back to summer
And the blossom tae the bee
But I'll win back never
To my ain countree.

The land of sweet Bordeaux
Is pleasant for tae see
But ne'er sae sweet as the land I left
And my ain countree.

(Alan Cunningham 1784-1842)

If the exile in the song consoled himself with wine, he was not untypical of the Jacobites at Court in Paris. One of their number, the Count of Hamilton, wrote French poetry in praise of King James addressed to a Miss Skelton, daughter of an Irish Jacobite in France:

Skelton, prens en main ton verre...
Et puis otant ton bonnet
Que tu jetteras par terre
Tu boiras comme je bois
Au plus aimable des rois.

A song popular at the French court of the period had the refrain *"Faridondé, Faridondé,"* a gallicisation of the Fair Dundee, a song made popular by the 150 Royal Scots who fought for France after the defeat of Claverhouse, Viscount Dundee, at Killiecrankie. Most of them died in Spain or Germany. One of the exiles who trusted Queen Anne's amnesty was David Lindsay, who had settled in the wine trade in France, like many Scots. He rued his decision to return as he was imprisoned immediately, suspected of plotting the return of James.

In Edinburgh, those plotting the same return joined the Auld Stuarts Club, the White Cockade Club, the Easy Club of the poet Ramsay, and the Jacobite Club, or met in Jacobite Howffs like Jenny Ha's in the Canongate. Before the '15 Rebellion, the Jacobite Club had 7,000 members but by the '45, its numbers had tripled. Meeting originally in Buchanan's Tavern in the West Bow, its Sunday evening carousals were initiated with three standing toasts: "The King ower the Water – may he soon have his own again"; "The Stuarts, may they flourish and never want a male stem"; and the last and most prophetic, "The Jacobite Club, may its numbers increase". That deadly serious political intrigue and outrageous drunkenness could co-exist within the same institution can be illustrated from two stories relating to the Club. Between the Rebellions, the Government tried to infiltrate the Club with its spies. One of them, Captain Stalker was discovered and exposed one night. When the clubbist with whom he had shared a fair quantity of wine, sentenced him to be "dipped in molten lead", he laughed, though somewhat nervously. It was only when he had one foot withering in the lead that he realised they meant what they said, and confessed his treason. The Government gave him a pension.

A more light-hearted and perhaps more typical version of life in the Jacobite Club, concerns "Singing Jamie Balfour" a popular member in the period well after the violence of the two Rebellions was over. An anecdote originally told by Chambers is included in an article on the Jacobite and Whig Clubs by Antiquary, an Edinburgh journalist in 1898.

> He was always in great request at the meetings of the club to sing *"The Wee German Lairdie", "Awa, Whigs, Awa",* and *"The Sow's Tail to Geordie".* He was a great drinker – a mighty bibber in fact, and was able to stand more drink than any two men, one beginning where the other left off. However, Jamie was sometimes "over-ta'en by Bacchus", as he called it. He would never give in that a man was drunk until he could neither stand or walk or run. When Jamie could not stand or walk he could often run, as the following anecdote tells: "Jamie going home from one of the meetings of the club, undertook to convoy a friend to Broughton. On arriving at the house of the latter they had another 'peg', and then Jamie set out home. But he was fearfully and wonderfully tipsy. At last, on reaching St. James' Square, then just beginning to be formed, he tumbled head over heels into the pit formed for the foundations of a house. A gentleman passing [says Chambers, who relates the story], heard his complaints, and going up to the spot was entreated by our hero to help him out. 'What would be the use of helping you out?' said the passer-by, 'when you could not stand though you were out?' 'Very true, perhaps, yet if you help me up, I'll run you to the Tron Kirk for a bottle of claret'. Pleased with his humour the gentleman placed him upon his feet, when instantly Jamie set off for the Tron Kirk at a pace distancing all ordinary competition. Accordingly he won the race, though at the conclusion he had to sit down on the steps of the Church, being quite unable to stand. After taking a minute or two to recover his breath, he cried: 'Well, another race to Fortune's for another bottle of claret'. Off he went to the tavern in question in the Stamp Office Close, and this bet he gained also. The claret, probably with additions, was discussed at Fortune's, and the end of the story is that Balfour sent his new friend home in a chair, utterly done up, at an early hour in the morning."

The Easy Club and Horn Club complete the *côterie* of influential Jacobite establishments. The former was eventually proscribed by the government, but for over 30 years it met in the Lawnmarket Tavern in Riddle's Close, combining original poetry and song with the traditional. Allan Ramsay was indebted to his sources there for *"The Tea Table Miscellany"* and *"The Evergreen"* collections of Scots songs, many of which had their airing at the Easy Club meetings. The Club had a strict constitution with fines of claret levied on those who broke the regulations. As a matter of course the regulations were frequently broken for the good of the club.

The Horn was an aristocratic gathering which included women in its revels. Women, of course played a great role in the Jacobite uprisings, producing heroines like Lady MacIntosh who opposed her husband and brought out Clan Chattan in the '45 and the Prince's saviour Flora MacDonald. At the time of the '45 it was reckoned that two-thirds of the Edinburgh ladies were Jacobite, one-third more than the men. Just before the '15 Rising the daughters of the Earl of Callander and Linlithgow, the Ladies Jean and Mary Livingstone, showed their mettle and powers of libation by leading astray a Whig messenger bound for London with vital anti-Jacobite information. The story is continued by Chambers:

> ... that evening as the messenger (a man of rank) was going down the High Street with the intention of mounting his horse in the Canongate and immediately setting out, he met two tall, handsome ladies in full dress, and wearing black velvet masks, who accosted him by name with a very easy demeanour and a winning sweetness of voice. Without hesitating as to the quality of these damsels he instantly proposed to treat them with a pint of claret at a neighbouring tavern. But they said that instead of accepting his kindness they were quite willing to treat him to his heart's content. They then adjourned to Geordie Hay's Tavern in Fleshmarket Close, and sitting down, the whole three drank merrily, plenteously, and long, so that the courier seemed at last to forget entirely the mission on which he was sent and the danger of the papers which he had about his person. After a pertinacious debauch of several hours the luckless messenger was at length fairly drunk under the table. It is needless to add that the fair nymphs proceeded to strip him of his papers, decamped, and were heard of no more.

Bumpers of the finest Bordeaux would undoubtedly regale the ladies when they recounted their success to their fellows of the Horn Club.

If the democratic nature of Edinburgh Tavern Club life was alien to the English, the sight of women socialising equally with men must have been anathema to a race whose gentlemen preferred to desert women as soon as dinner and decorum permitted port to replace them. If Ladies shared the conviviality with Lords in the Horn and Antemanum Club, they were also known to form their own *côteries* which met in the howffs of Lucky Wood and other tavern mistresses in the 1700's. One of the hundreds of clubs that existed was the Facers. Comprising members entirely

John Dowie's Tavern.

drawn from the gentle sex, their name was taken from the genteel tradition they had that anyone who left liquid at the bottom of her glass, automatically had the same flung in her face. Never was a fair complexion fouled by a drop, for local tradition had it that they would rather have spent a shilling on wine than tuppence on meat!

While he fails to mention the Facers, one Englishman who overcame his shock at the freedom of Scots women, and thoroughly enjoyed their company, was Captain Edward Topham. He recorded the social life of the Scottish capital during his stay in 1774, and in his *Letters from Edinburgh* he writes: "The virtue which is peculiarly characteristic of the Scotch nation is Hospitality. In this they excel every country in Europe ..." Much tavern life at this period was given over to oysters with porter or punch to wash them down. In the following passage, the Captain, positive that he has been invited to a private romantic assignation, tumbles upon an oyster cellar for the first time.

> ... when she mentioned the word Oyster Cellar, I imagined I must have mistaken the place of invitation: she repeated it, however, and I found it was not my business to make objections; so agreed immediately. You will not think it very odd, that I should expect, from the place where the appointment was made, to have had a *partie tête-à-tête.* I thought I was bound in honour to keep it a secret, and waited with great impatience till the hour arrived. When the clock struck the hour fixed on, away I went, and enquired if the lady was there: "Oh yes," cried the woman, "she has been here an hour, or more." I had just time to curse my want of punctuality, when the door opened, and I had the pleasure of being ushered in, not to one lady, as I expected, but to a large and brilliant company of both sexes, most of whom I had the honour of being acquainted with.
>
> The large table, round which they were seated, was covered with dishes full of oysters, and pots of porter. For a long time, I could not suppose that this was the only entertainment we were to have, and I sat waiting in expectation of a repast that was never to make its appearance. This I soon found verified, as the table was cleared, and glasses introduced. The ladies were now asked whether they would choose brandy or rum punch? I thought this question an odd one, but I was soon informed by the gentleman who sat next to me, that no wine was sold here; but that punch was quite "the thing". The ladies, who always love what is best, fixed upon brandy punch, and a large bowl was immediately introduced. The conversation hitherto had been insipid, and at intervals: it now became general and lively. The women, who, to do them justice, are much more entertaining than their neighbours in England, discovered a great deal of vivacity and fondness for repartee. A thousand things were hazarded, and met with applause; to which the oddity of the scene gave propriety, and which could have been produced in no other place.

Contemporary Edinburgh revellers may care to wander down the Cowgate to a howff which, though better lit, has the period feel of the oyster cellars of old, Bannermans. When Julian Bannerman set about converting the 18th century cellar into a pub, he first had to shovel thousands of empty oyster shells, left there since the great convivial era. Young men arranging to meet their dates there should however remember the fate of the deceived Captain!

Outwith the Oyster Cellars, Topham was invited to numerous suppers in taverns where he repeats his surprise at the women's capacity: "During the supper which continues for some time, the Scotch ladies drink more wine than an English woman could well bear." On his hosts in general, Topham writes: "They are extremely fond of jovial company ... and if they did not too often sacrifice to Bacchus the joys of a vacant hour, they would be the most entertaining people in Europe; but the goodness of their wine and the severity of their climate are indeed some excuse for them."

"To the King o'er the water".

Surviving alongside Edinburgh's Jacobite coteries were the Whig Clubs which entertained those on the other side of the political spectrum. The shortest lived of these clubs was "The Union" which lasted from 1706 to 1710. Whether it died because its support was unnecessary after the Union with England was well-established, or because after three years no one would admit to supporting the Union is left unanswered. Generally the Whig Clubs were not as numerous or long lived as the Jacobite ones. A cause may be the higher quality of the musical entertainment and wine among the latter. The Revolution Club and The Assembly of Birds were exceptions. Founded at the time of the Glorious Revolution which established Protestantism in Britain, the Revolution Club lasted from 1688 till 1794. A few of the distinguished Poker clubbists also belonged there, including the arch-British patriot Lord Kames. The Assembly of Birds, formed principally by Western Whigs residing in the Capital, tried to outdo the Jacobites in politics and in music. The poet Gay, designated like the rest with a bird's name, joined the society's warblings in the "Parrot's Nest" while in Edinburgh. His Club name was the

Nightingale and this political aviary was replete with a "Game Cock" preses, a Blackbird treasurer, a Gled clerk, and a Duck officer. In addition to adopting the persona of the bird, the members were expected to be experts at imitating the call of their particular winged favourite. In the wee sma' hours of a winter's night in 1725 the douce citizens of the High Street were awakened from their slumbers by the twittering of around thirty drunken "Birds" – "striving to excel in chanting and warbling their respective melodious notes". The High Street dwellers must have seen it all, or participated in it all, in their day.

That politics did not get in the way of the serious business of wine tasting, is more and more evident as the century progresses and the Jacobite/Whig divisions become blurred. However, even in the heart of the '45 Rebellion, when civilisation as they knew it was in danger of coming to an abrupt end, the Whig loyalists at least were torn between the battle and the bottle. The following are accounts of a future judge and future minister, and their attempts to have a go at the Rebels at the Battle of Prestonpans.

> The Jacobite rising of 1745 put Garden's patriotism to the test, but he did not emerge from the ordeal with flying colours … his love of strong drink got the better of his love of King and Country and he cut rather a sorry figure. Enlisting as a volunteer, he was despatched by the Royalist commander, Sir John Cope with a companion in arms, to watch the movements of the Highland army in the vicinity of Prestonpans. Passing through Musselburgh, Garden and his companion chanced to see a tavern where they had often regaled themselves with oysters and sherry and which they could not resist entering in order to renew old memories. The time passed merrily enough and the revellers thought no more of Sir John Cope and his instructions, till a straggling Highland recruit entered the tavern and took them prisoners. It was suggested that they should be hanged, but their helpless condition doubtless convinced the Highlanders that they were more likely to do valiant service for King Bacchus than for King George. At all events they were soon liberated.

Further east of Crystall's Inn where Lord Gardenstone was rejoicing, the future pillar of the Kirk, Carlyle, was rushing headlong to the fray in Lucky Vints just along from his father's house. Waiting till his two fellow loyalists joined up with them there, they then proceeded to his home:

> As we were finishing a small bowl of punch that I had made for them after dinner James Hay, the Gentleman I mentioned before, paid us a visit, and immediately after the ordinary civilities said earnestly that he had a small favour to ask of us, which was that we would be so good as to accept a small collation which his sister and he had provided at their house … We declined accepting this invitation, for fear of being too late. He continued strongly to solicit our company, adding that he would detain us a very short while as he had only 4 bottles of burgundy, which if we did not accept of, he would be

> obliged to give to the Highlanders. The name of Burgundy which some of us had never tasted, disposed us to listen to terms … and after one bottle of claret to wash away the taste of the whisky punch, we fell to the Burgundy, which we thought excellent, and in little more than an hour we were ready to take the road, it being then not long after 5 o'clock.

Carlyle, like Garden was taken prisoner before seeing action, and similarly was not ill-used by his captors. Burgundy, little known in Scotland for almost a century and a half, appears to have made a sudden re-appearance at the time of rebellion, probably as a result of Scots exiles returning from the channel ports, from where it was shipped. Although on different political sides, an indication of the homogeneity of Scots society in this divisive period is seen in the efforts of David Hume, a Whig to save Provost Stewart, a Jacobite wine merchant accused of delivering Edinburgh to the Prince. Hume published an anonymous pamphlet defending the Provost's integrity, which helped convince the Government and obtain his release. When Stewart found out who his benefactor had been he sent Hume a gift of a few dozen superb Burgundy. Hume wrote later "The gift ruined me. I was obliged to give so many dinners in honour of the wine."

SOBER AS A JUDGE 8

By far the most important group of people in the convivial history of 18th century Scotland, were her capital's legal fraternity. With no office space, and little living space, advocates conducted their business from their tavern, the place where a client was certain to find them. Being there, however, led to the tradition of sealing every bargain with a drink – "Tak a pint an gree" being the ritual end to any transaction. From that, the tavern extended itself into the very Court and judges were wont to sip claret while delivering men to the gallows. Boswell's father, Sir Alexander Boswell, summed up city life:

O'er draughts of wine the cit would moan his love
O'er draughts of wine the cit his bargain drove,
O'er draughts of wine the writer penned the will,
And legal wisdom counselled o'er a gill.

As the tavern was also where the advocate dined in the afternoons and supped at night, the boundary between business and pleasure was a narrow one.

If Edinburgh's inns lacked refinement, of atmosphere there was plenty. The Scots proverb "the clartier the cosier" – the dirtier the cosier – probably had its origin in the hostelries of Auld Reekie. An Englishman, Captain Burt, supped in one of the haunts off the High Street in the 1720's:

> Being a stranger I was invited to sup at a tavern. The cook was too filthy an object to describe; only another English gentleman whispered to me and said, he believed, if the fellow was to be thrown against the wall he would stick to it ... We supped very plentifully, and drank good French claret and were very merry till the clock struck ten, the hour when everybody is at liberty, by beat of the city drum, to throw their filth out at the windows. Then the company began to light pieces of paper and throw them upon the table to smoke the room, and as I thought to mix one bad smell with another.

Less clarty but infinitely cosier, Dawney Douglas's Tavern in Anchor Close was one of the best resorts in the city for food, home brewed ale and wine. Robert Burns, whose fame led to the howff's change of name, immortalised a visit to it when his friend William Smellie took him to a meeting of the Crochallan Fencibles, a club named after Douglas's favourite Gaelic air *"Crodh Chailein"*. The Willie of the song is the club "Colonell" William Dunbar, a Writer to the Signet who shared his conviviality with fellow legal men, Lords Gillies and Newton.

Pleydell playing High-Jinks at Clerihugh's.

As I cam by Crochallan
I cannily keekit ben;
Rattlin', roarin' Willie
Was sittin at yon board en',
Sittin at yon board en',
And amang guid companie;
Rattlin', roarin' Willie,
Ye're welcome hame to me.

Clerihugh's Tavern was one of the favourite haunts of the lawyers and their clubs. A typical night's entertainment is described by Scott in the Waverley novel, *Guy Mannering,* set in the early 1780's:

> ... the great bulk of the better classes and particularly those connected with the law, still lived in flats or dungeons of the Old Town. The manners also of some of the veterans of the law had not admitted innovation. One or two eminent lawyers still saw their clients in taverns, as was the general custom fifty years before; and although their habits were

> already considered as old-fashioned by the younger barristers, yet the custom of mixing wine and revelry with serious business was still maintained by those senior counsellors, who loved the old road, either because it was such, or because they had got too well used to it to travel any other. Among those praisers of the past time, who with ostentatious obstinacy affected the manners of a former generation, was this same Paulus Pleydell Esq. otherwise a good scholar, an excellent lawyer, and a worthy man.

Having been told by his maid that Mr. Pleydell is never in the house on a Saturday, the Englishman, Mannering, and Scots Borderer Dandy Dinmont set out for Clerihugh's:

> Dinmont descended confidently, then turned into a dark alley – then up a dark stair – and then into an open door. While he was whistling shrilly for the waiter, as if he had been one of his collie dogs, Mannering looked round him, and could hardly conceive how a gentleman of a liberal profession, and good society, should choose such a scene for social indulgence. Besides the miserable entrance, the house itself seemed paltry and half ruinous ... With some difficulty a waiter was prevailed upon to show Colonel Mannering and Dinmont the room where their friend, learned in the law, held his hebdomadal carousals. The scene which it exhibited, and particularly the attitude of the counsellor himself, the principal figure therein, struck his two clients with amazement.
>
> Mr. Pleydell was a lively, sharp-looking gentleman, with a professional shrewdness in his eye, and, generally speaking, a professional formality in his manners. But this, like his three-tailed wig and black coat, he could slip off on a Saturday evening, when surrounded by a party of jolly companions, and disposed for what he called his altitudes. On the present occasion, the revel had lasted since four o'clock and, at length, under the direction of a venerable compotator, who had shared the sports and festivity of three generations, the frolicsome company had begun to practise the ancient and now forgotten pastime of High Jinks. This game was played in several different ways. Most frequently the dice were thrown by the company, and those upon whom the lot fell were obliged to assume and maintain, for a time a certain ficticious character, or to repeat a certain number of fescennine verses in a particular order. If they departed from the characters assigned, or if their memory proved treacherous in the repetition, they incurred forfeits, which were either compounded for by swallowing an additional bumper, or by paying a small sum towards the reckoning. At this sport the jovial company were closely engaged, when Mannering entered the room.
>
> Mr. Counsellor Pleydell, such as we have described him, was enthroned, as a monarch in an elbow-chair, placed on the dining-table, his scratch wig on one side, his head crowned with a bottle-slider, his eye leering with an expression betwixt fun and the effects of wine, while his court around him resounded with such crambo scraps of verse as these:
> Where is Gerunto now? and what's become of him?
> Gerunto's drowned because he could not swim, etc. etc.

Such, O Themis, were anciently the sports of thy Scottish children! Dinmont was first in the room. He stood aghast a moment, and then exclaimed, "It's him sure enough – Deil o' the like o' that ever I saw" ... A large glass of claret was offered to Mannering, who drank it to the health of the reigning prince. "You are, I presume to guess," said the monarch, "that celebrated Sir Miles Mannering, so renowned in the French wars, and may well pronounce to us if the wines of Gascony lose their flavour in our more northern realm." Mannering, agreeably flattered by this allusion to the name of his celebrated ancestor, replied, by professing himself only a distant relation of the preux chevalier, and added, "that in his opinion the wine was superlatively good". "It's ower cauld for my stamach", said Dinmont, setting down the glass, (empty, however).

"We will correct that quality", answered King Paulus, the first of the name; "we have not forgotten that the moist and humid air of our valley of Liddel inclines to stronger potations – Seneschal, let our faithful yeoman have a cup of brandy; it will be more germain to the matter."

"And now", said Mannering, "since we have unwarily intruded upon your majesty at a moment of mirthful retirement, be pleased to say when you will indulge a stranger with an audience on those affairs of weight which have brought him to your northern capital."

The monarch opened Mac-Morlan's letter, and, running it hastily over, exclaimed, with his natural voice and manner, "Lucy Bertram of Ellangowan, poor dear lassie!"

"A forfeit! a forfeit!" exclaimed a dozen voices; "his majesty has forgot his kingly character."

"Not a whit! not a whit!" replied the king; "I'll be judged by this courteous knight. May not a monarch love a maid of low degree? Is not King Cophetua and the Beggar-maid, an adjudged case in point?..."

...So saying, he flung away his crown, and sprung from his exalted station with more agility than could have been expected from his age, ordered lights and a wash-hand basin and towel, with a cup of green tea, into another room, and made a sign to Mannering to accompany him. In less than two minutes he washed his face and hands, settled his wig in the glass, and to Mannering's great surprise, looked quite a different man from the childish Bacchanal he had seen a moment before...

After discussing the case seriously, Pleydell decides that he has conducted enough business for a Saturday.

..."But, hark! my lieges are impatient of their interregnum – I do not invite you to rejoin us, Colonel; it would be a trespass on your complaisance, unless you had begun the day with us, and gradually glided on from wisdom to mirth, and from mirth to – to – to extravagance. – Good night – Harry, go home with Mr. Mannering to his lodging – Colonel, I expect you at a little past two tomorrow."...

> ...In the morning, while the Colonel and his most quiet and silent of all retainers, Dominie Sampson, were finishing the breakfast which Barnes had made and poured out, after the Dominie had scalded himself in the attempt, Mr. Pleydell was suddenly ushered in. A nicely dressed bob-wig, upon every hair of which a zealous and careful barber had bestowed its proper allowance of powder; a well-brushed black suit, with very clean shoes and gold buckles and stock-buckle; a manner rather reserved and formal than intrusive, but, withal, showing only the formality of manner, by no means that of awkwardness; a countenance, the expressive and somewhat comic features of which were in complete repose, all showed a being perfectly different from the choice spirit of the evening before. A glance of shrewd and piercing fire in his eye was the only marked expression which recalled the man of "Saturday at e'en".

The childish High Jinks which were the staple divertissement of lawyers and judges of the age are all the more surprising when one considers the importance of the legal profession to Scottish life. Scots Law and the Presbyterian faith were the Scottish institutions untouched by the loss of the Scots Parliament in 1707. Law in particular attracted the best minds in the country, and became a vigorous intellectual forcing house in the 18th and 19th centuries. Rosalind Mitchison writes: "By the end of the 18th century the lawyers were the most effective group in her society. They were closely tied up in the economic advances and the intellectual excitement of the day, and their social position as the intelligent and professionalised section of the landed gentry kept Scotland together as a unity." As a group they were also aware of their history and culture, and while other groups of their class affected English manners, the lawyers deliberately retained their Scottishness, particularly in their use of the unfashionable Scots language. Claret was an integral part of their history and no professional body before or since has quaffed so deeply of that generous liquid as the Scots lawyers of the 18th century. They were also as kenspeckle a group of eccentric characters as ever graced a society. One such was Lord Monboddo (James Burnet) whose love of Ancient Greece and Rome extended to taking air baths naked in front of an open window and whose learned suppers attempted to revive the glory of the Attic banquets:

> The table was strewn with roses for did not Horace love to have it so at his beautiful home among the Sabine Hills? Similarly the master of the feast would garland his flasks of excellent Bordeaux, as Anacreon was wont to do at the court of Polycrate of Samos.

Monboddo also shocked the pre-Darwinian world by suggesting that man was descended from the apes. A contemporary Jacobite retorted, "Monboddo's got it wrong. We've no' come frae the apes, we're goin' back tae them wi' our imitation of the English."

Lord Monboddo

Lord Hermand

Lord Hermand (George Fergusson, 1743-1827) and Lord Newton (Charles Hay, 1747-1811) were friends in law and drink. Hermand believed that hard drinking ennobled mankind. Lord Cockburn wrote of him: "With Hermand drinking was a virtue; he had a sincere respect for drinking – indeed, a high moral approbation – and a serious compassion for the poor wretches who could not indulge in it, and with due contempt of those who could but did not." Once, horrified by the lenient sentence applied to a murder which developed from a drunken brawl, Hermand pleaded "Good God, my Laards, if he will do this when he's drunk, what will he not do when he's sober." Newton was famous for holding his liquor and could down three bottles of Médoc at a sitting, then dictate sixty pages of an important law paper without a hitch. Unlike his contemporaries, however, Newton felt that conversation spoiled wine appreciation and preferred his tastings, albeit surrounded by people, in total silence.

Lord Braxfield (Robert MacQueen, 1722-1799), the model for the hanging judge in R.L. Stevenson's *Weir of Hermiston,* has nothing to offer as a human being, except perhaps his sense of humour. Even that found expression in such a black way that the tyrannical image of the man who hanged or transported the Reformers in 1794 with heartless glee, is the true one. In one of the sedition trials, the prisoner Garrald "ventured to remark that all great men had been reformers – even our Saviour Himself". "Muckle He made o' that: He was hangit", was the profane reply of the man who prided himself upon being a "sincere Christian". As a judge and Tory, his drink was claret, and untutored in literature and the arts, his worldly knowledge was entirely based on law and its liquid accompaniment. W. Forbes Gray in his book *Some Old Scots Judges* writes:

> ... where claret was concerned, Braxfield's opinion was not to be traduced. Being entertained once at Douglas Castle, and observing that port was the only wine produced after dinner, his lordship with his customary rudeness, asked his host if "there was nae claret in the castle?" "I believe there is", was the reply, "but my butler tells me it is not good". "Let's pree it", said the senator. The claret having been produced and pronounced excellent, Braxfield, wishing to show that he was not ignorant of ecclesiastical phraseology, proposed that as a fama clamosa had gone forth against the wine, the parish minister (who was present) should "absolve" it. But his lordship had been a little foolhardy. "I know", said the clergyman, "that you are a very good judge in cases of civil and criminal law, but I see you do not understand the laws of the Church. We never absolve till after three appearances."

On a less latinate note was Braxfield's admonition of two young advocates with whom he had been carousing at night and who appeared in court with him the following morning: "Gentlemen, ye maun jist pack up yer papers and gang hame, for the ane o' ye's riften punch, and the ither's belching claret, and there'll be nae good got oot ye the day".

Lord Gardenstone (Francis Garden, 1721-1793), styled the Prince of Jolly Livers as a youth because of his stamina in worshipping Bacchus, also constructed one of Edinburgh's loveliest monuments over the health-giving spring water at St. Bernard's Well. The Doric Temple with the nymph Hygeia by the Water of Leith near Dean Village is perhaps built with thanks for a saved liver. Gardenstone was normal in almost every way but, like most judges, he had at least one quirk. He was into pigs. A plump suckling or ancient grunter was his constant companion, and he was known to take in strays. A friend arriving early at the judge's house one morning to waken his Lordship, stumbled over something in his bedroom which gave an audible grunt. Awakening and seeing the man's astonishment, Gardenstone yawned and said, "It's just a bit sow, poor beast, and I laid my breeches on it to keep it warm all night."

James Boswell was another legal wit who enjoyed every sensual pleasure the closes and wynds, laigh shops and oyster cellars, bawdy houses and claret howffs, the

Scottish capital had to offer. The diaries of his Edinburgh years from the late 1760's to 1779 are full of references to deep drinking, appalling hangovers, profound repentance ... and deep drinking.:

> September 1779. It is wonderful what joy there is in excess. I stood it better today than yesterday. I came home not drunk though I had about two bottles of claret.
>
> November 1774. Dined with the Colonel at his lodgings and as he was to be busy, just drank half a bottle of port ... I went to Fortune's, found nobody in the house but Captain James Gordon of Ellon. He and I drank five bottles of claret and were most profound politicians.
>
> March 1775. Mr. Digges and Colonel Stoppard and Miss MacLeod of Raasay dined with us. It was quite an easy, genteel dinner. We had two kinds of Greek wine, Port, Madeira, Mountain, Claret.

Boswell later remembered the society of these days, "Each glass of wine produced a flash of wit, like gunpowder thrown into the fire – puff, puff!" His mentor Johnson disagreed with his worship of Bacchus: "Drinking does not improve conversation. It alters the mind so as that you are pleased with any conversation."

In his cups Boswell frequently rounded off the night with a visit to one of the numerous bawdy houses of the High Street. During his Edinburgh years a remarkable little book was circulated privately among gentlemen entitled *Ranger's Impartial List of the Ladies of Pleasure in Edinburgh,* in which all the girls are listed along with physical descriptions and details of their specialities. Boswell spent a lot of time agonising guiltily over his excesses with both women and wine. One conjectures whether he ever sought out the following lady so as to compound the guilt in a one-off debauch:

> Miss Adams, alias Clayton, in Halkerston's Wynd – She is about 25 years of age, very agreeable, about the middle size, dark brown hair, fine eyes, remarkable good teeth and a tempting white bosom. She is likewise a firm votary to the wanton Goddess; and does not despise the god Bacchus, to whose rosy smiling cheeks she will often toss off a sparkling bumper...

One convivial club whose collective intellect might even have impressed Dr. Johnson, but for the fact they were Scots, was the Poker Club. Formed in 1762 to poke up Scottish national feeling to defend its rights within the Union it comprised some of the greatest minds in Europe and their friends; the philosopher Hume, the economist Adam Smith, the law lord Kames, the "founder" of the science of sociology Adam Fergusson, the minister and biographer "Jupiter" Carlyle and the dramatist Home.

For David Hume, the claret drinking tradition began in youth, and for quite unexpected reasons. To combat a severe bout of depression in his eighteenth year, his physician prescribed a regime of "long rides on rough country roads, a pint of claret per day and anti hysterical pills". While the anti-hysterical pills may have helped him in his battles against the clergy later on, it is likely that it was the claret which transformed him from a depressive youth to the jovial light of the city's suppers in later life. That being the case it is disconcerting to see him desert claret for port later on. Both he and Kames, while "poking" up national feeling, were also strong British patriots and the anti-French bias of the English obviously got through to them, so much so that Kames went against legal tradition and banished claret from his circuit court dinners. During the war with France in 1794 he asked Henry Erskine where he supposed D'Estaing and the French fleet in the Indies to be? "Confined to port, my lord, like ourselves", was the curt reply of one deprived of his claret. David Hume and his great friend John Home spent many's the evening drinking claret, with Hume trying to win his friend over to accepting port, at least as an after dinner drink. He never succeeded, nor was he any more successful in arguing the merits of Hume as the best spelling of the cognate name Home. Both disagreements are referred to in a humorous codicil to Hume's will: "I leave to my friend, Mr. John Home of Kilduff, ten dozen of my old claret at his choice; and one bottle of that other liquor called port. I also leave to him 6 dozen of port provided that he attests under his hand signed John Hume, that he has himself alone finished that bottle at two sittings. By this concession he will terminate the only two differences that ever rose between us concerning temporal matters".

The conviviality of the lawyers was not confined to the fleshpots of the capital, indeed the stories of advocates and judges on their circuit tours are perhaps even more outrageous than their antics in the city. Lord Hermand and his depute-advocate were once drunk from Ayr to Jedburgh in what was known as the "daft circuit". It should not be imagined, however, that the city wits were taking their excess to a "temperance" hinterland. Some of the scenes in the great houses they were entertained in astonished even the lawyers. Henry MacKenzie, author of the sentimental novel *The Man of Feeling* which made men and women affect tears during the rage for such material in the Age of Sensibility, recalled a circuit dinner at a noble house in the North. As a young advocate, he was having difficulty keeping up with the aristocratic topers around him, but the imposing will of the time insisted on constant drinking. Eventually he realised through an alcoholic haze that several places were empty at table, yet he was sure he had seen no one leave the room. It dawned on him, and looking under the table, he saw the proof. There, gentlemen lay in various stages of intoxication, sleeping the sleep of the innocents.

Realising that this was the only honourable way for a gentleman to retire, MacKenzie slipped from view and found a niche among the bodies. Within seconds, to his utter astonishment, he felt someone tugging at his neck. He opened his eyes to observe a servant kneeling in front of him, expertly removing his collar and saying "Dinna be feared, sir, it's me!" "And who are you?" "A'm the lad that louses the cravats" – the lad who stood by to prevent the intoxicated from asphyxiating themselves. Lord Cockburn got that story from MacKenzie and experienced exactly the same train of events himself at another house where "He lay quiet till the beams of the morning sun penetrated the apartment. The judge and some of his staunch friends coolly walked upstairs, washed their hands and faces, came down to breakfast and went into court quite fresh and fit for work". A young Englishman invited to stay at a castle in Angus at this time, either naively or deliberately ignored the custom of the house, and retired early from the drinking. The party pursued him to his very bedroom, where his memorable remonstrance to his host must have expressed what many a Scot left unsaid, "Sir, your hospitality borders on brutality!"

Scots humour, the blacker the better, rejoices in stories of inebriation and expressions boasting of degrees of drunkenness abounded then as much as they do today. A contemporary of Henry MacKenzie, Matthew Henderson stated that "no man could be called drunk, who had so much sense left as to draw in his leg from the wheel of a hackney coach". Many anecdotes of Circuit Dinners and aristocratic excesses are told in Dean Ramsay's couthy *Reminiscences of Scottish Life and Character;* the one of the two servants at Castle Grant who were on hand to carry the guests upstairs when they were paralytic, and who voiced extreme moral indignation when manners changed and drunkenness was no longer esteemed a virtue: "Ach, it's sair changed days at Castle Grant, when gentlemans can gang to bed on their ain feet!"; the other of the Galloway laird whose wife fell unnoticed off their horse when crossing the river Urr, after a night's debauch. On discovering his loss, the laird galloped back to find his lady lying in the shallows, water trickling into her open mouth, remonstrating: "No anither drap – neither het nor cauld!"

With so many people intent on destroying themselves with drink, it is no surprise that man's last journey, his funeral, was an occasion of orgiastic enjoyment. Stories of pall bearers going beyond the pale and forgetting corpses abound in every airt of a country where not to get drunk was to insult the departed. Boswell's father recalled a funeral visit to Lord Forglen's house where the clerk barred their departure after a few glasses with the words, "No, no, gentlemen, not so. It was the express will o' the dead that I should fill ye a' fou, and I maun fulfil the will o' the dead." One of the mourners later testified to the fulfilment of the last will: "Afore the end o't, there was na ane o' us able to bite his ain thoomb."

Safe in their clubs and howffs in Auld Reekie and generously soaked with claret in the great houses and inns during their circuit tours in the country, the one place the Scots lawyer was in danger of suffering claret withdrawal symptoms was England! Even with Leith merchants supplying the north of the country, it was always better to be sure and carry a sufficient supply of the *vin du pays,* when travelling in the land of port. In Smollett's epistolatory novel *Humphry Clinker* written in 1771, we are introduced to a "Scotch advocate" Mr. Michlewhimmen who is taking the waters, along with something more palatable, at Harrogate.

> For my part, I could not help thinking this lawyer was not such an invalid as he pretended to be. I observed he ate very heartily three times a-day; and though his bottle was marked stomachic tincture, he had recourse to it so often, and seemed to swallow it with such peculiar relish, that I suspected it was not compounded in the apothecary's shop, or the chemist's laboratory. One day, while he was earnest in discourse with Mrs. Tabitha, and his servant had gone out on some occasion or other, I dexterously exchanged the labels, and situation of his bottle and mine; and having tasted his tincture, found it was excellent claret. I forthwith handed it about me to some of my neighbours, and it was quite emptied before Mr. Michlewhimmen had occasion to repeat his draught. At length, turning about, he took hold of my bottle, instead of his own, and filling a large glass, drank to the health of Mrs. Tabitha – It had scarce touched his lips, when he perceived the change which had been put upon him, and was at first a little out of countenance – He seemed to retire within himself, in order to deliberate, and in half a minute his resolution was taken; addressing himself to our quarter, "I give the gentleman cradit for his wit (said he); it was a gude practical joke; but sometimes *hi joci in seria ducunt mala* – I hope for his own sake he has no drank all the liccor; for it was a vara poorful infusion of jallap in Bourdeaux wine; and its possable he may ha ta'en sic a dose as will produce a terrible catastrophe in his ain booels–"
>
> By far the greater part of the contents had fallen to the share of a young clothier from Leeds, who had come to make a figure at Harrigate, and was, in effect a great coxcomb in his way. It was a with a view to laugh at his fellow-guests, as well as to mortify the lawyer, that he had emptied the bottle, when it came to his turn and he had laughed accordingly; but now his mirth gave way to his apprehension – He began to spit, to make wry faces, and writhe himself into various contorsions – "Damn the stuff! (cried he) I thought it had a villanous twang – pah! He that would cozen a Scot, mun get oop betimes, and take Old Scratch for his counsellor–"
>
> "In troth mister what d'ye ca'um (replied the lawyer) your wit has run you into a filthy puddle – I'm truly consarned for your waeful case – the best advice I can give you, in sic a delemma, is to send an express to Rippon for doctor Waugh, without delay, and, in the mean time, swallow all the oil and butter you can find in the hoose, to defend your poor

> stomach and intastins from the villication of the particles of the jallup, which is vara violent, even when taken in moderation."
>
> The poor clothier's torments had already begun; he retired, roaring with pain, to his own chamber; the oil was swallowed, and the doctor sent for; but before he arrived, the miserable patient had made such discharges upwards and downwards, that nothing remained to give him further offence; and this double evacuation, was produced by imagination alone; for what he had drank was genuine wine of Bordeaux, which the lawyer had brought from Scotland for his own private use. The clothier, finding the joke turn out so expensive and disagreeable, quitted the house next morning, leaving the triumph to Michlewhimmen, who enjoyed it internally, without any outward signs of exultation – on the contrary, he affected to pity the young man for what he had suffered; and acquired fresh credit from this shew of moderation.

Moderation would have been understood by both Lord Cockburn (1779-1854) whose memoirs are one of the most valuable sources of Scottish social history of the period, and Lord Jeffrey (Francis Jeffrey, 1773-1850), the founder of the *Edinburgh Review.* They belong properly to the culture of Edinburgh's Golden Age of the early 19th century. However, like their contemporary Scott, they were alive in time to see the end of the old order at the Scottish Bar and the memory of it certainly informed their later work. Both joined the Antemanum club, favoured by Lord Newton, so called because its members always paid their wine bill "before hand", being incapable of doing it after a typical club night. In *Memorials of His Time* Cockburn described the Antemanum as a "jovial institution which contained, and helped to kill, most of the eminent topers of Edinburgh for about 60 years preceding 1818, when the degenerate temperance of the age at last destroyed it". The combination of the words "degenerate" and "temperance" could only come from one steeped in the conviviality of the legal life of the 18th century. Thomas Carlyle describes Cockburn's "rustic Scotch sense, sincerity and humour ... a bright, cheery voiced, hazel-eyed man; a Scotch dialect with plenty of good logic in it and of practical sagacity. Veracious, too. A gentleman, I should say, and perfectly in the Scotch type, perhaps the last of that particular species". That description commemorated by the firm founded by his brother, Cockburn & Co. of Leith, in one of their memorial claret labels in the 1970's, is a fitting epitaph to a man who straddled the old and the new. Both he and Jeffrey joined the Speculative Society, whose more restrained discursive meetings still take place today, a very different club from the Antemanum and a symbol of the changes in the culture of the legal profession.

Although drinking it in less orgiastic degrees, claret continues to be the favoured beverage among the doyens of Scots law today, and the awareness of tradition fostered by the dining clubs of the Writers to the Signet will ensure the continuation of the habit, established in the days of the Auld Alliance. In *The Scots Cellar* Marian McNeill concludes her chapter on wine by citing the love for it among lawyers:

> At the annual meeting of the Stair Society (for the study of Scots Law) held in Edinburgh in 1953, a suggestion that the society should hold a sherry party was opposed, says a newspaper account, by Lord President Cooper on the grounds that sherry and the history of Scots Law did not go together. There is but one wine for whose supremacy there will never be contending counsel at the Scottish Bar, and that wine is claret.

A sedate tavern scene. circa 1770.

KNEE DEEP IN CLARET 9

> I have heard Henry MacKenzie and other old people say that when a cargo of claret came to Leith, the common way of proclaiming its arrival was by sending a hogshead of it through the town on a cart, with a horn; and that anybody who wanted a sample or a drink under pretence of a sample, had only to go to the cart with a jug, which without much nicety about its size, was filled for a sixpence.

Lord Cockburn's description of claret carts rumbling through the Scottish capital as regularly as milk floats today, is all the more remarkable when one considers the probability that most of the wine sold so openly was obtained illegally. For throughout the 18th century, the continuation of the claret drinking tradition depended heavily on the success of smugglers. All sections of society indulged in drinking contraband wine; it was a way of rejecting overbearing English Government domination and it kept the cost of living down. The Scots had as many doubts as to the morality of the habit as someone enjoying duty free whisky, or watching a pirate video cassette today.

The success of the smugglers and the universal acceptance of the practice North of the Border has confused a number of wine writers who draw English conclusions from misunderstood Scottish data. Writing of the 1730's in his book *The Wine Trade,* A.D. Francis states, "In England, Spanish wines were well to the fore and still more so in Scotland. Scotland was a poor country and perhaps smuggled more than paid customs duty, but in these years it took over 1,000 tuns of Spanish wine, about 90% of its total imports of wine". Scottish records show however that of that 90% of Spanish wine, the probability is that three-quarters of it is Bordeaux claret passed as Spanish or Portuguese to escape the high duty. Two letters from merchants in Ayr and Inverness separated by a period of 50 years suffice to indicate how the claret was falsified. Often the claret was shipped to an *entrepôt* whence it could be smuggled more easily into Scotland. Writing to his agent in Rotterdam, Bailie Stewart of Inverness gives exact instructions concerning his, "four tun from Bordeaux, with two good white wine ... and 100 flasks best burgundy to be stowed among the wine in two chests ... I entreat, that in case any cruising sloops should meet the bark, that you make up invoice and bill of loading of the salt and wine as from London, borrowing some merchants name living there, since the ship is to report here as from Lisbon, and the wine to be entered as Portugal wine." The Isle of Man and Guernsey were great smuggling centres, especially later on in the century. The letter book of Alexander Oliphant, wine merchant and precursor of Whigham's of Ayr, has constant references to the illegal trade, including the problem of obtaining casks resembling the Spanish pipe rather than the Bordeaux *barrique* or hogshead, so as to ward off the gauger's suspicion.

To Thomas Barry, Guernsey, 14 January, 1767:

> ...you'll please ship on board his [Captain McGowns] vessel for our account 10 tuns of claret, the best you can afford at about 700 livres per tun and one tun of good malaga white wine. You'll please get the claret rack'd into Spanish casks – one half in pipes and the other in hogsheads and clear it out and ship under the denomination of Spanish Galicia; we must request you'll keep this to yourself, you need not even let the captain into the secret...

To Barry, Guernsey, 20th July 1768:

> If you can produce 20 or 30 good strong fresh empty pipes we would be glad if you fill them out of the hogsheads, provided it may be without prejudice to the wine ... from reason for getting the pipes is in order to be more reasonably dealt with in gauge here ... you may keep this to yourself.

A claret cart in Edinburgh

Not content with this arrangement, he tries to procure his claret nearer the source. Writing to Black & Co., wine merchants in Bordeaux, the family of Joseph Black, the great scientist at Edinburgh University, Oliphant speaks of a mutual friend having "Bordeaux claret for us at Bilbao or San Sebastian and which he entered here as Spanish wine ... Pray can you do this and what is the expense and disadvantage attending it?" The Bordelais were well aware of this practice and their Parliament turned a collective blind eye as a means of marketing their product during a trying period, ignoring "ceux qui ont souvent envoyé de nos vins dans les futailles d'Espagne et de Portugal pour le faire passer..."

The only person who voices any moral indignation at the smuggling custom is a Writer to the Signet, John Clerk of Penicuik, who in stating the obvious in 1730, could not have endeared himself to his claret-loving brethren at the Bar:

> ... this trade in French wines and brandies [is] founded on notorious perjury for it is well known that since the Union, when high duties in these liquors took place, the wines have been entered on the oaths of the importers as Spanish wines and have all payed the Spanish duties, and the Brandies were run without any duties at all.

The predilection for smuggling in Scotland was paralleled in her Celtic sister nation, Ireland. There too, huge quantities of claret, legal and illegal, were quaffed long after claret was reduced to the domain of the extremely rich in England. In Higounet's giant *Histoire de Bordeaux*, the volume on the city's economic history dwells on the relative importance of the different branches of the market in the British Isles.

> C'étaient l'Ecosse et surtout l'Irlande qui étaient en fait les principaux débouchées pour les vins de Bordeaux, car les droits de douane étaient moins élevé, moins prohibitif qu'en Angleterre, la consommation des vins français y restait relativement plus forte.

Official figures are quite inaccurate because at least double the amount would be imported illegally to the three countries, but for 1740, Bordeaux gives official amounts sent to Britain as 4,000 Tuns to Ireland, 2,500 Tuns to Scotland, and 1,000 Tuns to England. The divergence between Scotland and England is repeated nine years later when between January and June 1749, fourteen Scottish ships came to Bordeaux for wine, while England sent nine. When one considers the difference of population between the two countries, one can see the relative importance of the Scottish wine trade. Although drinking small quantities, England, however, was still an important market because it was willing to pay vast sums for named growths.

Yet correspondence between an innkeeper of Morpeth in Northumberland and a Leith wine merchant Edward Burd suggests both the deterioration of claret appreciation in England as early as 1735 and the unscrupulous Scot's desire to exploit the situation by supplying inferior wine. In a letter dated December 23 1735, Ann Smith of Morpeth complains to Burd that the last batch he sent was unfit for selling, yet orders five dozen more of

> your best tip-top claret ... for I shall never sell this [the last batch] unless I have something to commend it for I have nobody drinks wine here but gentlemen of the nicest pallats, and if I could get it in a fortnight's time I could put some of it off, for our sessions will be at that time and I shall have company who when they get merry may not distinguish the one from the other.

It is doubtful whether the later fame of Leith bottled claret was built on Edward Burd's Morpeth blend!

The principal base for smugglers operating in the West of Scotland was the Isle of Man. An indication of the universal acceptance of smuggled goods is revealed in the biography of a Border minister, Thomas Somerville. Here he refers to life in his father's Manse at Hawick in the 1750's.

> The South of Scotland was at that time, supplied with ample store of claret and brandy from the Isle of Man ... The usual beverage was strong ale, with a small glass of brandy, and at more formal dinners – often, indeed – claret – punch. Both rum and whisky were beginning to be introduced; but I remember my father protested against this practice as an innovation; and when any of his visitors preferred punch, he had to send to the grocers' for a single bottle of rum ... I have heard my father say that tea was prescribed by the physician to his mother when she was indisposed.

The clergy were the only group in Scotland whose influence could compare with the lawyers, and neither group allowed their respectable profession to affect their enjoyment. The Cloth did not keep the ministers from participating in the debauchery of the day, rather it gave them a screen to hide behind. Dr. "Bonum Magnum" Webster, Minister of the Tolbooth Kirk in Edinburgh, was confronted fou in the small hours one night and queried, "What would your parishioners do if they saw you in such a state?" "They wadna believe their een," was the reply.

The Temperance Movement of the 19th century practically cleared away toper ministers like Webster or his contemporary, Carlyle of Inveresk. Interestingly, so strongly was the comparatively recent phenomenon of whisky drinking considered the prime evil that claret was considered a temperance drink by some. Apparently in this century strictly religious Loch Fyne fishermen found it acceptable to drink claret at local howffs to take the chill from their bones, whereas whisky would have been anathema to them. The founder of the Temperance Movement in Scotland, John Dunlop, in fact based his anti-spirits campaign on a visit to wine-drinking France where he was surprised to see a Catholic people far more sober than his Presbyterian countrymen.

Claret Temperance of a sort was on the mind of Alexander Jupiter Carlyle, that pillar of the Kirk, in the later 18th century, when he tried to dry out an alcoholic teacher. Having been drunk for a week, no amount of holy persuasion could prevail on Mr. Purdie to sober up, so with ruin facing the man and his pretty daughter, Carlyle resolved on a desperate measure which recalls Hume's cure for depression – a pint of claret per day and long rides on rough country roads.

> When at breakfast, I thought of an expedient which I imagined I could depend upon for him, if it took effect. I communicated my plan to his daughter, and she was pleased. When I went to him again, I told him I was truly sorry I could not pass that day with him, as I was obliged to go to Stirling, by my father's orders, upon business, and that I had made choice of that day, as I could return without missing more than one day of College. I added that I had never been there, and had not been able to find a companion, for which I was sorry. "Nelly", said he, with great quickness, "do you think I could sit on a horse? If I could, I would go with him and show him the way." I cajoled him on this, and so did his daughter; and, in short, after an early dinner while the horses and a servant were preparing, we set out for Stirling about one o'clock. I having taken his word before his daughter, that in all things he would comply with my will, otherwise I would certainly return.
>
> I had much difficulty to get him to pass the little village public houses which were in our way, without calling for drams. He made this attempt half-a-dozen times in the first stage, but I would not consent, and besides promised him he should have as much wine as he pleased. With much difficulty I got him to Kilsyth, where we stopped to feed our horses, and where we drank a bottle of claret. In short, I got him to Stirling before it was quite dark, in the second week of April, old style: he ate a hearty supper, and we had another bottle of claret, and he confessed he never slept sound but that night, since he was taken ill. In short, we remained at Stirling all Sunday, attended church, and had our dinner and claret, and our walk on the Castle-hill in the evening. I brought him to his own house on Monday by five o'clock. The man's habit was broken; he was again of a sound mind and he attended his school on Tuesday in perfect health.

One habit broken and another begun more likely.

As a true Kirk man of the period, Carlyle's life was lubricated with wine. As a child he soon learned that calvinist disputation and red Bordeaux were not incompatible with the clergy and aristocracy in the person of his father and Lord Grange – "They were understood to pass much of their time in prayer, and in settling the high points of Calvinism; for their creed was that of Geneva … After these meetings for private prayer, however, in which they passed several hours before supper, praying alternately, they did not part without wine; for my mother used to complain of their late hours, and suspected that the claret had flowed liberally." As a divinity student in Glasgow his own taste for the grape was so mature that the meagre offerings of his local presbytery forced him to find an alternative source; "Whatever number there were in company they never allowed them more than two bottles of small Lisbon wine, [so] we bespoke a dinner for ourselves in another tavern." He also observed the greater sophistication attending dining and drinking habits as the century wore on.

> By this time even the second tavern in Haddington [where the presbytery dined, having quarrelled with the first] had knives and forks on their table. But ten or twelve years before that time, my father used to carry a shagreen case, with a knife and fork and spoon, as they perhaps do still, on many parts of the Continent. When I attended, in 1742 and 1743, they had still but one glass on the table, which went round with the bottle.

Gentlemen at the punch bowl

By 1756, in his mid-thirties, he was firmly established in Edinburgh's intellectual circle, with a knowledge of claret, which he put into good use for his drouthy cronies after the debates at the General Assembly of the Kirk of that year.

> It was during this Assembly that the Carrier's Inn, in the lower end of the West Bow, got into some credit, and was called the Diversorium … Home and I followed Logan, James

> Craig, and William Cullen, and were pleased with the house. He and I happening to dine with Dr. Robertson, at his uncle's, who lived in Pinkie House, a week before the General Assembly, some of us proposed to order Thomas Nicolson to lay in twelve dozen of the same claret, then 18s per dozen, from Mr. Scott, wine merchant at Leith – for in his house we proposed to make our Assembly parties; for, being out of the way, we proposed to have snug parties for our own friends. This was accordingly executed, but we could not be concealed; for, as it happens in such cases, the out-of-the-way place and mean house, and the attempt to be private, made it the more frequented – and no wonder, when the company consisted of Robertson, Home, Ferguson, Jardine and Wilkie, with the addition of David Hume and Lord Elibank, the Master of Ross, and Sir Gilbert Elliot.

Increasingly, men like Carlyle were laying down their wine, realising the subtlety of flavour careful ageing could impart to fine wines. In his diary of a visit to the Isle of Bute, still remote enough to be Gaelic-speaking in 1766, his diary entry reveals his appreciation of old wine and how it was revered outwith the centres of culture and fashion.

> The wine was excellent, and flowed freely. There was the best cyprus I ever saw, which had lain there since Lord Bute had left the island in 1745. The claret was of the same age and excellent.

A more detailed picture of the use of wine in the normal domestic situation among the middle and upper classes can be constructed from the Household Books which remain. Only those wealthy families whose loyalties and best interests lay with the Government would go to the trouble and expense of ordering wines whose pedigree was unquestionable. The Baillies of Mellerstain, a leading Whig pro-Union force, were such a family and nearly a quarter of their annual household expenses went on wine. The influence of English manners was felt earlier in families like the Baillies who spent much of their time in London. Port wine, which was only really established among the Scots upper classes by the turn of the 19th century, had already gained prominence at Mellerstain by 1749 when the following inventory of the cellar was taken:

Liquors	Bottles
Claret	26
Port	65
Hermitage	10
Canary	25
Shirrie	43
Modera	24
Frontiniac	4

Seraionse........................ $4^1/2$
Strong Ale...................... 152
Second Ale..................... 572
Bottled small Beer.......... 217
Orange wine.................... 33
White wine...................... 15
Cotrottee............................ 5
Punch besides shrub......... 34

Unfortunately no such definitive inventories exist for the same household in its pre-Union years but by examining individual entries over the years a pattern emerges in which claret is by far the most common beverage in their Scottish years while contact with England introduced other more expensive wines.

1707. June 6th: For a hogshead clarit laid in from
Plummer at Edinburgh
For corks and bottling it at Lieth and cariing the bottles 1s. duson cariing doun emty and 2s. per pice duson full there being 19 duson of chapin bottles and 3 duson of muchkins, and drink mony ....£ 4 0 0

1715 in London	Sterling
For 6 botles champyne at 7s.,	2.14.0
2 botles Harmtage (Hermitage) 12s.	
Dutchs	
For 10 duson botles port wine	
from Bonnet.	9. 0.0.

Given that the Pound Scots was worth 1/8d. Sterling, one can see the relative cheapness of wine in the North. Over a period from 1693 to 1718 the prices of claret paid by the Baillies in Scotland and England ranges from £5 to £25 (Sterling) in Scotland and from £27 to £47 in England. The vast difference in prices is to do with the cheapness and availability of French wines in Scotland while any product of that enemy country was anathema to the English. The prohibitive duties imposed on claret in England also resulted in specialisation, by the few that could afford it, in the very finest claret – wines whose excellence made the duty worthwhile. The rise of the named growths is explored fully in the Bordeaux chapter, but certainly until the second or third decade of the century, the Scots were drinking *en masse* the generic wine "claret" while the English were spending fortunes on small quantities of "Pontac", "Hobryon", "Margaux", or other emerging growths. Interestingly the only reference to Chateau wine in Lady Grisell's accounts is the following in 1716: "For a Hogshead Pontack wine bought at Bordaux by my Lord Stairs all expences came to (St) £34 16 7⁹/₁₂". In other words, she takes it on the advice of a fellow Scots aristocrat, rather than the numerous London merchants who could have supplied it, along with the "Modera", "Champyne", "Harmtage" and other expensive wines she imported.

"Confined to Port". Fullerton of Carstairs and Captain Lewis. Circa 1800.

While the Scots aristocracy rushed to adopt English manners, they retained a traditional distrust of their sister nation, and preferred the company of their countrymen. In her instructions to her family about to leave on the Grand Tour, she draws on her personal experience to give sound advice:

> At Rotterdam. Avoid the English house the most impertinently imposing of any we met with. If Mr. Baillie the banker be alive, send for him, for Mr. Knaughten a banker, both Scotsmen, either of them will be useful to you, when they know who you are.
>
> At Florence. A French house in the Via Magia is the best to lodge at, where we are well used. Collins's an English house there, is generally full and not the most reasonable. All English houses or any English body you employ abroad for anything are generally the first and readyest to impose upon you, therefor to be avoided, or at least be much upon your guard.
>
> At Boulogne, A good place to be at, inquire for Mr. Smith, a wine merchant, a Scotsman; we had wine from him; he is very sivil and servisable to all his country folks.

At home, Lady Grisell presided over Mellerstain with the same exacting care. The hour of dining in the 18th century was generally 2 in the afternoon, gradually receding to 4 by the end of the century, then to 6 and even 8 in the 19th century. Still today, it is very much a movable feast, depending on hours of work and social class. A typical dinner at Mellerstain, chosen from the many recorded by Lady Grisell, could be the following:

> 1st Course: soup; relief cod's head with alle sauce; fricasey of rabits; natle cale; 3 boiled chickens; boyld ham.
> 2nd Course: a roasted fillet of bief, larded, with a ragout of sweet breads under it; tansy; crawfish; lemon pudding; rague sweetbreads; 8 roast ducks; sparagus
> Deseart: ratafia cream and gellies; chestnuts; cheese and butter; oranges; confections; apples; sillibubs; pistoches.

The Victorian habit of having many separate courses with a wine for each had not yet arrived, so you just took your fancy in any order you liked with food and wine. Lady Grisell does not include lists of wines with the menus, as it is understood there would be a selection offered by the butler from the claret, canary, champagne or sack. The good Lady has left us her *Memorandums and Directions to Servants.* Her instructions to the Butler number some 37 items, of which the following show how seriously she regarded the care of the wine.

> 1. You must rise airly in the morning which will make your whole businness and household accounts easie.
> 8. Stand at the sideboard and fill what is called for to the other servants that came for it, and never fill, nor let any other do it in a dirty glass, but as soon as a glass is drunk

out of, range it derectly in the brass pail which you must have there with water for that purpose, then wype it.

15. (at the end of the meal) Then take away the cloath and set down what wine is cald for, with the silver marks upon them, in bottle boards, and a decanter of water, and glasses to every one round.
17. As soon as the company leaves the dining room after diner and super come immediately and lock up what liquors are left, clean your glasses and set everything in its place and in order.
26. Every morning clean all the bottles that have been emptyd the day before, and set them up in the bottle rack, this will save much trouble and make cleaner bottles, than when the dirt is allowed to dry in them, if any has a bad smell or sedement sticking to them, to make them as sweet and clean as new boyle some wood ashes in watter and make a strong Lee, and put the bottles into it befor it is cold, let them soak in it all night, next day wash them well in it, then in clean water, a few hours standing in the Lee may do for those not very dirty, and hang them in the bottle rack with their heads down, the most necessary thing for having good wine and ale is clean bottles and good corking, every bottle must be ranced with a little of the Liquor that is bottling, and one bottle of it will do the whole.
28. You must keep your self very clean.

The use of wine was so common that it entered the folklore of home-made recipes against illness. "Daffy Elixir" was just the thing for the colic – a mixture of Lisbon wine, brandy, caraway, fennel seeds, aniseed with saffron, orange peel, and snake root. Hartshorn jelly was another delicacy esteemed by invalids, made from hartshorn, lemon, cinnamon, sugar and white wine. If you were really sick you graduated to hartshorn Flummery which consisted of the original medicine, the jelly, with the fortification of cream, nutmeg, cinnamon, lemon peel and laurel leaves. This was sweetened and boiled, strained and served cold with sugar, cream and wine. Certainly a more interesting concoction than the ubiquitous whisky toddy today, but probably guaranteed to float you into sweet oblivion just the same.

Much attention has been focused on the claret v. port debate because it reflects on the relationship between the new partners in the United Kingdom. However much more apposite to the social history of Scotland is the changeover from wine and ale to whisky among men and to tea among women. Tea, introduced at the end of the 17th century began as a breakfast beverage among the aristocrats but gradually spread throughout the day and throughout society till by the end of the century, Presbyterian ministers were bemoaning its effect on the masses in the Statistical Account of 1797. Whisky, which had remained in its East Highland fastness gradually made inroads into Lowland taste from the middle of the century onwards and by the 1780's and 90's Burns is more liable to praise Glenlivet than Lafite. Glenlivet was difficult to obtain, however, and writing from Dumfriesshire in 1788, Burns describes whisky's place in local society: "The whisky of this country is a most rascally liquor, and by consequence, only drunk by the most rascally part of the inhabitants."

The ministers regarded tea and whisky as equally injurious – the minister of Currie writing:

> The introduction of those baneful articles to the poor, tea and whisky, will soon produce that corruption of morals and debility of constitution … which must materially injure the real strength and population of Scotland.

The Minister of Coldingham (with an obsequious qualification for his social superiors) was of the same persuasion:

> The numbers of the poor are increasing which may be ascribed to the too common use of tea and whisky … The only extravagance they (the generality of the people) are guilty of is their breakfasting upon tea in place of porridge, the constant morning diet of their more athletic ancestors which debilitates them (here I do not include the principal families) and the immoderate use of whisky which too many of the lower class are guilty of, which destroys them.

In the parish of Gargunnock, tea was definitely regarded as the more dangerous of the terrible twosome. There it was the custom to add a gill of whisky to the last cup from the pot "to correct all the bad effect of the tea".

By the end of the 18th century then, claret was under threat in Scotland – British Government imposts were being more strictly applied, smuggling was more carefully controlled and cheaper port, tea and whisky competed for favour among different elements in society. Yet claret drinking was so much a part of the life of the country's middle and upper classes that it survived, albeit in a more exclusive social stratification than had been the case in other periods of its history. The social stratification of claret drinking reflects growing English cultural and economic influence which became more and more pervasive as the 18th century and 19th century progressed, particularly among the upper reaches of society. Often more North British than Scottish, the English phobia for the French and their phobia for revolution rendered port more *à point* for the age than the traditional claret. For the masses, whisky, and the old alternative to wine, ale, took over completely.

Not only drink was divided by caste. For the first time in its history, Edinburgh itself was dividing into Auld Toun for the lower and New Town for the upper ranks. The homogeneous nature of tenement life was broken and in the separation of the classes into their respective ghettoes we have a potent physical symbol for the changes wrought in Scottish society as a whole. Claret had been a symbol of continuity shared, albeit intermittently, by all the classes from the days of the Auld Alliance through till the end of the 18th century. We can see in it too a symbol for a Scotland that would never return. Scotland was a more divided society than at any other period in her history. Astonishingly, the conflicts produced the country's most creative age since the 16th century, and if the Enlightenment was North British and port drinking, the Vernacular Revival in literature was Scottish and claret coloured.

It is too easy to over-simplify a complex age to make a point, and certainly the symbols of different movements within society break down when we examine individual personalities. For many, Robert Burns personifies the age with all its contradictions. All the warring factions in the culture surfaced at some point in Burns' personality and found expression in his poems and songs: Scot/North Briton, Jacobite/Whig, French Revolutionary/British patriot, Enlightenment/Romantic, Scots Vernacular/Augustan English, Bawdry/Propriety. A poor farmer, he wrote mordant satirical poems against privilege and authority, whether vested in the landed gentry or the Kirk. Yet he was close enough to the older rural society to enjoy the friendship and patronage of the Ayrshire aristocracy.

His ambivalent attitude is expressed in two of his works referring to wine. His great hymn for mankind, *"Is There, for Honest Poverty"* contains the lines

Gie fools their silks, and knaves their wine
A man's a man for a' that
For a' that and a' that
Their tinsel show and a' that
The honest man, though e'er sae poor,
Is king o' men for a' that.

Here wine symbolises the conspicuous consumption and opulence of the aristocracy compared to the honest poverty of the people. In *"The Whistle"* however, Burns can write with warmth and humour of an aristocratic claret drinking contest to which he was invited. Conspicuous consumption was far from his mind when he wrote the following introduction and poem:

As the authentic prose history of the *'Whistle'* is curious, I shall here give it :- In the train of Anne of Denmark, when she came to Scotland with our James the Sixth, there came over also a Danish gentleman of gigantic stature and great prowess, and a matchless champion of Bacchus. He had a little ebony whistle, which at the commencement of the orgies he laid on the table, and whoever was the last able to blow it, everybody else being disabled by the potency of the bottle, was to carry off the whistle as a trophy of victory. The Dane produced credentials of his victories, without a single defeat, at the courts of

Copenhagen, Stockholm, Moscow, Warsaw, and several of the petty courts in Germany; and challenged the Scots Bacchanalians to the alternative of trying his prowess, or else of acknowledging their inferiority. After many overthrows on the part of the Scots, the Dane was encountered by Sir Robert Lawrie of Maxwelton, ancestor of the present worthy baronet of that name, who, after three days and three nights' hard contest, left the Scandinavian under the table.

And blew on the whistle his requiem shrill.

Sir Walter, son of Sir Robert before mentioned, afterwards lost the whistle to Walter Riddel of Glenriddel, who had married a sister of Sir Walter's – on Friday, the 16th of October 1789, at Friars' Carse, the whistle was once more contended for as related in the ballad, by the present Sir Robert Lawrie of Maxwelton; Robert Riddel, Esq., of Glenriddel, lineal descendant and representative of Walter Riddel, who won the whistle, and in whose family it had continued; and Alexander Ferguson Esq., of Craigdarroch, likewise descended from the great Sir Robert, which last gentleman carried off the hardwon honours of the field.

I sing of a whistle, a whistle of worth,
I sing of a whistle, the pride of the North,
Was brought to the court of our good Scottish King,
and long with his whistle all Scotland shall ring.

Old Loda, still rueing the arm of Fingal,
the god of the bottle sends down from his hall –
"This whistle's your challenge – to Scotland get o'er,
And drink them to hell, sir, or ne'er see me more!"

Till Robert, the lord of the Cairn and the Skarr,
Unmatch'd at the bottle, unconquer'd in war,
He drank his poor godship as deep as the sea,
No tide of the Baltic e'er drunker than he.

Thus Robert, victorious, the trophy has gain'd;
Which now in his house for ages remain'd;
Till three noble chieftains, and all of his blood,
The jovial contest again have renew'd

Three joyous good fellows, with hearts clear of flaw
Craigdarroch, so famous for wit, worth, and law;
And trusty Glenriddel, so skill'd in old coins;
And gallant Sir Robert, deep-read in old wines.

Craigdarroch began, with a tongue smooth as oil,
Desiring Glenriddel to yield up the spoil;
Or else he would muster the heads of the clan,
And once more, in claret, try which was the man.

"By the gods of the ancients!" Glenriddel replies,
"Before I surrender so glorious a prize,
I'll conjure the ghost of the great Rorie More.
And bumper his horn with him twenty times o'er."

Sir Robert, a soldier, no speech would pretend,
But he ne'er turn'd his back on his foe – or his friend,
Said, Toss down the whistle, the prize of the field,
And, knee-deep in claret, he'd die ere he'd yield.

The dinner being over, the claret they ply,
And every new cork is a new spring of joy;
In the bands of old friendship the kindred so set,
And the bands grew the tighter the more they were wet.

Gay pleasure ran riot as bumpers ran o'er;
Bright Phoebus ne'er witness'd so joyous a core,
And vow'd that to leave them he was quite forlorn,
Till Cynthia hinted he'd see them next morn.

Six bottles apiece had well wore out the night,
When gallant Sir Robert, to finish the fight,
turn'd o'er in one bumper a bottle of red,
And swore 'twas the way that their ancestors did.

Then worthy Glenriddel, so cautious and sage;
No longer the warfare, ungodly, would wage;
A high ruling-elder to wallow in wine!
He left the foul business to folks less divine.

The gallant Sir Robert fought hard to the end;
But who can with Fate and quart-bumpers contend?
Though Fate said – A hero shall perish in light;
So up rose bright Phoebus – and down fell the knight.

Next up rose our bard, like a prophet in drink:
"Craigdarroch, thou'lt soar when creation shall sink!
But if thou wouldst flourish immortal in rhyme,
come – one bottle more – and have at the sublime!

"Thy line, that have struggled for freedom with Bruce,
Shall heroes and patriots ever produce:
So thine be the laurel, and mine be the bay;
The field thou has won, by yon bright god of day!"

On receiving the invitation to be present at the contest, Burns replied:

The king's poor blackguard slave am I
And scarce dow spare a minute;
But I'll be with you by and by,
Or else the devil's in it!

The King's work he alludes to is that of exciseman, and the irony of his situation did not escape this great *bon vivant.* In the space of May 1788 and November 1789 he could write two very different letters:

> ... I engaged in the smuggling trade, and God knows if ever any poor man experienced better returns – two for one!! but as freight and delivery has turned out so dear, I am thinking of taking out a license, and beginning in fair trade...

> ... I am now appointed to an Excise Division ... there to flourish and bring forth fruits – worthy of repentance – I know how the word Exciseman, or still more appropriate Gauger, will sound in your Ears – I too have seen the day when my auditory nerves would have felt very delicately on this subject, but a wife and children are things which have a wonderful power in blunting these kind of sensations.

Burns then, was part of a profession gradually gaining control over the smugglers, and thus depriving the people and the poet, of their cheap supply of wine and brandy. As a poet, Burns had to send himself up and *"The Deil's Awa Wi' the Exciseman"* is very much wishful thinking on Burns the Exciseman's part. For Burns the man there were no contradictions in his enjoyment of drink, he could be equally happy replete with tippenny ale, brandy, whisky or ... knee deep in claret.

At the dawn of the 19th century, a friend from Burns' Edinburgh days in the coterie of the Crochallan Fencibles, uttered a famous *cri de coeur,* directed not against excisemen, the high duty or the port drinker, but the growing aversion to serious drinking which the "Tea faced generation" were now adopting: "What shall we come to at last, I believe I shall be left alone on the face of the earth, drinking claret."

At least as far as his own professional colleagues were concerned, Lord Newton's fears were groundless.

GAE BRING TAE ME 10

Gae bring tae me a pint o' wine
And fill it in a silver tassie
(Burns)

Cadboll Cup, a Highland drinking vessel.

Supplying Scottish conviviality remained the responsibility of the home-based wine trade. However, in order to secure supplies of the precious liquid, Scots left to establish colonies of wine dealers in the areas of production. Not surprisingly the greatest of these colonies was in Bordeaux.

How cosmopolitan Bordeaux must have been in the 17th and 18th centuries! When the fleet arrived in the late Autumn for the new wine, the quays buzzed with merchants, skippers and dealers of all nationalities. The flags sported by the ships which filled the harbour would reveal at a glance which nationalities were represented and among those of the low countries, Scandinavia, Ireland, England and the Baltic States, the St. Andrew's Cross would certainly be seen. At the height of the shipping season, a constant stream of small boats laden with wine from vineyards upstream or on the shores of the Gironde estuary would be arriving at the quays. Landed on the quayside the wine would barely have time to settle before being snapped up by traders with orders for so many tuns of claret and so many white. Once bought and a ship bound for the appropriate port found, wine destined for the Scottish market would soon be secure in the waterside cellars of Leith, Perth, Dundee and Glasgow.

When the wines available in Bordeaux were hardly differentiated other than into "Haut Pays" and "Vins de Ville" or claret and white, its purchase was a fairly simple affair. Home-based wine merchants would charge the skippers of ships bound for Bordeaux with the task of obtaining their wine on the quayside there. It was simply a matter of placing an order with the skipper and agreeing to buy at the going rate. However, as different qualities, growths and wine-types emerged there was the need for a greater degree of sophistication and a new breed of middle-men established themselves – the expatriate négociant based permanently in the city. They came to Bordeaux to arrange the export of wines to their home countries and perhaps elsewhere, but also carried on a brisk export trade in commodities which could be offered in return for claret. One of the earliest Scots merchants in Bordeaux was Alexander Bezet who, as we have seen, arrived around the middle of the 16th century. The growth of the Scots colony in Bordeaux was mainly from the early 1600s and by the mid-18th century Scottish names became familiar in the city's wine trade. There were Gordons, MacLeods, Blacks, Pringles, Sandilands and many more. The Scots who came to learn the trade were in the city temporarily. One such apprentice, the Invernessian Alex Stewart, spent a brief sojourn in Bordeaux around 1730. Others such as Alexander Gordon came with the intention of staying to organise the Bordeaux end of the wine trade for merchants in Scotland. Others came and left prematurely, having failed to create a niche for their enterprise. One of the Roses of Kilravock was forced to return home, his attempt to establish a business in the city having met with little success.

The constant coming and going of compatriots must have been of comfort and support to the Scots permanently based in Bordeaux. Already there was a Scots church there – one Peter Gilbert Primrose was its minister in 1602 and sometime later we hear of another Scots minister called John Welsh who was advised by Primrose to seek permission to preach in Bordeaux "To theme that cums to this place, because bayth of yere greitt number and the long abode of 8 or 9 moneth and ignorance of ye French toung". The "great number" of Scots in Bordeaux was hardly sufficient consolation to the Edinburgh-man Walter Pringle who had left his native city for Bordeaux at the age of 18 and many years later had not overcome his homesickness. This he confessed in correspondence with the Leith merchant Edward Burd in 1724.

> I wish with all my heart I could be in Edinburgh tomorrow, provided I could return in a day or two. I would not desire more, I assure you this would give vast pleasure, for I don't imagine I shall be there again…

Pringle was clearly torn between returning to Scotland and staying in Bordeaux to

Port of Bordeaux, 18th century

continue his successful enterprise. For the next eight years at least his commercial instincts overcame nostalgia – there is evidence that he was still trading in the city in 1732.

Many of the Scots dealers were based in the suburb of the "Chartrons" with most of the other foreigners in the city. Originally they had been forbidden by the authorities to live within the city boundaries and having established themselves in this suburb, the tradition continued long after the regulation banning them from residence in Bordeaux was removed. Pringle was lodged there, sharing his accommodation with an Irishman called Brown. Here Pringle would have had some office space for storing his purchases until such time as they were dispatched to Scotland.

From the correspondence of expatriates with their clients in Scotland an impression is given of the nature of the work undertaken. At this time wine quality was a prime consideration and differences in it were reflected in the selling price. Négociants as a result were ill-advised to sit around Bordeaux awaiting the arrival of new wines before reporting on the vintage to prospective clients at home. They made it an integral part of their work to visit wine-producers in the country for some advance information on how the vintage was shaping up. George Gordon in his letter to Edward Burd on 11 October 1727 provides a brief prognosis and promises more detailed information once the country visits have been made.

> Shall have almost as much wine as last year and will be very good but dear. Not green as was much feared but really better than has been this long time. As my father is in the country with my uncle tasting and I go myself tomorrow shall at our return give you a more particular account…

Having visited, sampled, discussed and compared the wines of the district, the next task of the dealer was to despatch full "Vintage Reports" as a guide to merchants in Scotland. Pringle's findings on the 1733 vintage were forwarded to John Baird, shipmaster in Leith, and an exact copy was received at Edward Burd's establishment. Presumably several other merchants were on Pringle's mailing list and received this assessment of that year's vintage.

> I take the liberty of giving you my opinion of this vintage … The clarets in Graves have in general a very good and lively colour and those which are sufficiently mature have good body and flavour but many are green and have not the body which might be expected from the colour, and in general there is less than last year … In Medoc the colour is also generally good and the wines are attended by the same good and bad qualitys as in Graves but I think the quantity in Medoc is somewhat larger in proportion. Tis my opinion that in general in the countrys above mentioned the clarets are better than any since vintage 1727. There is a great scarcity of the white wines of high and low Prignacs, Sauterne, Barsac and these countrys. They are clear and well tasted but green and no great body. The Graves Blanquefort and other white wines thereabouts are also green, otherways pretty good in taste. Most part of the great growths vis Pontac, Chateau Margeaux and Lafite is sold at £2000 per ton, Latour which is of the same class was so ill used last summer by storm of hail that what remains of it is good for nothing. My advices from Frontignan, Cotte Rotti and Hermitage bear that scarcity there is very great, but the wines are generally good. The great scarcity and goodness of the wines all over this country will no doubt make them sell a good deal dearer than last year especially the small wines which are usually distilled now are bought up and loaded off at ct per ct. dearer than last year. But the better wines fit for our countrys cannot rise near so much. Brandys have risen vastly, they were at £120 and if there is as much demand as usual they'll soon gett to £150.

There is no evidence of how impressed Burd was with this glowing report and whether orders for wine followed. Certainly the report for 1730, by all accounts a lesser vintage, must have caught Burd's imagination since a large order for which the

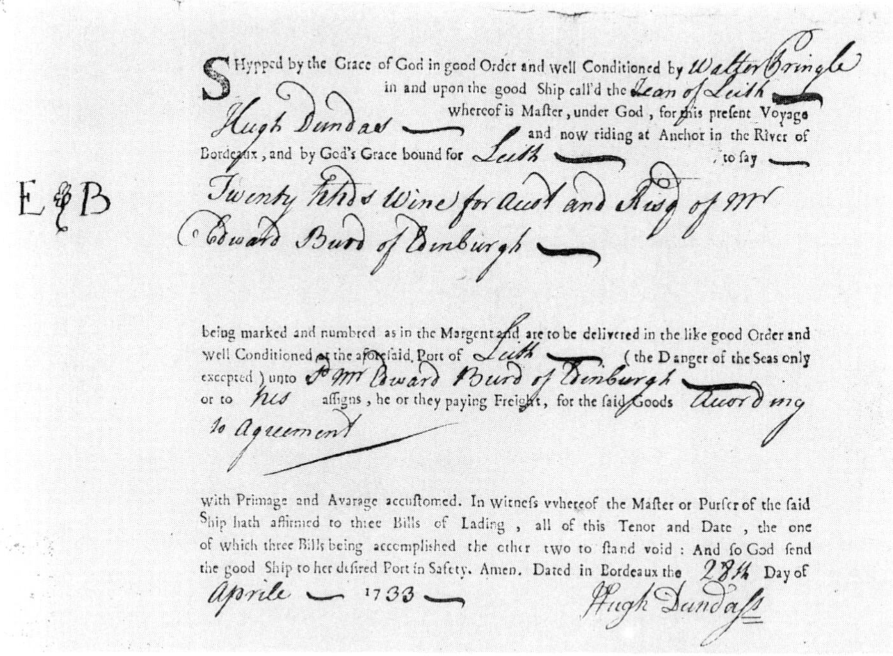

E & B

SHypped by the Grace of God in good Order and well Conditioned by *Walter Pringle* in and upon the good Ship call'd the *Jean of Leith* whereof is Master, under God, for this present Voyage *Hugh Dundas* and now riding at Anchor in the River of Bordeaux, and by God's Grace bound for *Leith*, to say *Twenty hhds Wine for Acct and Risq of Mr Edward Burd of Edinburgh*

being marked and numbred as in the Margent and are to be delivered in the like good Order and well Conditioned at the aforesaid Port of *Leith* (the Danger of the Seas only excepted) unto *Mr Edward Burd of Edinburgh* or to *his* assigns, he or they paying Freight, for the said Goods *According to agreement*

with Primage and Avarage accustomed. In Witness whereof the Master or Purser of the said Ship hath affirmed to three Bills of Lading, all of this Tenor and Date, the one of which three Bills being accomplished the other two to stand void: And so God send the good Ship to her desired Port in Safety. Amen. Dated in Bordeaux the *28th* Day of *Aprile* 1733

Hugh Dundass

Burd's order from Pringle 1733.

invoice still exists was elicited from him.

2 hhds	Margeaux Claret fine	@ £840	per tun	('fine' = after fining)
4 "	Graves " "	@ £525	" "	
2 "	Montferan " "	@ £390	" "	
6 "	Graves " "	@ £350	" "	
2 "	Graves white wine	@ £220	" "	

There were several locally produced commodities other than wine which interested Scottish importers and Pringle was willing to supply them. One of his circulars ends with an allusion to other celebrated products of south-west France:

> The prunes are pretty good and sell at £5.15.0 to £6 per ct. the chesnuts and wallnuts in Blaye are also good and sell chesnuts at £10.5.0 per bushl and the wallnuts at £9.5.0.

Doubtless there would have been interest in the prices some of the Scottish exports might achieve in Bordeaux. Again Pringle supplies the requisite information: "Best wheat at £8.15.0 to £9 per bushl. Coal at £260 last prices".

The orders for wine placed by Shairp of Houston, another Leith-based merchant, with the Bordeaux firm of Sampson and Sandilands were of much the same magnitude as Burd's. Shairp clearly was not interested in being delivered any old plonk as he stresses in his letter of 13th September 1716:

> You'll load of any account on board of Mr Patrick Aitkenhead four tuns good Graves Claret and one tun white wine. I doubt not your care only most entreat it be amongst the best. I grudge not two or three crouns extraordinary on the first cost it being only the quality of my wine that will bring customers, for I am altogether unable to force a trade by drinking which is too much the practice here…

Two months later he was ordering more wine, probably on the basis of favourable vintage reports. Thus Sampson and Sandilands were instructed to:

> please load aboard the next ship ten tun of the best ordinary claret wine that's sent to this country, deep and well body'd, three tun Strong Claret wine (the tun Margeaux I had last year proved good) and one tun of the very best white that comes for this country … I hope you'll take care in choosing the wine.

Early in the new year Shairp had an opportunity to sample wine of that vintage which had been imported by Aitkenhead. Immediately he wrote to Sampson and Sandilands declaring that Aitkenhead's claret "is in my oppinion as good as any yet comed". Inspired by this favourable tasting Shairp ordered more wine from the Bordeaux firm. No sooner had the letter been posted than Shairp began to have serious doubts about the vintage and five days later on 15 January 1717 he dispatched another letter to Sampson and Sandilands, who by this time must have been reeling in confusion, in which he reported: "This day [I] tasted Mr. Clark's strong wine which he says is Margeaux, I find it appalling small, I hope the three tuns I commissioned will be better else it will not answer …" Then, hedging his bets, Shairp orders half a tun of Cahors "black wine", possibly because he knew that at least its quality would be fairly predictable. One can appreciate why Shairp was concerned. Wine merchants in Scotland were torn between soaring demand for quality clarets in the home market which pressured them into buying supplies at all costs and on the other hand a natural resistance to buying too much of a commodity for which only the seller's recommendation was available. Shelling out anything up to £1000 per tun for wines was not a matter to be treated lightly by the home-based merchant.

There was similar concern on the part of the négociant in Bordeaux to off-load any wines purchased as quickly as possible. In order to secure an order their sales talk had to be good and there was no better proponent of this art than Pringle. His descriptions and recommendations were lavish, generous and elaborate. Merchants operating in blissful ignorance from Edinburgh would have been hard put to ignore such examples of Pringle's patter that formed part of a letter received by Burd at his Leith premises in 1733:

> These six hhds old Claret are I think excellent, but I could not get any of the low priced

that pleased me, however I am persuaded that you'll like the new, else I assure you I'll quit all manner of pretentions to knowledge in wines, and seek out some other trade...

Transporting wine by sea from Bordeaux to Leith and other Scottish ports was relatively cheap, largely because there was no necessity to tranship cargoes into vessels of varying draughts and there was little recourse to overland carriage. Claret could be landed more cheaply in Scotland than in London because of the disparity in import duties payable, and because of the comparative ease of sea transport it was also cheaper there than in Paris and other inland cities of France. Its landed price in Leith was barely one-eighth more than the price prevailing in Bordeaux, even after a range of different charges and expenses were taken into account. In this respect the details of an invoice issued by Pringle in 1733 are of some interest:

Invoice of Goods Ship'd aboard the Jean of Leith, Hugh Dundas Master, by order and for account and risque of Mr Edward Burd of Edinburgh.

To	3 Hd Claret Vintage 1731	@	510 Livres per tun	£ 382.10.0
	3 " " " "	@	400	300.00.0
	8 " new " drawn fine	@	315	630.00.0
	6 " Prignac White Wine	@	200	300.00.0
				£1612.10.0

Charges

Duty	£117.5.0		
Brokerage	15		
Cooperage	30		
Rolling and Coach Hire	10		
Stowage and Drinkwine	10		
Advance freight 5/- per hhg		Total	£1820.16.0
		commission 2½% =	45.10.4
			£1866. 7.0

Chateau bottling was exceptional at this time. It was as late as 1800 before Bordeaux-bottled clarets were beginning to appear in significant numbers, but even at that the practice was not widespread. Excepting the few bottles brought back on the homeward journey the claret which so enriched the lives of 18th century Scots was all *mise en bouteille en Écosse.* The wine was shipped in wooden hogsheads and bottled at the place of consumption – the prospect of Bordeaux-bottled claret rattling and clinking in the holds of ships bobbing like corks in the Bay of Biscay and the bilge water being gradually converted into a rich mixture of some Medoc growth or other, was one which hardly appealed. So unusual was it for the Scots dealers in Bordeaux to arrange for the bottling of wine, that in 1733 Pringle was writing home for Jamie Rannie's (an Edinburgh merchant) "recipes as to how to make the best brown and white wax for waxing the corks and necks of bottles". Not that shipment in hogsheads was entirely risk-free. Edward Burd took Walter Pringle to task on one occasion for a hogshead of claret of which he had recently taken delivery, being "prick'd". There was little Pringle could do about the condition of the wine and, without offering to replace the defective product, he simply went on to suggest reasons as to why it might have deteriorated in the hogshead. Bad cooperage, he offered as one reason, or bad stowage, or "a hard squeeze of a crow iron", brandished by a clumsy stevedore in trying to manhandle it into the ship. Whichever was the cause the sad fact of the matter was that the equivalent of 300 bottles of claret were now unfit for drinking.

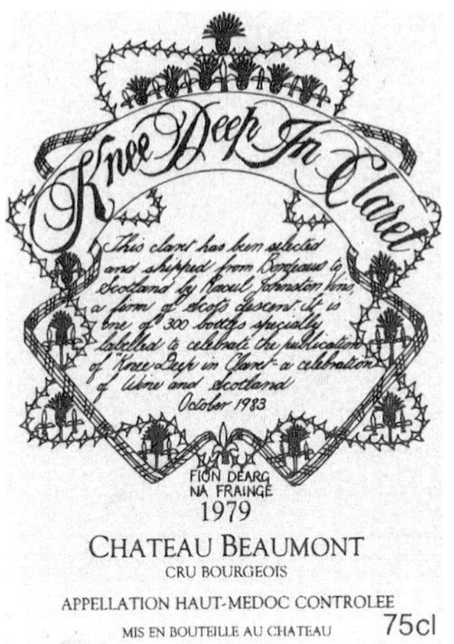

Claret shipments hit a couple of peaks within the "wine year". The first came a few weeks after the harvest was complete when wines were ready for transportation. Over the New Year period there was a lull in trade, but activity accelerated soon afterwards with the return of the Northern Fleet. By May the flow of wine from Bordeaux was reduced to a trickle and thereafter until the next harvest, négociants busied themselves preparing their premises for the influx of new wine in the Autumn and in "bringing up" the ones they had retained in their cellars to be sold at a later date as "old" claret. To "bring up" claret there were a range of treatments to be performed. Hogsheads had to be topped up to replace the volume lost to evaporation, they were racked off the lees or sediment, and fined. At this time a publication from claret-crazy Edinburgh, the *Encyclopaedia Britannica* of 1797 could go into some detail as to how the latter process was effected:

> The forcings proper for claret are the whites of a dozen eggs, beat up with a tea-spoonful of salt, and well worked with a forcing rod. Take care to use no bad egg. This is for one hogshead.

The hiatus in shipping activity also allowed dealers ample opportunity to "strengthen" their clarets. This practice was ostensibly to improve the transportability of delicate wines though there is evidence to suggest that its main purpose was to "round off" or soften the hard, tannin-charged clarets. The clientèle in Scotland would have been aghast if they realized how widespread this practice was, particularly since mixing and adulterating wines in Scotland would have cost the offender his life and because the wine-drinking public which had maintained so much loyalty to "fresche fragrant clairettis" never dreamed that part of the freshness and fragrance resulted from liberal dollops of foreign material being administered to the wine. Not that the Scots were without warning that this was the case, Sir John Lauder of Fountainhall in a 17th century account of his journey to Orléans and Poitiers made some critical observations about the manner by which the commodity arrived at its overseas customer:

> There is no vine out of France to foreine country, save that which they brimstone a little, otherwise it would not keep on the sea, but it would spoil. It's true the wine works much of it out againe, yet this makes the wine much more unwholesome and heady than that we drink in the country wheir it growes at hand.

Brimstone and all, claret continued to be put away with as much alacrity as before. In the following century imbibers would have derived some consolation from the fact that it was at least a species of wine which "strengthened" claret. The finest wines were bulked out with Hermitage – the full-bodied and deeply-coloured Rhône wine. Even in a good year the Bordeaux négociant Johnston was convinced that his Chateau Lafite needed "hermitaging". The lesser growths were topped up and strengthened according to a strict code of practice, the details of which are preserved in Johnston's "Livre de Chai" for 1765.

> It is not necessary to ullage with their own wines provided you do it with good wines of other prices. Gravs wine if good may do for Medoc wines or Medoc for Gravs wines but would not choose to ullage with Palus, Cahors or strong wines but with some that will not alter the quality much as anything perceivable except when much ullage is required.

> On tasting wines I have found the Alicantes always smoother and finer than Benicarlos which have generally better color but when the latter are good they will do very well to mix one half the other which I generally did for ease, by running off half the hogshead and filling up with the other...

> When I found Rivasalt (Rivesaltes) good I have some years put half of them and no

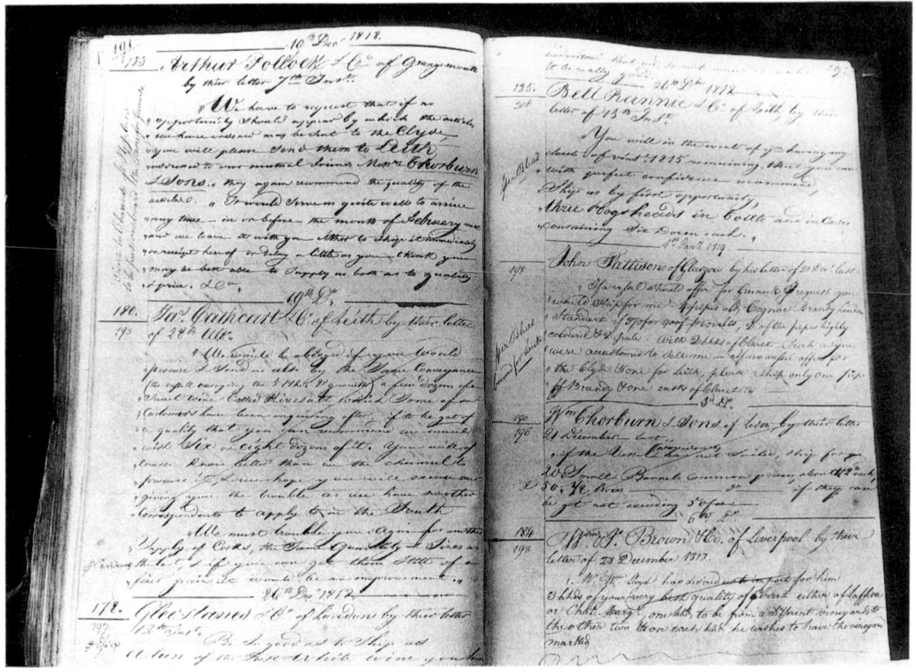

Wines for Leith, Grangemouth and Glasgow in Johnston's order-book, 1818.

> Benicarlo … I have always altered my quantities in proportion to the years, its body and colour … I have given from 4 or 5 to 7 or 8 of Spanish in a middling years or as far as 15 or 16 gallons to the hhg. when the year was very bad and wines thin and green.

So, unknown to them, the Scottish palates' resistance to Iberian wines was being constantly undermined, as Alicante and Benicarlo wine laced their claret. What is more, Scottish négociants were as guilty as any in perpetrating this adulteration. The Johnston whose "instructions for wine" have been given was in fact of Scottish extraction. William Johnston who came to Bordeaux in 1716 was the namesake of his grandfather who moved from Moffat to Armagh some 90 years earlier. In Bordeaux William Johnston became involved in the wine trade and his direct descendants carry on the tradition under the names of Nathaniel Johnston et Fils and Raoul Johnston Vins. The Johnstons were among the first foreign négociants to take French citizenship, but despite this and the fact that they arrived from Scotland indirectly through the Ulster Plantation they still consider themselves to be Scots. One of the few French representatives at the International Gathering of the Clans in Edinburgh in 1979 was Jean-Marie Johnston, a wine dealer based in Pauillac. When he donned the kilt at his wedding, Jean-Marie was in fact reviving a family tradition. In the early 1900s his grandfather Nathaniel Arthur as a boy used to suffer the embarrassment of being teased for wearing a kilt on Sundays in Bordeaux.

William Johnston's business was founded on the export of wine and brandy. Having gone into partnership with his brother Nathaniel in 1765, affairs increased meteorically and in 1788-89 it was noted by the future United States President Thomas Jefferson, that the Johnstons had the foremost trading company in the city. At the time they were shipping large quantities of Chateau d'Yquem, the Sauternes growth, and in 1785 they were the most important of the merchants dealing in Chateau Latour. For a period of ten years around 1790 the Johnstons together with another merchant called Forster took the *abonnement* of Chateau Margaux – they bought the entire production! Perhaps because they were able to establish such firm connections with the *grand crus* and indeed in later years to buy into one in particular, Chateau Latour, the Johnstons remained and still remain the sole modern testimony to the once substantial Scottish involvement in the Bordeaux wine trade.

As if to constantly remind themselves of their Scottish origins, the Johnston *Maison* was exporting considerable quantities of claret to Scotland in the early 1800s. The firm's letter-books chronicle this trade in some detail and reveal much about the way in which Scotland's links with wine and the wine trade were evolving. The Johnstons did business with what appears to have been an entirely new breed of home-based merchants. Gone were Burd, Oliphant, Shairp and Baird, replaced by names, some of which are familiar today, Bell, Rannie and Co., Lyndesay, Bruce, Cockburn, all of Leith, Robertson and Aughterson and Hugh Crawford of Greenock, and many more. Their orders reflect an increased interest in particular growths and vintages. Cathcart and Sons of Leith, ordering in January 1818, provide a typical example. Their requirements were:

4	hogsheads	Lafitte	of	the	1815	vintage
4	"	Latour	"	"	"	"
4	"	Leoville	"	"	"	"
3	"	Kirwan	"	"	"	"

The home market which saw claret becoming less the wine of the people but instead the reserve of the Scottish upper classes, was concentrating increasingly on the *Grands Crus.* Thus in addition to the order detailed above there were many others liberally sprinkled with famous names. One of Bell, Rannie and Co.'s orders in 1818 was for 5 hogsheads each of Latour, Leoville and Lafitte. Lyndesay's order a year earlier was made up of Leoville and Pichon; the Leith merchants, Graham and Son, specified Latour and Lafitte; and so on…

Bell, Rannie and Co., one of the favourite suppliers to the Edinburgh clubs, was a regular customer of the Johnstons in the second and third decade of the 19th century. They had only recently come into the Johnston "fold" having shifted their commercial allegiances with the stock of their previous contacts in Bordeaux – Forster and Chalmers, when it was taken over by the Johnstons in 1812. Judging by the size of their introductory order, Bell, Rannie and Co. must have been quite a catch for the Johnstons.

Edinburgh, 12 November 1812

> We beg leave to avail ourselves of the information we have received from your Mr William Johnston, over in this place, regarding the stock of wines which belonged to our friends Messrs Forster and Chalmers and are now at your disposal, and to request that when proper licences are granted by our Government and opportunity of shipping by a vessel for this port, that you will ship for our account of the above stock:
>
> 2 Tuns Latour
> 5 " Lafitte
> 4 " Bergeron
> 2 " Cauvale
> 2 " Duluc
>
> and that you would purchase also for our attention and ship by the same conveyance
>
> 2 hgs Hermitage of the 1st class
> 2 " Vin de Grave
> 2 " Frontignan
> 2 pieces Cognac Brandy
>
> Although we have mentioned particular growths in our order we request that you will attend to the body and flavour of what you can ship and in consequence we leave to you to find such as attains this description of your own stock or that of Messrs Forster and Chalmers.

For not the first time in the history of the Bordeaux wine trade, there were impediments in linking consumer with the producer as a result of deteriorating political relationships. This time the impediments were in the form of import licences to which Bell, Rannie and Co. refer – the claret trade was once again suffering because France and England (now Britain) were flexing their military muscles at each other.

From then on, however, the records of Bell, Rannie and Co.'s orders are prominent in Johnston's letter books. Not only were orders placed frequently, generally once every other month, but also they were characterised by an inordinate concern for the quality of the wine delivered, to the extent that the Johnstons found them tiresome, "for no wine, (they say)," reported the younger William Johnston in

1817, clearly exasperated, "except those of strong body and high flavour ensure their market." However demanding the firm was of the Johnston's patience, it certainly did not prevent a healthy commercial relationship building up between them. But there was not the remotest possibility that Bell, Rannie and Co. would be rewarded for their patronage in the same way as Lyndesay and Co. were for theirs. Clearly Lyndesay was the Johnston's favourite and an annotation by one of the Johnstons to a letter from Lyndesay in 1814 suggests that their commercial loyalty should be recognised.

> Nothing can exceed the real attachment this friend has always shown us. I have no doubt but that when the fruit season is in you will send him some plumbs, olives and apples for his own use as a small proof of our attachment in our past.

Claret was easily the most important wine traded, though substantial quantities of growths from outwith the Gironde figure in orders placed with the Johnstons. Most of these were from the lower Rhône Valley and Languedoc. By this time the privileges of Bordeaux had been swept away and nothing other than distance and convenience prevented "foreign" wines being shipped through Bordeaux.

A Johnston wedding, Bordeaux 1982.

Vintage-consciousness was sweeping the Scottish wine-drinking public in the early decades of the 19th century and demand for claret tended to fluctuate violently depending on how the vintage was regarded. Poorish vintages in the period

1811-14 were reflected in a lower turnover of the wine, to the extent that as Lyndesay reported in 1816 "There is a great deal of Claret unsold at Leith." When Lyndesay made this observation the 1815 vintage had not been properly assessed. As it turned out this vintage proved exceptional and gradually news about the quality of the 1815's filtered home and generated a spate of orders whose tone gives an impression of a gathering momentum of frenzied purchases. Graham and Sons wrote Johnston in October 1817 to stock up their cellar with this highly recommended wine: "We have now to request you will lay aside for us 30 hgs claret of vintage 1815." In March 1818 Bell, Rannie and Co. were after 5 hogshead each of Latour, Leoville and Lafitte 1815. In May 1818 Cochran and Sons of Leith wrote, "requesting to inform them if we could afford them from 50 to 60 hgs of 1815 in equal proportions of 1st and 2nd growth." By the beginning of 1819 little of this highly sought after vintage remained and orders reflect a certain feeling of vain hope. Cathcart asks Johnston to ship 5 hogsheads of "Latour and Lafite if any are to be had". Another order from Lyndesay pleads that, "if you can spare 10hgs more of the Ducasse please ship them at the first opportunity", and Hagart, forsaking any preference for growths, simply instructs them to load "any spare claret of 1815".

There was still no sign in 1815 of bottled clarets being exported from Bordeaux. Despite the attendant risks – "pinches from crow irons", and their vulnerability to all sorts of adulteration before reaching the customer, claret was invariably dispatched from the Quai des Chartrons in hogsheads. A little more than twenty years later there is some evidence of the *grands crus* in particular being bottled prior to loading at Bordeaux. The consignment of Johnston's wine which left for Leith on the *"Catherine et Ann"* in 1837 was typical of the "mixed" cargoes of claret for the remainder of the century.

30 hogsheads	Latour
16 "	Lafite
17 "	Margaux
20 "	Mouton
360 bottles	Haut Brion
750 "	Leoville
396 "	Rauzan

Today few clarets leave the chateaux unbottled.

By 1820 Scotsmen had achieved a high degree of penetration into all facets of the wine trade. They were firmly established in Bordeaux throughout the 18th century and were now beginning to move into other wine-producing districts in large numbers, even into those of Iberia. There were even Scots based in London who were arranging insurance for wine shipments. When Robertson and Aughterson of Greenock sent for 5 hogsheads of Johnston Claret in 1812 they specified that the insurance should be arranged through Messrs. Stirling and Robertson in the City. The "network" was a dispersed one, covering most of Western Europe, but nevertheless it was tight and close knit. For example, Johnston in 1816 was supplying French wine to the Scottish merchants Newton, Gordon, Murdoch and Scott, then based in Madeira and dealing in local wine. The Lisbon firm of Brown and Reid also took delivery of wines shipped directly by Johnston.

Scots were reluctant partners in the Union, but during the 19th century were certainly making the best of what they considered a bad job. They were to the fore in the expansionist waves of Britons throughout the century and, where the wine trade was concerned, wheedled their way into all aspects of it, in widely scattered regions. Theirs was a significant, albeit underestimated contribution to the development of the wine industry of Europe and the Empire.

Jacobite claret glasses.

FION DEARG NA FRAINGE 11

Just as the remaining stocks of the 1815 vintage were drying up, men with familiar names – Arthur Bell, Johnnie Walker, and others – were blending whiskies which would eventually conquer the world and seriously undermine wine drinking in Scotland. Over the ensuing 150 years, during which these blends became household names, the popular image of whisky as the drink of Celtic civilization with a tradition in the Highlands reaching back into the mists of history has been fostered. So effectively has this association between product and place been implanted on consumer consciousness that we Celts are as guilty as any of believing the stereotype of the traditional whisky-drinking Highlander. The association is spurious since long before the first trickle of neat *uisge-beatha* ever issued from Highland stills, a surprising range and quantity of wines were being drunk the length and breadth of the *Gaidhealtachd.* The history of wine drinking north and west of the "Highland Line" is both long and auspicious.

Perhaps the earliest reference to the use of wine in this area dates from the 6th century A.D. – about the same time as the Scots were spilling over to Dalriada from their native Ireland. Adamnan, St. Columba's biographer, reports that at this time it was in daily used in Iona for sacramental purposes, and records what is likely to have been the Highlands' first transaction involving wine when Columba sailed south to "Land's Head" (Kintyre) to meet "Gallic sailors coming hither from the provinces of Gaul".

Gaelic songs, poetry and oral tradition make mention of wine literally centuries before whisky makes a similar appearance. One mention in particular which suggests the Gaels early penchant for the grape comes in a poem by Dubhghall Mac an Ghiolla Ghlais dedicated to one of Clan Gregor, Eoin Mac Phadruig who died in 1519. In this Dubhghall draws a comparison between Eoin and Fionn MacCumhall, a figure in the oral tradition from an even earlier date, not only for their blue eyes, but also for a good conceit of the cellar

"Math as cubhaidh a rosg gorm
re mac Cumhaill na gcorn bhfhiar
ionann a n-uabhar fá fhion
agus a rùn ag dhìol chliar."

[Well doth his blue eye
match Cumhalls son of the
curving goblets; like their
pride over wine, and their good-
will in requiting poets.]

By way of contrast the earliest references to *uisge-beatha* date from around 1650 and even in these it generally foots a list of more prestigious drinks. Mary MacLeod's song *"Mairi"* from the turn of the 18th century, which describes the pattern of drinking amongst the MacLeods, is typical of the way in which whisky is introduced in texts.

Dhomhsa b'aithne
Beus nan Leodach
Fion ga ligeadh
Beoir 'ga h-ol ac'
Is treas tarruing
Ga cur an stopa
Cobhair fheumach
Riarach beoshlaint'

[Well did I know
the custom of the MacLeods
Wine they broach
and ale they drink
And the thrice-brewed liquor (whisky)
they fill the stoup
A timely aid
To a feast's enjoyment.]

To judge from the numerous allusions to it in literature the use of wine by Gaels reached something of a plateau during the 17th century. Being the nearest source of wine, and because of the continuing political and commercial links between France and Scotland, French wine had become very popular in the *Gaidhealtachd. "Moladh na landaidh"* (In Praise of Islay) written by Iain MacPhaideir during the century supports this early preference.

'S'n uair a shuideamaid mu'n bhord
Cha b'e 'm buideal beag ar leóir
Ach togsaid do'n fhion dhearg ar coir
A tighinn a stór na Frainge

[When we sit about the table
A small flask is not sufficient
Rather a hogshead of red wine
From the French store.]

But French wine did not have the monopoly. It was with Spanish wine and brandy that Iain MacPhaideir drank the health of his love, despite adding, somewhat apologetically, his fear of the consequences.

Dh'olainn, a ghaoil, do dheoch-slainte
a dh'fhion no bhrandaidh na Spainnte
Ged a dh'fhagadh e mi tinn

[My love I would drink your health
On Spanish wine or brandy
Though it may leave me poorly.]

Mairi Nighean Alasdair recalls a love song in which a Spanish ship was seen breaking up on the shore, its cargo of hogsheads being smashed by the waves and the wine tainting the sea water.

Gaelic mythology reckons the Celts to be a pure-blooded race of Spanish origin which migrated northwards. With pure-blooded being given as "wine blooded" in Gaelic *(Fion-fhuil)* we can only wonder whether all the wine imagery in literature actually concerns the product of the Spanish vine or whether it is a re-affirmation of the origin of the species! Most of the wine came from France so it may be that the bards were confusing their geography for poetic and historic effect.

However much wine was drunk in the *Gaidhealtachd* it is unlikely that it was ever the drink of the commonality. The lower classes of the time eked out a meagre existence on what meat was available locally and on products of corn such as bread and ale. Wine drinking was a symbol of status associated with clan chiefs and their entourage and in Highland society only they had the wherewithal to barter for wine. That in itself was yet another indication of social status. A song in praise of Allan the chief of Clan Ranald among other things uses the idea of being able to pay for and consume wine in large quantities to underline his nobility.

Ceannard air sluadh an uair fairechais
Cha b'e 'm buideal beag bu mhath leat
Cha b'iad na stoip ach na galain
Togsaidean fion' air an ceannaibh ruit
Mar dh'oladh cach phaigheadh Ailean.

[Chieftain of hosts in hour of manliness
A flask would not do him
neither stoups nor gallons
Rather brimming hogsheads of wine
And whatever others drank Allan paid for.]

Reinforcing this association of wine and social standing is the claim during a dispute between a South Uist woman and a Barra woman about the relative merits of their respective clan chiefs – Clan Ranald and MacNeil – that one of the symbols of the latter's glory is his practice of giving his horses wine as their morning dram.

In another fantastic context wine is again used to eulogise a clan chief, or rather his *birlinn* (galley). A song said to have been composed by the nurse of Donald Gorm Og, the first baronet of Sleat in Skye, describes the luxurious equipment of the vessel the Baronet would build:

Tha stiuir oir orr' tri chruinn sheilich innt'
Gu bheil tobar fion innt'
Agus tobar fioruisg' shios an deireadh innt'

[She has a golden rudder and three willow masts
With a well of wine in her
And in the stern a well of pure water.]

The Highlands' bards, dependent on the chief's bounty, became in the interests of job preservation professional flatterers, many of whose descriptions were barely realistic. Were the history of wine drinking in the area to be reconstructed simply from their obsequious offerings, the place of wine within this society might reasonably be doubted. Fortunately the evidence incorporated in the verse and song of the time is supported by official registers, which in particular provide proof that the passion for wine at the beginning of the seventeenth century was so strong that the Government found it impossible to restrain.

The first official attempt to curb the use of wine in the islands came as part of the "Statutes of Iona", enacted in 1609. Here Commissioners for the Isles were charged with discretionary powers from the King himself to begin the "civilization and improvement" of that part of Scotland. The Bishop of the Isles, whose task was to communicate the decisions of the Commissioners, set sail for Iona in July 1609 to meet with almost all the principal islanders. There the chiefs were presented with, and agreed to abide by, nine statutes designed with "improvement" in mind. They agreed *inter alia* not to encourage bards and other "idlers of this class", not to use any description of firearms, to give proper obedience to clergymen, to establish inns at appropriate places for the convenience of travellers and to have the eldest sons of certain classes of Highland gentlemen educated in the Lowlands. The fifth statue, relating to wine drinking, proceeds on the narrative that one of the chief causes of poverty, cruelty and inhuman barbarity practised in the numerous feuds and skirmishes, was their inordinate love of strong wine and aquavitae, procured from local dealers and mainland merchants. As a result it was decided that any attempt to import wine or aquavitae for sale by local dealers would be punished by seizure without compensation. Similarly, attempts to buy from mainland suppliers were to be dealt with mercilessly – a fine of £40 to be paid for the first offence, £100 for the second and, for the third, the loss of all "possessions and movable goods". The chiefs themselves did not have their wine supplies jeopardised, perhaps as a means of securing their agreement to recognise the "Statutes". They, along with all other barons and wealthy gentlemen, were allowed to buy sufficient wine and other drinks required for their own private use, but only from Lowland dealers.

Whether because of the loophole allowing the gentry relative freedom to buy wines, or for other reasons, the improvements which the Statutes were supposed to engender never materialised, and by 1616 the Scottish Privy Council was obliged to apply stricter regulations. This time not only the sale of wine but also its use in the Islands was prohibited under heavier penalties. To make this prohibition effective locally, half the penalty raised was to be paid to the landlord or chief. He in turn was formally bound to restrict his own wine-drinking and to ensure that none of his tenants should buy or drink any wine whatsoever. This stricter control on wine-drinking was based on the Privy Council's belief that

> The grite and extraordinar excesse in drinking wyne commonlie vsit amangis the commonis and tennentis of the Yllis is not onlie ane occasioun of the beastlie and barbarous cruelteis and inhumaniteis that fallis oute amangis thame to the offens and displesour of God and contempt of law and justice bot with that it drawis numberis of thame to miserable necessitie and povertie sua that thay ar constraynit quhen thay want of thair awne to tak from thair nichtbouris.

The 1616 legislation defined how much wine could be used annually in the households of island chieftains. Smaller chiefs such as MacKinnon of Skye, MacLean of Coll, and MacLaine of Lochbuie in Mull were restricted to one tun or four hogsheads. Those of a higher rank such as Clan Ranald were permitted three tuns or twelve hogsheads, while chiefs of even greater standing – MacLeod of Dunvegan, MacLean of Duart, Donald Gorm of Sleat – were allowed four tuns each for their household's annual use. One can only wonder what the "normal" ration of wine was in these households, if a restricted supply was set at four tuns annually. At a constant rate of consumption this would be equivalent of up to 10 litres of wine per day!

It appears that the regulations of 1616 were hardly more effective than the Statutes of 1609, and in 1622 new legislation was introduced. This proved to be even more stringent, making it illegal for ships masters to carry more wine to the Isles than was allowed to chiefs under the 1616 Act. Again the link between excessive drinking, internecine feuds, acts of violence and the stunted development of civilisation was quoted as justification for this measure:

> Forasmekle as it is understand to the Lordis of Secreit Counsell that one of the cheiff caussis whilk procuris the continewance of the inhabitants of the Ilis in thair barbarous and incivile forme of living is the grite quantitie of wynes yeirlie caryed to the Ilis with the insatiable desire quhairof the saidis inhabitantis ar so far possest that quhen thair arryvis ony ship or other veshell thair with wynes, thay spend bothe dayis and nightis in thair excesse of drinking and seldome do thay leave thair drinking so lang as thair is ony of the wyne restand sua that being overcome with drink thair fallis oute mony inconvenientis amangis thame to the brek of his Maiesteis peace.

If the memorable skirmish between the MacLeods of Raasay and the MacKenzies of Gairloch is something to judge by, the efforts of the authorities to restrain wine drinking, were perfectly justified. This particular episode came at the end of a period in which the two clans were constantly at loggerheads over the possession of parts of Torridon. Murdo MacKenzie, the son and heir to MacKenzie of Gairloch, sailed for Skye with a number of his followers, spoiling for a fight. Their galley however was forced by the severity of the weather to shelter off Raasay, and in time the young laird of Raasay, curious about the presence of this strange ship, boarded her with twelve men. After having had a good look at the ship and her company, under the pretext of buying wine, he left again with his retinue. Later he came back to buy more wine. The transaction complete, MacLeod invited the ship's company to join him and his now enlarged retinue to share the wine purchased. Naturally there were few who could pass up so magnanimous an offer and presently with MacLeod making the wine move quickly, most of the MacKenzies became drunk and retired below. MacLeod, seizing the opportunity, declared Murdo MacKenzie a prisoner. Despite being disabled through drink Murdo resisted and in the fight that ensued the few sober MacKenzies gave a good account of themselves. They managed to effect their escape but not before many of their number, including the Gairloch heir, were killed.

Wine was also to the fore in peacemaking. For many years during the 17th century the MacDonalds and MacLeods of Skye had been engaged in the so-called *"Cogadh na Cailiche Caim"* – the War of the One-Eyed Old Woman. Hostilities had erupted when after a handfasting arrangement the one-eyed sister of the MacLeod chief was returned unwanted by his MacDonald counterpart. In itself this was sufficient reason for animosity but the circumstances of her return – on a one-eyed horse, led by a one-eyed servant and followed by a one-eyed dog – was too great an insult for the MacLeods to contain their bellicose instincts. But however spectacular the war was it could hardly have upstaged the celebrations in Dunvegan Castle which marked its conclusion. For this party, hosted by Rory Mor their chief, the MacLeods were joined by MacDonalds from various parts and together they made a considerable dent in the Castle's annual wine allowance. Judging by the descriptions of MacMhuraich, the hereditary bard of the MacDonalds of Clanranald, no one was in a hurry to leave:

Se hoidhce dhamhsa san Dun
Nior bhe an coinmhe fallsa fhùar
Cuim lionmhur ga hibhe ahor
Fionbhrugh mor is lion mhur sluagh

[Six nights I have been in the Dun (Dunvegan Castle)
Plenty of ale was drunk at the table
There was a large wine-hall and a numerous host.]

MacMhuraich continues to depict a scene in which the company drank deeply of "generous wine that would overcome the hardiest heroes" and admits that

Fiche misge lin g'laoi
No char leigse lin no le

[Twenty times drunk we were each day
Nor did we rebel against it anymore than he.]

He himself fell victim to the wine that flowed and concluded one evening prostrate in a lobby surrounded by a pack of licking dogs. The MacLeod bard who witnessed the scene, confirms that there was no professional solidarity among poets in the early 17th century:

Tha bard Mhic Dho'uill air a dhruim
'S e cur as a chionn a chorr
'S am fear thug dhasan a dhiol
Thug e biadh do choin 'ic Leoid

[The MacDonald bard is on his back
He who is throwing up in excess
The one (ie wine) who gave him his problem
Is now giving the MacLeod dogs a feed.]

For Rory Mor and other chiefs the unstinted hospitality, shown on occasions such as these, was probably the heaviest drain on their resources. Perhaps MacAulay had Rory Mor in mind when he marvelled at the capacity of the chiefs of Skye to extend hospitality on a grand scale, despite relatively spartan domestic circumstances. They would, he opined, *"often do the honours ... with a lofty courtesy worthy of the splendid circle of Versailles"*. But there was little evidence of the civility and dignity of Versailles in Martin Martin's description of the "Manner of drinking us'd by the chief Men of the Isles", during the 17th century:

> Among persons of distinction it was reckon'd an affront put upon any company to broach a piece of wine, ale or aquavitae and not see it all drank out at one meeting.

Nor did Versailles have anything to compare with the arrangements for transporting to bed the revellers who had succumbed to strong drink:

> There were two men with a barrow attending punctually on such occasions. They stood at the door until some became drunk, and they carry'd them upon the barrow to bed, and return'd again to their post as long as any continued fresh, and so carry'd off the whole company one by one as they became drunk.

The need to impress through lavishing wine and food on guests seems to have been a fairly consistent feature of the MacLeod line. One of Rory Mor's ancestors, Alasdair Crotach, who died in 1547 played this part to perfection. Once at the Royal table in Holyrood he was taunted by a Lowland noble that Skye could never match the magnificent and spacious halls, the ornate candelabra and the richly laden tables of the Palace. Unperturbed, Alasdair rose to the challenge and asserted that on all these counts Skye could better Holyrood, at which the Lowland noble announced that he would visit Skye to judge for himself.

It was late in the evening when the nobleman eventually arrived at Dunvegan. He was conducted, not to the castle, but up the slopes of Healaval Mor, one of the flat-topped "MacLeod's Tables" – and eventually to the summit which, for the occasion, was edged by torch-bearing clansmen and covered with an extravagant feast of extraordinary quality and variety, complemented by copious supplies of claret. While still bemused by the scene before him the Lowland laird's attention was drawn by Alasdair Crotach to the size and magnificence of his hall, the star-spangled sky, the feast, and the lighting arrangements, all of which upstaged anything Holyrood could offer. Suitably chastened the Lowlander made apologetic noises and returned south forthwith.

As if to reiterate their penchant for wine in every succeeding generation, the 17th century MacLeod chiefs initiated the practice of having every heir to the chieftainship prove his manhood, on coming of age, by quaffing without pause for breath, the contents of a large ox horn, filled to the brim with one and a half pints of claret! Suitably, this silver mounted horn, has taken the name of one of the clan's greatest topers – Rory Mor.

The MacLeods did not have the monopoly of conviviality in Skye. Not so many miles from Dunvegan is the MacDonald stronghold of Duntulm Castle:

Dun tuilm an talamh deagh-mhaiseach
Am biodh ceir 'ga las' as coinnleiribh
Is fion 'ga ol gu saoibhir ann
Am piosa glasa soillsichte

[The lovely country of
Duntulm wherein waxen
candles blaze, and
wine is drunk freely
from worn and gleaming
cups of silver in a
mansion wide and joyous
and full of music.]

Duntulm Castle.

Duntulm Castle regrettably is now ruined having been abandoned because, among other reasons, Donald Gorm Mor, one of the MacDonald chiefs, persisted in returning as a ghost to throw boozey parties with similarly deceased friends.

Glimpses of the wine drinking traditions elsewhere in the *Gaidhealtachd* abound. For example Brahan Castle in Ross, stronghold of the MacKenzies, was noted for the richness and variety of its feast table and equally for the diversity of liquors available:

Gheibhteadh gu leoir, pailteas mu d'bhord
Deoch de gach seorsa dh'aimichteadh
Rum, portair a's beoir: fion, branndaidh ri ol
A chuireadh fir og fo mheamnachd.

[You would get plenty,
A table of variety, drink of every
sort you could name, Rum, porter,
Wine, brandy to drink, inspiring
Thoughts in young men.]

The Clan Ranald possessions in Moidart also found repute in the wealth of the fare available.

Tir tha doannan a cuir thairis
Le tuil bhainne, meal, a's fion.

[A land that is always overflowing
With floods of milk, honey and wine.]

And over in those in the Outer Hebrides

Steach gu Uibhist an eorna
Far an olte fion ceannaich

[To Uist of Barley
Where imported wine is drunk.]

Imported wine? Every last hogshead of it was imported – the possibilities for local production being somewhat limited. But as to how it was imported, through whom and from where only a little can be said. Some of the wine came through local middlemen to the Highland customer from the continental supplier. Rory Mor MacLeod certainly received wine from a merchant based in Lewis. Evidence in the *Book of Dunvegan* – the published records of the MacLeod household – confirms this in reproducing letters of horning issued against Rory Mor for the non-payment of a wine bill. The first letter, dated 5th April 1610, was raised by Robert Campbell the merchant in Stornoway who was owed 100 merks for "Certaine sufficient wynes bocht and ressavit fra ye said complenar…" Discharging this debt was not one of Rory Mor's priorities and the unfortunate Campbell was obliged to issue another letter in 1625 for the sum of £509 Scots due on the same "Certaine wynes ressavit be him with quhilk he wes weill pleased". Pleased or not with the wines supplied Rory Mor made no attempt to pay off this 15-year-old debt before his death in the following year. Campbell realistically cut his losses and made no further claims for payment against the MacLeod estate. Presumably Rory Mor's treatment of his local wine dealer was not typical of the general attitude of Highland chieftains to those who provided their tipple, since there is evidence at this and later dates of wine merchants actually remaining in business.

Smuggling was an import "option" to which the topography of the north-west coastline lent itself. More will be said about this activity during the 18th century when it boomed, but from the narratives accompanying the Statutes and Regulations the fact that more wine than could be effectively controlled by the authorities was being brought to the north-west in the early 17th century, is clearly implied. The *Gaidhealtachd* was in effect limbering up for the great era of wine running which was to establish itself in the final decades of the century.

The concept of "importing" seems to have been interpreted with a fair degree of latitude by some chiefs and clansmen. An example of one of the more dubious "importing" techniques practiced involves the ill-fated voyage of the barque *"Suzanne".* She left St. Malo for Limerick in December 1634 with a cargo of wine and other merchandise to the value of £1000 sterling. Fearful weather drove the *"Suzanne"* further north than was intended and eventually she took shelter off South Uist. The assistance of local people was asked and a deal in which a barrel each of Spanish wine and raisins was paid, had to be struck before the islanders would conduct the ship to a safe anchorage. The latter had no intention of accepting just one barrel of the wine aboard for their rescue service, and when beached, the *"Suzanne's"* cargo was plundered with the active involvement of Clan Ranald and Ragnall Mor, Laird of Borve Castle in Benbecula. The volume *Les Ecossais en France* in which this incident is recorded, describes the scene

> Un grand nombre d'individus…tirèrent et burent le vin jour par jour, emportèrent toutes les marchandises, ne laissant pas même aux malheureux marins leurs effets de corps.

Having appropriated her cargo the Uist wreckers added insult to injury by giving the *"Suzanne's"* captain an offer he could not refuse – to sell the *"Suzanne"* for £8. Her true value was close to £150.

The mistaken impression may have been given that the only wine-drinking that went on in the Highlands occurred within sight of the Minch. In reality a strong wine-drinking tradition obtained throughout the whole of the area. Certainly wine was as easily available in other parts. As early as 1557 the Burgh Court of Inverness was discussing arrangements for the payment of outstanding wine debts. On this occasion a group of Invernessians were being asked to settle the debt of "…the sowme of fowyer skoyr sex pundis fyf schillingis and that for thre towne thre puntionis wyne ressaid be tham" – a debt which they had incurred with the merchants Patre Crommy and James Robertson. A little over half a century later, Taylor the London water poet on his "penniless" journey in Scotland fell in with a hunting party of Scottish noblemen, gentlemen and camp followers in the Braemar area and was invited to take part in an al fresco feast of breathtaking extravagance, lubricated by "good ale, sacke, white and claret, tent or allegant with the most potent aquavitae." Already the eastern Highlands displayed a diversity in the choice of wine available unmatched at that time in the west.

Still during the 17th century, Robert Gordon of Gordonstoun was shipping barley from the Earl of Sutherland's estate south to the Lowlands, and taking wine and a variety of other commodities in exchange. One particular shipment in 1678 Robert Gordon insisted, was to be paid for thus:

> halfe the price of the vituall, in money, and the other halfe in goods, namely, two halfe butts of Sacke, at twentie-one pound sterling the butts; three hogshead of French wine, att twentie-foure pound sterling the tunn; three hundredth stane of iron.

The Highlands of the 18th century were much better documented than in the previous one and from contemporary accounts it appears that wine in the area's social life had reached an unprecedented prominence. Trade in wine was much better organised (but not so well organised as to interfere with the considerable wine smuggling activity which was developing). At Inverness, for example, wine was imported directly from Bordeaux and Spain by Bailie John Stewart, and from there was redistributed through the coastlands of the Moray Firth and to further flung parts of the Highlands. By the middle of the 18th century General Wade's roads threaded along glens and over mountain passes, "opening up" the Highlands and facilitating the control of the Jacobite natives. Coincidentally, Wade's roads made the transport of wine from merchant to customer considerably easier. Captain Burt who accompanied Wade to Inverness in 1725 as one of the road-building squad, described in his *Letters from the North of Scotland* how difficult transporting wine was before properly paved roads were introduced.

> There is little need of carts for the business of the Town (Inverness) and when a hogshead of wine has been to be carried to any part not very far distant, it has been placed upon a kind of frame among four horses, two on a side, following each other; the ways are so rough and rocky that no wheel ever turned upon them since the formation of this globe; and therefore if the townsmen were furnished with sufficient wheel carriages for goods of great weight, they would be seldom useful.

Better roads, which Burt helped design, eventually eased this problem, no doubt to the delight of Highland wine drinkers.

The wine biber of the 1700's also found more outlets for his favourite beverage than was the case a generation before. At most of the Highlands' recognised fording points, crossroads and road ends, wherever there was a certain amount of passing trade, inns and change-houses now tempted the thirsty traveller. Captain Burt was clearly impressed by what such establishments could offer:

> We have one great advantage, that makes amends for many inconveniences, that is, the wholesome and agreeable drink – I mean French claret, which is to be met with almost everywhere in Public Houses of any note, except in the heart of the Highlands, and sometimes even there.

An inn without wine was then somewhat exceptional judging by the reactions of contemporary travellers when it was unavailable. Severe disappointment was expressed by Bishop Forbes of Ross and Caithness, while on an episcopal visitation to Caithness in 1762 when he discovered wine could not be had. He complained that "in all the publick houes we halted at ... we could have no kind of drink but small ale and whiskie". Only days before, Forbes had been delighted by the quality and cheapness of the claret on sale at Mathieson's Tavern in Fortrose.

Disappointment was also in store for Johnson and Boswell during their peregrinations in the Highlands *en route* for the Hebrides. Making for Skye they passed through Glenelg where, at last, after a long rain-sodden day of travelling, Johnson and his colleague

> came to our inn weary and peevish, and began to inquire for meat and beds. Of the provisions the negative catalogue was very copious, there was no meat, no milk, no bread, no eggs, no wine. We did not express much satisfaction. Here however we were to stay.

The poverty of the fare at Glenelg was unusual. The traditional Highland inn was certainly rough and ready but could be relied upon to provide reasonable food and excellent wine. In her *Memoirs* Elizabeth Grant of Rothiemurchus pens a sketch of the typical hostelry in the 18th and early 19th centuries.

> No carpets on the floor, no cushions in the chairs, no curtains to the windows. Of course polished tables, or even clean ones, were unknown. All the accessories of the dinner were wretched, but the dinner itself was excellent; hotch-potch, salmon, fine mutton, grouse, scanty vegetables, bad bread, but good wine.

The "good wine" was generally claret, but not invariably. Travellers in the mid-18th century might happen upon inns such as the "British Arms" in Elgin where a wide range of wines in addition to claret were on sale. The bills presented by the landlord,

Robert Gordon, to a local gentleman, Dunbar of Thunderton, reveal the choice available: Rhenish, Champagne, Port, Sherry, Frontignac, Mountain, Madeira, Malaga, Lisbon, Claret, Sack as well as whey, tea, coffee and cider. This impressive list was somewhat wasted on Dunbar for he, more often than not settled for claret. One bill dated 1769 was for 35 bottles of claret, all for the sum of £4.7.6. Dunbar's only digression from his normal drinking pattern was when be bought, by way of a change, a bottle each of Port and Lisbon at a total cost of 4/-.

Like Dunbar most Highlanders of the time displayed a strong preference for claret. This wine's popularity was not simply because it was considered a superior drink to any others, but also because it was consistent with the general interest in France and things French which obtained in the north. French influence in the Highlands was pervasive. Many young lairds and gentlemen received their education in France, and the area's priests were likely to be products of the Scots Colleges in Douai or Paris. Other Highlanders such as Cameron of Lochiel and Neil MacEachan spent time in France, the former in exile since the first Jacobite Rebellion, and the latter as an agent of the French government. The French traveller of the later 18th century, Faujas de St. Fond, reported that French was spoken at the Duke of Argyll's table "With as much purity as in the polished circles of Paris". It was fashionable to emulate French cuisine, or as Burt scathingly puts it, dishes were "disguised after the French manner" and the appropriate accompaniment for any meal would have been claret.

In 18th century Britain claret was generally the drink associated with the pro-French and Jacobite factions. Apparently denying any consideration of relative quality, the Whigs preferred drink was port, which by all accounts was then a raw and coarse liquor. In two fundamental respects the Highland Jacobite differed from his Lowland counterpart. The former remained deeply imbued in French culture and civilisation up until the mid-18th century whereas generally throughout the Presbyterian south, French influence had been on the wane since the time of the Reformation. Maintaining the bond between the French and the Highlanders was their Catholicism. The other distinguishing feature was that while Lowlanders by and large were content to express their Jacobitism through proposing numerous toasts to the "Pretender" in large draughts of claret, the Highlander displayed a willingness to translate his pro-Jacobite sentiments into actually doing battle for the cause. Highland chiefs had little to thank the Stewart line for, but nevertheless were hopelessly caught up in a fever of Jacobitism generated in particular by the charismatic character of Bonnie Prince Charlie.

A victim of this fever was young Clan Ranald, one of the Prince's most loyal followers who had already been honoured by his commission in the French Service

A *Highland wine-merchant.*

MacDonald of Boisdale's wine-bottle seal, circa 1780

for his efforts to recruit Highlanders to the "Ecossais Royale" – a regiment raised in France by the Drummond Dukes of Perth. Another Uistman Neil MacEachan, was similarly bitten. Having received most of his education in France he returned to the islands in 1738 to help in one such recruiting drive. MacEachan's exile in France following the '45 was marked by his auspicious success in the French military, a tradition carried on by his son Alexandre Jacques Josephe Etienne MacDonald who was to become the Duke of Tarentum and one of Napoleon's twenty-six marshals. (Whether as a cover for Neil or to simplify pronunciation for the French the family had changed their name to MacDonald). Both MacEachan and Clan Ranald, in keeping with their political leanings, were great *amateurs* of French Wine. MacEachan on his retiral, chose to remove to Sancerre in the Loire district for the simple reason that there, living was cheap and the wine good. Clan Ranald and his cousin Boisdale imported claret to their South Uist homes by the hogshead and there had it racked into bottles specially manufactured with their personal seal.

It was one such bottle that Clan Ranald brought to the tired and dispirited Prince on his arrival in Benbecula following the disaster at Culloden. Wine in fact, was a constant accessory of the Prince throughout the fruitless campaign. Having arrived in Eriskay on the wine-laden barque, *"La Doutellay"*, to express his claim to the throne more forcefully, there were very few occasions over the next few months when the Prince was deprived of his daily ration of claret. The accounts submitted by James Gib, the Master of Household, detail how much liquor was bought. A merchant in Airth supplied a hogshead for £18 and another, Mr. Don, received upwards of £50 for the wine he provided. Close on £8 was spent on it in Glasgow and at the Prince's lodgings in Inverness before the fateful battle a record of the wines laid in by the merchant Alasdair Fraser still remains.

22 February 1746	Claret 3 dozen	£3. 0. 0.
	Lisbone 1/2 "	10. 0.
	Sherry 1/2 "	10. 0.

The Young Pretender's liking for wine was widely known. Indeed there is some dispute as to whether the words of the song, *"Bha do phog mar fhion na Frainge" (Your kiss was like French wine)* were more literal than metaphorical. The many presents of wine which were sent to the Prince whilst in hiding from Government troops would have been gratefully received. Waiting at Rossinish in Benbecula before embarking for Skye a messenger brought him a roasted chicken and a couple of bottles of wine from Clan Ranald. Having gone "over the sea to Skye", Kingsburgh greeted him with a bottle of wine and some biscuits sent by Lady Margaret MacDonald. However his chivalry prevented him from imbibing the paltry ration of claret he had in his possession on the sea journey.

> Lady Clan Ranald had but one half bottle of wine (there being so many demands on her particularly from parties of the military) which she likewise caused to be put on board the boat. The Prince in the passage would not allow any person to share in this small allowance of wine, but kept it altogether for Miss (Flora) MacDonald's use, lest she should faint with the cold and other inconveniences of a night passage.

Despite having led the second disastrous Jacobite attempt within 30 years, Bonnie Prince Charlie has not been forgotten in the *Gaidhealtachd.* Today glasses are still lifted in his praise. Perhaps more surprisingly even the most ardent Unionist from the south, using what little Gaelic he might have, inadvertently toasts the Prince with *"Slainte Mhor!"* To the uninitiated this would simply mean "Great Health", but to the Gael it is "Health to Marion" – *Mor,* the Gaelic for Marion, being the by-name used by the Prince while in hiding.

THE PETTY SNUFF BOX 12

In the eastern Highlands where Burt claimed port could not be had for "love nor money", politics hardly seems to have influenced drinking patterns. There is no clearer testimony to this than the case of Duncan Forbes of Culloden, Lord President of Scotland for some time during the 18th century, and perhaps one of the Highlands' most fervent Whigs. Despite his political leanings Forbes' propensity for claret was legendary. Whilst among his colleagues in Edinburgh's legal circles claret drinking would have been mandatory, and at Culloden House, his country residence, he would have had to continue claret-assisted carousals to maintain appearances and influence among Highland dignitaries. Though Forbes was reputed to have had a head capable of standing claret in copious amounts, his constitution sometimes succumbed to the repeated assaults it had to bear. At one such juncture in 1716, Forbes, in a rather delicate state, wrote to one of his jovial Edinburgh friends in rather despairing terms

> For my own part I am almost wearied of this wicked world; one wish, and but one I had when I left you concerning myself, that I might enjoy eight days free of company and Claret. How I have succeeded, you may guess by this, that though today it be just a month since I saw you, I have not yet buckled a shoe, that is, I have not been one day out of my boots.

Forbes' reputation for tremendous hospitality was somewhat bolstered by the practice at Culloden House to prize off the top of each successive hogshead of claret and place it in a corner of the hall to be emptied by the pailful when guests required. When visitors arrived at the house another bacchanalian ritual took place. Burt who had first-hand knowledge of it described what happened:

> It is the custom of that house, at the first visit or introduction, to take up your freedom, by cracking his nut (as he terms it) that is a cocoa-shell, which holds a pint, filled with champagne, or such other sort of wine as you shall choose, you may guess by the introduction at the contents of the volume. Few go away sober at any time, and for the greatest part of his guests, in the conclusion they cannot go at all.

The social ethos of the time prevented the polite guest from leaving parties so long as the host was still willing or able to provide hospitality. This generally constituted his liquor in breathtaking quantities. In such circumstances few could retire from revelries under their own steam, and thus for the evening's casualties

Duncan Forbes and his cronies at Culloden House

Forbes had made special provision:

> As the company are disabled one after another, two servants, who are all the while in waiting, take up the individuals with short poles in their chairs, as they sit (if not fallen down) and carry them to their beds.

According to Burt, Forbes kept

> a plentiful table and excellent wines of various sorts and in great quantities, as indeed he ought, for I have often said, I thought there was so much wine spilt in his hall as would content a moderate family.

The focus of so much conviviality in Culloden House was the massive hall table, itself so deeply saturated on so many occasions by copious libations of claret that the wood from which it was constructed could not be identified. Little wonder then that research into the house's account books revealed that for a single nine-month period, purchases of wine alone would have cost Forbes £2000 sterling at prices prevailing at the time of the survey. That was in 1812!

Perhaps even more guilty than Duncan Forbes in instigating bacchanalian excesses was his brother whose by-name – "Bumper John" – leaves no doubt about his bibulous inclinations. He was a celebrated toper whose expenditure on liquor by 1716 had reached such a level that there were serious doubts about his ability to pay for the claret he quaffed so liberally. In March, 1716, while John was in London at Parliament, he wrote his brother, then the Lord Advocate's Depute in Edinburgh, to pass on a Brigadier Grant's best wishes. Grant's greeting having been communicated he continues with what turns out to be the main purpose of his correspondence with Duncan.

> He [Grant] tells me Mr James is to send wine. If you can prevaill with Mr Innes to send me a gross of bottells of his best and strongest wine in companie with the Brigadiers it would be oblidgeing and I shall pay him thankfully att meeting.

Neither John Forbes' elevated position in society nor his promises to settle up for the wine impressed Innes, and this he appears to have made plain, for in John's next letter of the 12th April, 1716, he tells Duncan

> I am sorrie to find my credite runs so low with Mr Innes as not to afford me a gross or two of his wine.

Undaunted John adopts another approach, to use his brother's undoubted influence to procure the requisite liquor

> I desyre you may cause some other of your acquaintance doe it and I shall pay them honestly.

Clearly Duncan was unwilling to become involved in any of John's dubious transactions and omitted to do anything about this request. By May 1st, John was rather exasperated by his vain efforts to secure a supply of wine, and in a further letter to his brother he cannot disguise his pique –

> your periwig will be sent to you next week, tho' you have sent me no wine.

As to whether he thought that a periwig in exchange for 144 bottles of claret was a reasonable deal, John does not specify. Doubtless Duncan didn't!

The hospitality and conviviality of Culloden House may have been unusual, but it certainly was not unique in the Highlands of the 18th century. Bishop Forbes on his way to Caithness came across another gentleman, Sutherland of Langwell, who was recognised for the same qualities of generosity. According to the Bishop if any gentleman traveller passed by Sutherland's house, he would allow him to continue for a while before dispatching servants after him and

> though none of his acquaintance in any shape, to take him prisoner back to his house, there to be entertained with many good things for several days, if by any means he can be prevailed upon to stay that long.

Among the "good things" would have been claret, Sutherland of Langwell was "a jovial hearty man who liked a good glass of claret at home and abroad, and was exceedingly merry over it". He was equally generous in lavishing wine on others as he was in providing for his own needs. On one occasion when a small company dined with him his whispered instructions to a servant were overheard:

"John, slack a dozen corks of wine, then go down stairs and take your dinner, and when you have done, come up and slack another dozen."

Travellers, if their constitution would allow, might stray for 20 miles off their route just to sample the generosity of the Langwell household. Sutherland's skill as a host was widely recognised, and it was this that prompted Lady Jane, wife of Ulbster to invite him to be "landlord" at a dinner in her Thurso residence for Lord Duffus, Sir William Dunbar, Durran, and Scotscalder. She reckoned that her visitors were on the scrounge for "a sett of drink" rather than being sociable and instructed Sutherland to "make an example of them". This he executed with his usual deftness, to the extent that those of the party who managed to leave, did so only by virtue of being "oxter-handed" from the house.

Wine appears to have graced the tables of most of the Highland aristocratic households. Boswell and Johnson, whose journals provide an embryonic *Good Food Guide* to the Highlands and Islands of the 18th century, were rarely offered less than the best of wines during their travels. At Talisker House in Skye, for example, while dining with Magnus MacLeod and MacLeod of Bay, Johnson records that they "had admirable venison, generous wine; in a word all that a good table has". Among their other visits in Skye, Ullinish House and Dunvegan Castle also received the travellers' seal of gastronomic approval. So also did Corrichatachin's table, though in Boswell's case, the memories of the wines tasted may not have been among the most pleasant. He and the host had been drinking long into the night, and the next morning Boswell was full of remorse.

I awaked at noon, with a severe head-ache. I was much vexed that I should have been guilty of such a riot ... When I rose, I went to Dr Johnsons room and taking up Mrs MacKinnons prayer book, I opened it at the twentieth Sunday after Trinity, in the epistle for which I read 'And not be drunk with wine, wherein there is excess'. Some would have taken this as divine interposition.

The choicest wines and the best food were reserved for the most distinguished visitors and doubtless Boswell and Johnson, being of the rare breed of genteel travellers, were given the full treatment by their hosts. Inferior wines and fare were provided for visitors of lesser social standing and so on down the echelons of society. At Lord Lovat's seat, Castle Dounie, the correlation between class and the quality of sustenance offered could be clearly distinguished within the same sitting. Lovat's biographer, John Hill Burton, describes this remarkable arrangement.

At the head of the table where there were neighbouring chiefs and distinguished strangers, Claret and French cookery graced the board. The next department was occupied by Duihne Wassels, who enjoyed beef and mutton, with a glass of some humbler wine. The

> sturdy commoners of the clan would occupy the next range feeding on sheeps heads, and drinking whiskey or ale. In further progress the fare degenerated with the feeders, and clustering on the castle green in sunshine, or cowering in the outhouses in foul weather, were congregated the ragamuffins of the clan to gnaw the bones and devour other offal.

As was the case with their neighbours in the Lowlands, Highlanders did not restrict their wine drinking to happy, joyful occasions. On the contrary no laird's or gentleman's funeral took place without plentiful supplies of good cheer for those who attended. Sir Alexander MacDonald of Sleat's funeral in 1746 was no exception – the largesse accompanying the ceremony having reputedly cost his estate £2645. With so much wine flowing this solemn event soon degenerated into riotous merry-making. In the brawling which ensued many were seriously injured. Comparing it with a similar event some time afterwards, MacDonald of Ord remarked

> There has not been a funeral like it since that of Sir Alexander MacDonald, when three men were killed, and fifty were taken out of the Churchyard with the breath just left in them.

At funerals where such quantities of wine were being lavishly dispensed there was a real danger that the reverence of the occasion would be forgotten and important details of the funeral arrangements be overlooked. It seems particularly apt given his track record, that this was the case at the funeral of Duncan Forbes' mother. He was responsible for entertaining the mourners who had assembled, and in Forbes' *Memoirs* published after his death the circumstances leading to a variety of indiscretions which resulted are graphically described.

> The Lady of Culloden … being dead, a very grand entertainment was prepared, and her funeral obsequies were intended to be performed with the utmost solemnity. On the day appointed a prodigious multitude appeared, consisting perhaps of 10,000 [sic] people. The noblemen and gentlemen present drank most plentifully, and the care of the entertainment was devolved upon him, her younger son, who played his part so well that, forgetting his grief, he made the company drink to such an immoderate excess, as even to forget what they were doing; at last it was moved to proceed to the place of internment; they quickly rose up and rode out of the church yard; but unluckily for them, they had neglected to give orders for the lifting of the corpse … When at the grave, the main thing is wanting, and while all the friends are crowding to perform the last duties to the deceased behold the subject is no nearer than the place in which she died. A messenger is instantly sent off to hasten up the corpse, which was done with all imaginable speed, and the lady was laid in the grave with all the decorum and decency that could be expected from gentlemen who had fared so sumptuously and drank so plenteously at her house.

While the greater part of Highland clansmen were pledging their allegiance to one or other of the "Pretenders" to the throne, the Magistrates of the "Highland Capital", Inverness, were using the birthday of the German who actually occupied the coveted throne as an excuse for an annual binge. Here as in every Scottish burgh, the monarch's birthday celebrations implied an evening of dissipation at the Cross or Town Hall. Town Council Accounts from 1730 record expenditure on these. The King's birthday celebrations of 1732 is a typical example –

$4^1/2$ dozen bottles Claret	= 18/-
2 bottles 'Zerie' (Sherry)	£1.16. 0
To the Kirk Officer for ringing the bell	12/-
A Door Keeper	12/-
Candles	£1.10. 0

and lastly an item which might have distinguished this celebration from others elsewhere in Scotland,

Peat for the bonfire	11/-

By 1736 the liquor ration for Magistrates on such occasions had been increased to 6 dozen bottles of claret. The "extra" 18 bottles in that year appears to have had an adverse effect on their behaviour since the Burgh Treasurer was required to stump up for the ten bottles of wine and 17 glasses which were either stolen or broken in the frolic. The celebrations following the Battle of Dettingen in 1742 were characterised by similar recklessness by the councillors and this time the casualties were 6 glasses and a "bottle screw". For a change, behaviour at the King's Birthday celebrations in 1745 was exemplary – no breakages or thefts were recorded, a fact which might not be unrelated to the presence of ten soldiers of the Earl of Loudoun's Regiment charged with the task of "guarding the table and the bonfire". On other occasions there were minor incidents, but none more serious than the breakage of yet another "bottle screw" and a chamber pot in 1764 when the burgh entertained Colonel Stewart. There is nothing to suggest how the latter item came to be broken at this event, but those with fertile imaginations might think of a few plausible reasons.

Another of the Council's obligations was to entertain Circuit Judges on their visits to Inverness. This they carried out without stinting on the claret. In 1759 their visit was honoured by disposing of 70 bottles of the wine in the Town Hall. Three years later when the advocates Dundas and Crosbie were in town, something akin to a "wine and cheese party" was arranged. In addition to the 56 bottles of claret bought for the occasion, $3^1/2$ lbs Gloucester Cheese, 4 lbs Raisins, 4 lbs rock almonds, 12 biscuits and $3^1/2$ mould candles were purchased.

Though they were only too happy to share the contents of the town's wine cellars with the Councillors, the Lords of Session were not willing to risk their culinary offerings. Instead they brought a cook with them from Edinburgh, who was made responsible for the preparation of their meals while in Inverness. This cook was the creator of a celebrated *fête champêtre* on the islands in the River Ness at which Councillors and Judges became totally insensible on the accompanying wine. At the time it was remarked that had the small craft the party used to reach the island overturned on the return journey, through the uncontrolled, inebriated lurch of an individual succumbing to excessive drinking, the consequent drownings would have dislocated the Scottish legal system for some time.

Inverness's acquaintance with French wine has spanned many centuries. The Exchequer Rolls of 1460 record one of the first purchases made by Magistrates on behalf of the burgh. The transaction involved the purchase in Aberdeen of 4 pipes of wine from Gascony and elsewhere at a cost of £25 Scots. This was shipped along the Buchan and Moray coast to Inverness before being dispatched southwards to Leith for the King's household. After the first leg of the journey the four pipes required a considerable amount of "topping up", for which the sum of 26/- was paid for the 6 flagons and 3 quarts used. There was the suggestion that the Aberdeen suppliers short-measured the Inverness Councillors, but evaporation and leakage aboard ship are the most likely causes of the loss.

In maintaining Inverness's acquaintance with wine in more recent history, the "Wine Shop" on Bridge Street was of great import. Opening in 1727 the "Wine Shop" continued business in the same premises until they were demolished in 1886 during the construction of the suspension bridge over the River Ness. The proprietors, Francis & Wilson and Co., who were also involved in the "Grocery" and the Hemp Factory, enjoyed a virtual monopoly on retail wine sales in the town. Despite the absence of competition they built up a solid reputation for service and quality. Once after bottling a large quantity of wine for a customer, the proprietors discovered that the bottles used were a little small and did not contain the requisite measure. Immediately they reclaimed every bottle from the customer and other sufficient ones were sent in their place. One of the "Wine Shop's" more respected patrons was Francis Humberston MacKenzie who later became Lord Seaforth. Before embarking on his regular Highland jaunts from his Grafton Street home in London, orders for wine were forwarded to Francis & Wilson. If that of May 31st, 1725, is typical, then it can safely be assumed that Mr MacKenzie was not given to temperance.

I shall be obliged to you on receipt of this to send to Brahan wines as below, with direction

> not to unpack the crates 'till I arrive, which will be abt. 10 days after you get this. I trust you will send no wines but the best, and if you have not good, rather send none...
>
> | | |
> |---|---|
> | Claret | 50 doz |
> | Port | 30 doz |
> | Sherry | 25 doz |

Underneath the "Wine Shop" were arched cellars of some antiquity. Tradition has it that Queen Mary of Scots lodged there when refused admission to the castle.

Nearby, and also a victim of the suspension bridge's construction, was the tavern popularly known as "Castle Tolmies". Together they would have constituted a focus for the wine *amateurs* and connoisseurs of the town. If the advertisement in the *Aberdeen Journal* of 21st August, 1750, which announced its opening is to be believed, then the citizens of Inverness could enjoy services and facilities in "Castle Tolmies" of a more metropolitan quality and standard:

> William Tolmie from London, vintner has opened a publick house at the sign of the Castle in Inverness, where gentlemen and ladies, travellers may expect the best accommodation and entertainment for themselves and horses in the English manner. N.B. Ready Service.

The garrisoning of the Highlands by Government troops during the 18th century introduced a new wine-drinking class to the north. In the early 1700's claret had been banished from English tables as a result of prohibitive import duties and anti-Gallic feelings. Under the Methuen Treaty of 1703 port wine and other Iberian products were given import preference over French goods. These political machinations did not seem to have affected the palates of the Government soldiers stationed in the Highlands where claret was still freely available. Doubtless it was personal preference overcoming political unacceptability which in 1728 allowed General Seaburg of Fort William to include a tun of claret in an order placed with Bailie Stewart of Inverness – an inclusion which would have raised more than a few eyebrows south of the border.

Imports of wine into the Highlands and Islands were organised by merchants such as Bailie Stewart. These merchants tended not to be shopkeepers, as the restricted sense of the Scots word would imply. Stewart had no shop, in fact, and such goods as required stocking were kept in his wine cellars or in an out-building which he called, the "Barn". He and his colleagues simply organised the export and import of commodities between producers and consumers and rarely saw the bulk of the commodities in which they dealt. Stewart's exports included the main "cash crops" of the Highland agricultural and fishing economies, and their destinations were various and sometimes exotic. Barley was delivered to the Lowlands and

Holland, oats went to London and on one occasion as far as Venice, oatmeal was delivered to the Hebrides and west coast, salmon to the south of Scotland and to continental parts; and herring and cod to the ports of the Baltic, Low Countries, the Mediterranean and Bordeaux. Naturally Stewart endeavoured to lade his ships with foreign goods on the return leg, and amongst the goods he brought home, claret and other French wines figured prominently. The arrangements for the purchase and handling of claret at the Bordeaux end were made by Robert Gordon or his brother Alex, Scots *négociants* resident in the city. Alternatively, this work was done by Stewart's son Alex, who spent some time there learning the wine trade. Stewart, being a shrewd businessman, left little to chance in placing orders with his Bordeaux agents. His instructions to them, as in this letter, were both detailed and strongly worded:

> To Messrs. Alexr. Gordon & Copy (Bordeaux) Inverness 1728.
>
> You are to ship for our Acct. on the said ship [*"Margaret"*] four tun of the best and strongest new Claret, and two tun of good old Claret. If can be had, two tun Brandy in greater casks and a tun of Barasack [Barsac] white wine in hogsheads. You'll notice that we desire the Claret be better than ordinary sort that comes to this country; and if it is not good and such as you think will not keep, we incline you send none. We earnestly intreat that you take care our wine be good.

His correspondence with customers reveals the tastes of a wide cross-section of the Highland wine-drinking fraternity of the time. Among his biggest customers in the Inverness area was "Bumper John" Forbes, the Earls of Moray, Lord Lovat, MacIntosh of MacIntosh, and further afield the Earls of Caithness, Sinclair of Ulbster, and Lord Reay. On the west coast the customers he supplied through his Fort William-based agent, Duncan MacIntyre, were characters such as Stewart of Ardsheal, MacDonald of Kinlochmoidart, Sir Alexander MacDonald of Sleat, MacLeod of MacLeod and sometimes Clan Ranald in South Uist. Rarely, in fact did Stewart supply anyone of lesser station than chiefs, lairds or gentlemen, not that he would have been averse to doing so. Though a committed Jacobite, this did not interfere with his brisk trade in wine with Hanoverian soldiers, Colonel Lie, whose regiment was stationed in Inverness, General Guest, Governor of Inverness and Major Gordon of the Bernera Barracks at Glenelg were all patrons – but so also were many celebrated Jacobites.

The Highlands were not short of households which in themselves could account for a reasonably big shipment of claret, but despite this potential market Stewart often encountered difficulties in getting rid of speculative imports of wine. Two such inconveniences were identified in a letter to his son in Bordeaux, dated July

1728. Sales, he explained, were slow because of the lack of ready cash on the West Coast and because of a glut of wine, particularly in the Lochaber and Appin areas, occasioned by excessive shipments by Summerville, a merchant from Renfrew. But Stewart was unworried for "if we sell as cheap as any other, I find we will be preferred to any".

In early 1723 it was the Moray Firth's turn to be over-supplied in wine. Stewart wrote his son advising him to avoid going too deeply into debt because the current glut made wine sales difficult, and there was the risk of financial embarrassment for the firm. Happily his salmon sold well in Gascony that Spring and by March his son was being instructed to "ship four tuns good Claret for my accot, with the oyr goods formerly ordered but pray take care that the Claret be prime good and rackt of the lees..." His trade in claret rarely meant a direct shipment from Bordeaux to Inverness. Often Claret was shipped via Dutch ports – perhaps because trading with France directly was discouraged by the British government and ships engaging in it risked seizure. French wine re-exported from Rotterdam or Amsterdam stood a better chance of evading the vigilant customs vessels. Sometimes more specific reasons necessitated the use of the triangular route – Bordeaux – Holland – Scotland. Stewart's letter to Robert Gordon in 1718 quotes one such instance:

> This serves to advise you that your friend Alex Steuart and ye ship Alexander of this pleace were designed to have gone your way for a loadning of wine etc. but the surprising news of the war with Spain had diverted this project, and he now proceeds for Rotterdam in Holland with a loadning of Salmon: therefor we desire that how soon this comes to hand youl enquire if can find any occasion of any ship on freight to Holland, bound for Rotterdam ... then you are to ship for our accots ten tuns of excellent good strong claret wine, 2 tuns white wine ... We hope youl take the most proper method to secure this wine from dammadge in the passage to Holland ... We entreat you take care to ship good strong wine for us, since small does not doe with us...

Neither was Inverness always the eventual destination for Stewart's claret shipments as the following letter reveals.

> Inverness 28 March 1730
>
> Mssr. Alex & James Coutts (London)
>
> I desire how soon this comes to hand you will insure for my accot, on the said barque *["Christian"]* and her carrgoe of wine, etc, £150 ster. againest all hazards, wt privilege to said barque to return hither by the Eirish Channell, and call in the Sound of Mull, near Fort William, and from Hence to this pleace by ye Orknies...

In another important respect the trade in wine between the Highlands and Bordeaux was not entirely "straight". Smuggling, particularly during the 18th century, was rife along the Highland coasts and throughout the islands. Johnson had not been long on his "travels" before discovering that the wine he and, more particularly, his colleague Boswell were drinking had been brought in illicitly.

> Their trade is unconstrained; they pay no customs, for there is no officer to demand them; whatever therefore is made dear only by impost is obtained here at an easy rate.

It was this "easy rate" that pleasantly surprised Bishop Forbes, when at Mathieson's Tavern in Fortrose he was offered claret at two shillings sterling per chopin bottle. Exploring the question further with the proprietor it was explained that the reason for the claret's cheapness was the fact that Mathieson had arranged its import himself so as to avoid paying duties.

Smuggling – or as it was popularly called, "Fair Trading" – was universal in the Highlands as it was in Scotland ... especially following the Union. The most convenient smuggling option was to bring claret ashore secretly, avoiding detection by customs officials. This generally required some detailed planning involving a merchant – who rarely had any scruples about indulging in this form of crime; the customer in whose interests the "crime" was being committed; the skipper of the vessel involved, and the Bordeaux-based shipper. A letter to Dunbar of Thunderton in 1710 from William Sutherland, a merchant in Elgin, details the elaborate arrangements required to ensure the secret landing of the claret shipment.

> I have ventured to order Skipper Watt, how soon it pleases God he comes to the firth, to call at Caussie [Covesea] and cruise betwixt that and Burgh-head, until you order boats to waite him. He is to give half of what I have of the same sort with his last cargoe, to any having your order. Its not amiss to secure one boat at Caussie as well as the burgh boats. The signall he makes will be all sails furled, except his main Topsaile; and the boats you order to him are to lower their saile when within muskett shott, and then hoist it again; this, least he should be surprised with catch poles. He is to write you before he sails to Bordeaux...

Petty Bay, four miles to the east of Inverness, was a favourite spot for landing contraband wine. One of the town's merchants operated an ingenious system by which he knew of the arrival of an illicit cargo and could communicate with the crew of a ship involved, without arousing the suspicions of Customs officials. Whenever a ship carrying the requisite wine hove to in Petty Bay, a runner set off for Inverness brandishing an empty snuff box. This he handed to the merchant as a sign of the cargo's arrival. If the merchant passed the box back full this was a signal that he was ready to take delivery of the illicit goods. However should there be any risk of detection the box was passed back half-full, and the runner returned to Petty Bay to warn the ship to remain out of sight for a day or two. For years the "Petty Snuff

Box" system was operated without a rat being smelled. In fact on one occasion the runner arrived with the snuff box and handed it to the merchant who was at the time engaged in conversation with a Customs Officer. The merchant half-filled the box, tossed the runner a sixpence by way of change, sent him on his way and continued his conversation.

A claret bottle recovered after 200 years at the bottom of the Kyle of Shuna.

With large businesses to protect and respectable customers to humour it would have been reasonable to expect merchants such as Stewart not to have risked smuggling. From his letter book, however, it is clear that Stewart was as active a smuggler as anyone. One instance, involving the ship *"Christian"* reveals how risky smuggling could be. In early 1730 the *"Christian"* left Bordeaux with a cargo of wine and brandy, and under his instructions, she was to proceed directly to the north-west coast of Scotland. Some of her cargo of brandy was ear-marked for Stewart of Ardsheal – the Governor of Fort William, Captain Campbell was to take 5 hogsheads of claret and thereafter the remainder of the cargo was to be offered to MacDonald of Kinlochmoidart. What was left after he had taken his share was to be disposed of in South Uist, Skye and Lochalsh. A letter from Stewart to the skipper of the *"Christian"* after she had arrived in the Sound of Mull, calls for a rapid change of plans following his getting wind of there being imminent danger of discovery.

I am apprehensive there may be great danger in your laying any time in the Sound of

Mull, and therefore, I hope my friends will order matters so that no time be lost. Let all you are to unload there to put to shoar together, so as your lying makes no great noise. And I think fitt yourself and sloop take borrowed names, and that it not be known the shipe belongs to this place.

Despite these precautions the *"Christian"* was discovered by the Customs Official based in Fort William, and had to effect a hurried escape, her cargo being dumped in the Kyle of Shuna. It may be some consolation to the luckless characters who over the years have struggled in vain to find the gold-laden Spanish Galleon in Tobermory Bay, that they could always turn their attention to the Kyle of Shuna for another sunken treasure!

If smuggled wine was intercepted by customs officials it was confiscated without compensation. For the would-be smuggler such eventualities were hard to accept. Not only was there the loss of the wine itself but also considerable amounts of money might have been involved in the unsuccessful venture. In some cases the confiscation of wine was so unbearable that attempts were made to retrieve the impounded cargo. Archibald Dunbar, Provost of Elgin around 1710, was one unfortunate whose claret shipment had been seized. He, however, was able to use his position to ensure its safe return, as this letter of protest to him from the local customs official reveals.

25th Aprile 1716
Alexr. Erskine, Collector of the Customs att Inverness, protests against Archbald Dunbar of Thunderton, Provost of Elgine, ffor all damage and loss that has happened to seven hogsheads of rede wine, imbezled without payment of duty, and seized by Alexr. Cummine, tydsurveyor att Inverness, in the sellar of William Crombie, vintner in Elgine, one of the keys of the said sellar being in custody of the said Archbald Dunbar, and delivered to him by Alexr. Cummine fforesaid, which key he refused to me, the said Alexr. Erskine, on the 16th att night, and next morning the hanging lock of the said sellar of which the said collector had the key, was brock off, and the other lock of which Thunderton had the key was intire and close lockt up, which he himself opened, and upon tapping, the fforesaid seven casks was found with nothing in them but water, a little colloured with wine, whereas they were all left by the fforsaid Alexr. Cummine fful of good and sufficient rede wine upon his delivering up the key to the said Archbald Dunbar, and thereffor protests that he shall by lyable in the fful value of the fforsaid seven hogsheads of rede wine, conforme to eighteen pound per hogshead; and also protests against the fforesaid William Crombie, vintner, ffor the value of said wine being imbezled by him and taken in without paying the duty, and also carried out of his said sellar and the cask ffilled up with water.
Alexr. Erskine.

Having had no change from Dunbar as a result of this letter, Erskine approached him, the perpetrator of the crime, and the local Justice of the Peace requesting a warrant to search "such houses, kilns, barns etc of the town of Elgine and adjacent places in that countrie", with a view to recovering the wine. Not surprisingly this was refused. Erskine then tried to pursue the matter with individuals in higher authority, but it was eventually smoothed over as a result of the intervention of Charles Eyre, Solicitor to H.M. Customs, who himself was a great lover of claret, and probably not averse to accepting cheap contraband wine when it came his way.

When the safe passage of illicit wine could not be guaranteed, elaborate precautions were taken to deceive customs officials in event of its discovery. Convincing them that the wine was not destined for the local market was one of the tricks pulled by Stewart. In 1726 he wrote to Alexander Todd, the Master of the Leith barque *"Catherine"* instructing him thus:

> You are to proceed without loss of time to St. Martins (probably St. Martins de Ré, Ile de Ré off La Rochelle) and you are to address yourself to Mr. Alexr. Gordon, Mercht. there, and deliver him the letter herewith given you, who will furnish you in what quantity of salt your ship can take in, and the liquor which Mr. Robert Gordon of Bordeaux is to ship for our accot. which will be about 12 tunns. And sd. Mr. Gordon is to provide you in foreign clearances. Yull endeavour to gett as much as possible, and notice that when, Please God, you return, in case you meet or is taken up by any Coustome House yatches, to declare yourself bound for Riga in the Balticke, and be shure you be well furnished with clearances accordingly. If you gett safe to the firth yule endeavour to call off Causea where orders will attend you. We beg your utmost care and dilligence.

The posting of two Government Cruisers to the Moray Firth in 1725 was a vain attempt to eradicate smuggling along that coast. Their presence may have been an added nuisance but smuggling continued much as before. With the men of power and influence of the Highlands, such as Duncan Forbes of Culloden, if not actively involved in the activity, then certainly turning a blind eye to it, feeble gestures of this sort were doomed to failure. Cheap claret, free of duty, retained its privileged position on Highland tables for the remainder of the century.

DON, CLYDE AND TAY 13

Whyche water of Tay is so navigable
From the East sea to Saynt Johnstowne
For all such shippes bee able
Fortie tunne of wyne to carry up and downe
For vitallying and keping of the toune.

These lines are taken from the Chronicle of John Hardyng, an Englishman who in the 15th century spent three-and-a-half years in Scotland. He was then under instruction from Henry V to obtain there certain deeds and information which might confirm England's superiority over the Scots. Clearly he was on a fool's errand, as he himself must have realised since on his return he presented his report to the monarch in metre form. Notwithstanding the serious nature of his task Hardyng sacrificed a certain amount of accuracy in his account for the sake of rhyme and rhythm. History does not relate how useful Hardyng's slightly fanciful descriptions were to the English realm, but at least he may have been consoled to learn that this extract does inspire a murmur of excitement in the student of the Scottish wine trade. Just consider, for instance, how Hardyng chose to measure the River Tay's navigability. Even if only one shipment of 40 tuns of wine were to be landed annually, St. Johnstowne [Perth] would have been a significant market for the liquor. In fact, Hardyng would have chosen to describe navigability this way because wine shipments were commonplace and not unusual events in the "Fair City's" life at the time.

Besides Perth there were a number of coastal and estuarine burghs boasting a healthy involvement in the wine trade during the Middle Ages. The Fair at Dundee for example, could offer the 13th century consumer a wide range of luxury and exotic goods as well as wine. It was to this burgh that King Alexander's wain, drawn by oxen, was sent from his castle at Forfar to stock up on casks of Gascony wine for his "summer drink". Wine was also circulating in the town of Aberdeen. The Burgh Accounts record presents of wine being made to local dignitaries. In 1453 the Countess of Huntly was gifted a hogshead of red wine at a cost to the burgh of 5s 4d. Around that time the Bishops of St. Andrews and Aberdeen were similarly honoured. However the Abbot of Arbroath and the Prior of Whithorne were less fortunate, receiving less than half the quantity the town set aside for their ecclesiastical superiors. In fact the quarriers who brought the stones for the construction of the Brig o' Balgownie had almost the same amount of wine lavished on them by the burgh as had the Abbot and Prior. Still on the east coast, but nearly a century later, St. Andrews and Burntisland figure among the ports to which the Bordeaux-based merchant Gilbert Balfour shipped claret. Berwick, at the time one of Scotland's foremost sea ports, also had a healthy wine trade. Her commerce which was so well developed during the 13th century as to earn the description "Alexandria" in the Chronicle of Lanercost, was protected and encouraged by local Guild Laws and in an indirect fashion by wine. An act of the Guild Law in 1249, attempting to prevent speculation and to ensure fair trading, decreed that no Guild brother was allowed to buy fish or any other merchandise brought to the port until the vessel was moored and her oars taken out. Thus no one could sail out to meet a ship and do a quick deal. Contravention of this regulation was punished by banishment from the Burgh for a year and a day or forfeiture of a cask of wine to the Guild. Most serious breaches of Guild regulations were similarly dealt with. Given penalties such as these, how many Guild brethren could honestly deny secretly praying for a local "crime wave"? Furth of Edinburgh the import and sale of wine was the preserve of Royal Burghs, largely as a result of the monopolistic privileges their burgesses had amassed.

On the west coast the Firth of Clyde provided a secondary focus for the early wine trade. Dumbarton, rather than Glasgow, figured most prominently in the records of early shipments, particularly from Bordeaux. In 1546 two merchants from the Fronsadais (near Bordeaux) loaded about 60 tuns of wine for Dumbarton and a short time later a certain Guillaume Audiene was responsible for the cargo of 100 tuns of Bourg Claret which arrived in the Clyde port. The bulk of the wine dispatched on the *"Guillemette"* by the agents of Robin de Saugues, a burgess of Bordeaux, was for Dumbarton and in this burgh a small colony of French merchants connected with the trade established themselves during the 15th century. Glasgow was not totally eclipsed by Dumbarton as a wine port. Jhone Leslie in his history of Scotland written in 1596 associated Glasgow with a considerable coastwise trade in the commodity:

> Bot till Argyle in the Hilande Iles, and lykwyse to the outmost iles in Ireland it [Glasgow] sends baith vine and ale and sik kinde of drink as natiouns have plesure off.

Beyond the Clyde very few towns on the west coast had dealings of any consequence in the wine trade. Occasionally batches of claret would arrive at the Galloway burghs of Wigtown, Kirkcudbright and Dumfries. In Ayr however, wine probably played a more integral role in burgh life at the time. The Sheriffs of Ayr's records for 1246 include accounts for wine provided to the garrison in the local castle and throughout this and the succeeding century mention is made of an annual gift of one hogshead of wine by the burgh to the Grey Friars of Ayr.

Provision of wine for ecclesiastical purposes seems to have been fairly standard practice in Scottish burghs. Belying its reputation, Aberdeen furnished very generous presents of wine to the clergy and Glasgow, according to her records, made frequent donations of wine right up until 1750 for use in the sacrament. Ecclesiastical establishments along with palaces, castles and the houses of the nobility accounted for a considerable proportion of the wine drunk in Scotland's Middle Ages. Melrose Abbey, at the height of its prosperity, supported 200 monks and used annually 20 casks of wine in its guest house and another 18 for the divine service. A drought of wine in such places was neither expected nor easily accepted. The Annals of Dunfermline tell how William Malvoisan, Bishop of St. Andrews, deprived the Abbey of its presentations to the churches of Kinglassie and Hailes, because during an official visit to the town in 1203, the Abbots and monks had neglected to provide him with enough wine for his collation after supper. The hosts protested, claiming that there would have been ample had the Bishop's own attendants not been secretly tippling, but the punishment stood.

The right to import, buy and sell wine was a jealously guarded privilege among the "freemen" of Scottish burghs. Anyone attempting to muscle in on their activities and who could not produce his "burghal credentials" found the going more than a little tough. Burgh councils were made up of freemen, many of whom were deeply embroiled in the wine business, and this ensured that their monopoly remained unthreatened. In fact the council had ultimate control over which wine was drunk, when, and at what price. Furthermore these august bodies managed to account for more than a reasonable proportion of the wines drunk locally. In Aberdeen the burgh magistrates made it their business to ensure a fair distribution of wine among citizens. All shipments brought to Aberdeen for sale were first bought by the Provost and the magistrates who then controlled its re-sale. Most of the time this arrangement proved financially satisfactory both for the burgh and for the council members but on several occasions they found themselves with an embarrassing amount of unsellable wine on their hands. In 1561 they imprudently bought the entire cargo from two French ships, and after failing to find buyers for it amongst vintners and taverners, had to resort to an early form of sales promotion, promising the merchants who relieved them of their dubious bargain preference in future transactions. Salutary lessons were learned from such experiences and when in early 1650 a shipmaster called John Anderson arrived with 80 tuns of French wine, the Council issued this warning:

> If it sall please God that John Anderson's shipe come heir full with wynes ther will be also much provisone as will serve for the nixt yeir and this yeir also.

The warning was heeded and for the remainder of the season only a few cargoes of wine were landed in the port, and these were immediately re-loaded on smaller vessels and ultimately "dumped" on Peterhead, Fraserburgh and Dundee, for their authorities to deal with.

Wine could only be sold within Burghs but before it could be released onto the market its quality had to be assessed locally, a requirement which created what must have been the most sought-after post in mediaeval Scotland – the "taster" or "sampler". In 1523 the burgh records of Dundee mention two such *gustatores vinii* – George Pollock and Andrew Barry. As with other tasters their job was to check that newly landed wine was fit for the market, and whatever the 16th century equivalent of "job satisfaction" was, they surely had a fair share.

The wine having been proved, its selling price was fixed. For this purpose the authorities in 16th century Elgin distinguished two types of wine – "Bordeus" and "Scherand" (more than likely, Charente, the region in which cognac is now produced) and both were to be sold at 7d per pint. Barely an elbow could bend in this burgh without it having to be reported to the Council. All purchases, sales of wine and its cellarage were reported in fine detail in a section of the council minutes labelled "Ventonaris of Wyne". Thus posterity benefits from such inconsequential facts as:

> Betuix November 1635 and November 1636, Isobell Hardie, spous to William Lesly declarant that sche ventit and brocht to hir cellar ... tua tun of french wyn and ane pype of spaynis wyne.

Not content with encumbering the retailer with such bureaucratic impedimentia, the poor drinker was also bound by rules and regulations in this and other burghs. For instance, the *amateur* of wine in Elgin found drinking after 10 o'clock could land a fine of £5 on his taverner. Only one condition could exempt the taverners from enforcing this premature curtailment of imbibing, that was "in case of necessitie to seik folkis." There are some places in which such a loop-hole would produce spontaneous epidemics after 10 p.m. Whether or not this happened in Elgin in the early 1600s was not recorded, nor was the answer to the question of whether topers who had become "seik folkis" through excess were allowed to administer more wine as medicine after this hour.

Aberdeen's town council of the time were not convinced that their citizens were using wine for medicinal purposes. Rather the reverse, they imagined! Extravagant feasting and over-indulgence in the convivial glass had become so marked a feature of the town's social life that in 1623 the Council passed an act which ordained that no more than six men and six women could take part in any dinner, supper, afternoon drink or baptism. This enforced reduction of the number of participants in any binge clearly had no effect on the per head consumption of wine, for two years later another step was taken to curb the Aberdonian excesses. This time the council enacted that no person was allowed to compel his neighbour at table with him to drink more wine or beer than he pleased, and to be caught doing so would result in a £40 fine. There is the theory that over-sensitivity to this ruling produced a marked reluctance in Aberdonians to "put their hands in their pockets" when rounds were to be bought, and consequently gave rise to the alleged meanness of the city folk. Such speculation can be nipped in the bud since their reputation is undeserved, indeed there is sufficient proof of Aberdeen's generosity, manifest through extravagant gifts of wine and other luxurious items to visitors and dignitaries, for it to be categorically denied. In 1630, for example, Sir James Skeyne and Sir Andrew Fletcher, President and Senator of the College of Justice, were provided with wine and "dessert" by the town to mark their visit, and a year later the Earl of Perth received "wine and sugar".

By any standards the magistrates of Aberdeen were most lavish with wine but in comparison with Glasgow their largesse pales into insignificance. Time and again throughout the 17th and 18th century the burgh coffers were "assaulted" in order to finance cavalier and extravagant purchases of wine for use in "treating" guests and rewarding benefactors. The entry in the Burgh records for 12th May 1684 is typical of these. This permits the town's treasurer to pay £41.5.6 sterling for

> ane butt of seck sent be the town to his grace the Duke of Hamilton and ane rubar of seck given be the town to Barron Bailyie for good service to the town.

Other beneficiaries of the town's generosity included Lord Blantyre, who received two hogsheads of claret, and James Bowman, the burgh Provost who in 1717 was provided with a hogshead of wine for his own use. Some of the recipients remain anonymous for one reason or another. Three hogsheads of French wine were given in 1691 "to some persones of quality on the toun's accompt", and in 1695 one hogshead was gifted to a "friend of this town whom it is not fitt to name"? Few visitors of any standing who came to the "Dear Green Place" were allowed to leave without being honoured by the "toune treit". According to the bills presented for "treats" they involved little else but wine. Claret was bought for General Wade's visit in 1728, and for those of the Duke of Hamilton and Earl of Portmore in 1733. The Marquis of Graham also visited and five dozen bottles of claret and half a dozen "preniock" (prignac) were consumed. To what extent the Glasgow magistrates were treating themselves during these visits is a matter of debate, but there is other evidence to suggest that they were not averse to self-entertainment. The King's birthday sparked off a round of celebrations in which magistrates were heavily involved. In July 1734, £5.12.0 sterling was paid to a William Gordon for wines provided "for the use of the toun on the Kings birthday in May last". This was a perennial spree, but other incidental opportunities were also taken. During the same year a payment of £24.10.6 was made to a tavern owner, Annabel Dennie,

> for reckonings in her house by the Magistrates and other gentlemen with them the time of electing of the Member of Parliament of this district and in treating about the touns affairs with respect to the said member.

A few years later a similar amount was paid out for wine to celebrate the "news of the Princess of Wales being brought to bed..." The records reveal that the birth of a young prince was another excuse for a binge and the burgh finances were tapped accordingly.

Another use of wine common to most Scottish burghs from the late Middle Ages into the 18th century was for public revenue raising. Until the Union of 1707 attempted to mould the Scottish wine market into a form consistent with England's anti-French and pro-Iberian inclinations, Scots generally imported wine free from punitive duties, and as a result were able to buy their claret and sack at prices well below those prevailing south of the border. For the wine drinker these happy circumstances were marred by one major encumbrance – the local "imposts" levied by Burgh Councils. These taxes generally applied to the retail sale of wine or ale within burghs and effected an increase of a few pence per pint in their "over the counter" prices. Burgh councils often acquired the right to levy "imposts" from a reigning monarch eager to curry favour, or to reward and even "buy" loyalty. Charles II in 1678 was to grant Aberdeen's council the right to £50 Scots on every tun of French wine, and on every butt of sack, Spanish and Rhenish wine sold in the town for a period of eleven years because of the

> deplorable and sad condition of our ancient burgh of Aberdeen and its citizens ... owing to the heavy burden of debt due by them to their own mortifications and other pious uses, incurred by them in constructing their harbour, restoring their churches and the bridges of Don and Dee, and diverse other public works.

Some years later this concession was renewed because of Aberdeen's loyalty to the crown and

> particularly at their being insulted and opprest since the late happy Revolution by the Highland Rebells under the commands of Major-General Buchan.

Glasgow was similarly rewarded in 1687 for having been the place where the same rebels encountered the greatest resistance and for "supplying fire and lights to ranks of the [King's] Forces".

For the townsfolk of Aberdeen and Glasgow who were rewarded for their loyalty in a way which inflated the price of their wine, speculation on what would have happened if their allegiance was in the opposite direction might not have been unreasonable. Indeed there may have been some Glaswegians who felt that in such circumstances "setting-fire" rather than "supplying fire" should have been the option chosen.

Don

> There is lately imported, directly from the places of growth, and to be sold by public roup in small lots of butts, half butts and quarter butts as purchasers incline, a parcel of old Mountain, Malaga, Zerry and Lisbon wines, all quite fine, and of the very best quality; which will begin to be set up at very low prices, on Wednesday the 29th current, at Convener Sims fishhouse, near the shore, where the wines presently lie, and may be viewed and tasted on any lawful day, from 11 to 12 in the forenoon, and from 3 to 4 in the afternoon.
>
> *Aberdeen Journal,* August 14th, 1750

The Port of Aberdeen

There was nothing unusual in public auctions of batches of wine arriving in Britain's ports during the 18th century. In London the genteel surroundings of Lloyds or Garraways coffeehouses would have been the venue for similar sales. In Edinburgh the head of Gray's Close, opposite the Fountain Well was a favourite site for exposing newly arrived wines to public scrutiny. Appropriately in Aberdeen the auctions were in fishmongers' premises.

As a market for wine the North-East was on a par with anywhere beyond Edinburgh, and Aberdeen was the focus of most of the wine imported to the area. A certain amount of this wine was transhipped and dispatched along the Buchan coast to such towns as Cullen, Fraserburgh and Peterhead. Some went southwards to Stonehaven, Dundee and occasionally as far as Bo'ness on the Firth of Forth. Periodically Danzig and other foreign ports figure amongst the destinations for re-exported wine.

Outside the city there were the large houses, castles and the better-to-do elements of the north-east's rural population to supply. The papers of the Monymusk Estate for 1735 reveal the lifestyle of Alexander Grant, a typical north-east country gentleman of the period. Drink of different sorts was a large item in Grant's budget. He possessed a brewhouse and employed a brewer for his estate workers' ale rations. Wine which he had delivered from James Brebner in Aberdeen and a few other merchants, including Bailie Forbes in Banff, was the largest single item in Grant's household expenditure, the bill for 1736 being about £60 sterling. Sherry, Malaga and Madeira were frequent purchases but claret was clearly his favourite. In February 1736 he spent over £6 sterling on "duty – fraught – carriage – filling up – couperage and facring (fining) of a hhd of Claret by James Brebner", and in May of the same year he sent for another dozen bottles of the wine from the same merchant. Andrew Dyce supplied him with another hogshead of claret in July 1737 and in between times pipes of "Cherry Malaga and Madera" were being delivered.

However, most of the wine landed in Aberdeen never left the burgh. Aberdeen, with a population exceeding 10,000 souls in the mid-18th century; with its two colleges, and their respective academics; a number of change houses, inns and hotels; and a town council not noted for frugality particularly where it concerned the purchases of wine, could account for prodigious quantities of the liquor on its own. The Town Council's cellars boasted an excellent stock of vintage wines which was raided whenever the occasion arose or when the council agreed to make gifts of wine to individuals. Generally those incursions into the town's wine stocks accounted for little more than a quart of claret here and a quart there. Periodically, however, massive quantities of wine were involved. Hector Boece, the historian of Angus origins who taught at King's College in 1528, was the lucky recipient of one of the council's more attractive offerings. The occasion was his being awarded the degree of Doctor of Divinity – a relatively rare occurrence in Aberdeen, which the magistrates recognised by voting him a present of a "tun of wine whenever the new wines arrived, or, if he preferred, £20 to buy a new bonnet". History does not relate which Boece chose, but if modern Scottish mortals are to be judged by, it would be a rare individual who would admit a preference for a "bunnet" over the equivalent of 1000 bottles of claret!

If an opportunity presented itself the magistrates themselves showed little compunction in delving into the "toun's wine" cellar for their own use. Nor was there much attempt made to disguise the fact that they had been at the wine. The eagle-eye of an *Aberdeen Journal* reporter caught them in the act during the general rejoicing after peace had been declared in February 1749. He described the scenes of dissipation thus:

> At twelve o'clock the Provost and Magistrates, with the Officers Civil and Military, made a procession from the town houses, preceded by drums, trumpets, the town musician and officers bare-headed, and mounted the cross. Peace was declared in due form and several loyal toasts were drunk, while two companies of Lord Ancrum's Regiment, well dressed, were drawn up in proper order and fired six volleys amidst the loud acclamations of the innumerable crowd of spectators. Then the gentlemen on the cross threw bottles of wine and glasses among the populace – The day was concluded with the ringeing of bells, bonefires, etc....

Had there been an Aberdeen Ratepayers' Association at the time, the merry-making at the community's expense would have been an obvious target for criticism. Of course there wasn't and in any case the wily magistrates had ensured that the possibility of reproach for their prodigal use of wine was lessened, by setting up a separate account from which their "courtesies" and bills for "potatiounes" were financed. On becoming burgesses, 16th century Aberdonians were obliged to gift one tun of wine to the burgh. In later centuries the "gifts" were commuted into a cash payment of £4 by the newly-elevated citizens. Initially this money was paid into the "Casualties Account", where it secured the continuation of Council-sponsored binges. However, if the participants in these revelries had been fully aware of the other uses to which this account was put the enthusiasm of their merry-making may have been curbed. If there was money left in the account after purchases of claret had been made, the residue may well have gone into defraying the expenses of burning witches and hanging pirates – such was the flexibility of the "Casualties Account". In 1616 a new account was opened in which the £4 payments were lodged. This, the Guild Wine Account, was used to maintain stocks in the Town House cellar.

The scene of many magisterial revelries during the 18th century was the Lemon Tree Tavern in Huxter Row. This also was the haunt of many of the burgh's merchants. Those of more noble and gentle rank were to be found in the New Inn on Castlegate. Other refuges for topers included Affleck's Tavern in Exchequer Row, Skipper Anderson's House and the Bonny Wife's Inn. An impressive range of wines was on offer in Aberdeen's hostelries, and with prices being very moderate, the patrons were many and the bills lengthy. Examples of bills presented in one of the taverns – probably the New Inn – testify to the level of trade such places were attracting. On 15 April 1783 the Duke of Gordon entertained 31 to dinner and in the process disposed of 44 bottles of claret, 3 of madeira, 19 of port, 4 of sherry and about 50 bottles of different types of ale, all for a little more than £15. The same evening there was an entertainment of 19 military officers in which 10 magnums and 19 bottles of claret, 8 of port, 3 of sherry and 45 bottles of beer were emptied!

Among the devotees of tavern life were the professors of Marischal College. The University Accounts of the time reveal the staggering frequency with which they visited such establishments. The taste for wine of the Professor of Moral Philosophy in the late 18th century – James Beattie – is clearly seen in the entries in his day-book kept between 1773 and 1798. In 1775 he noted the clearing of a wine debt with his main supplier, William Brebner. This had mounted to over £11, the bulk of which had been spent on two-thirds of a hogshead of white wine and 84 bottles of "Red Port".

A north-east wine-merchant

Before 1707 many of the ports along the Buchan coast had a brisk trade directly with wine producing countries. The Union however saw its demise, there being established in Aberdeen a Customs House to extract duties on wines imported anywhere between Cullen in the west and Todhead to the south. Cargoes of wine landed anywhere between these points had henceforth to be declared in Aberdeen, a ruling which proved less than convenient for importers in the burghs distant from the city. The Provost of Banff, in the memorial of 1785 he laid before the Convention of Royal Burghs requesting aid in an application to the Lords of the Treasury for having a Custom House in Banff, explains:

> The importation of wine, which sometime ago was considerable upon this coast is now entirely stopped. Owing to the importer or merchant being under the necessity of going such a distance to the Custom House to make oath as to the identity of the wine before he can obtain a permite to transire or even to send a cask but a few miles by land carriage, which is a burden and expense, considering the high duties which he cannot afford...

Banff did in fact get her Custom House in 1801 to serve the coast between Cullen and Fraserburgh, but not particularly because of the Provost's plea. In response to the memorial it was reported by a Customs official that the revenue paid in 1785 on cargoes landed at Fraserburgh, Banff and Portsoy amounted to £1356 of which £735 was paid for wine, and that he suggested, was hardly sufficient to justify a Custom House.

Little wonder that the revenues were so low, most of the wine was being run illicitly on the coast. In fact John Forbes, an official at Aberdeen's Customs House, indicated in 1786 that it was only by virtue of the fact that ships employed in the Revenue Service were forcibly escorting ships in, that any duty was paid at all. It was clear to the Customs officers that ships discharging at all places along the Buchan Coast registered significantly smaller cargoes than vessels of equal burden landing at ports where they could be supervised by officials. The "lost" cargo, they knew full well was wine, but there was little they could do to prevent its smuggling along a coast which provided such ideal opportunities. Even in Aberdeen under their very noses, the Customs officials had extreme difficulties in preventing high-duty goods being landed clandestinely. In January 1747 for example, the *"Anne of Aberdeen"* skippered by James Ferguson arrived in the harbour with a cargo of 150 tuns which on inspection was found to include wine and other goods upon which duties should have been paid. Ferguson protested that these goods were bound for Bergen and not for import, but when asked to produce bills of lading and clearance papers could not, because he claimed the precaution of throwing them overboard had been taken in case of being stopped by privateers. A search warrant was issued and while all the legitimate goods for Aberdeen were being off-loaded the Customs officials remained at hand scrutinising operations. The vessel left for Bergen in April carrying the remaining cargo of wine, rum, tea, coffee, soap and despite the close interest of Customs officers the *"Anne"* changed her course and landed the goods at Kirkwall. No one ever found out how much wine was landed on the Buchan coast and at other jetties in Aberdeen while the *"Anne"* occupied the attention of the Customs officers.

Clyde

Dumbarton stole a march on Glasgow at an early date by permitting the establishment of a colony of French merchants within the burgh and as a result fostered conditions in which wine imports were landed there in preference to its rival further up the Clyde. It says a lot for the enterprise of Glaswegians that they strove defiantly against Dumbarton's initial advantage in the wine trade. They met foreign vessels at landing places within the Firth and after concluding deals, transferred the casks of wine into vessels with shallower draughts so that the valuable cargo could be brought through difficult waters upstream to Glasgow. Naturally the burgesses of Dumbarton were not too enamoured of this dodge and in retaliation interceded and forcibly prevented the completion of a deal in 1469 between Glaswegian representatives and the master of a French vessel carrying large quantities of wine which moored in the Firth. The Auditors of Causes and Complaints were brought in to sort out this debacle and after investigation found in favour of Glasgow as the "first byars of the wyne". Dumbarton's magistrates were formally admonished with the threat that behaviour of that nature would not be tolerated in the future, and with that, the wine trade in Glasgow was given space to develop.

And develop it did. A century or so later there were few burghs in Scotland which could boast the level of trade in wines which Glasgow had. Between April and May 1597 the Burgh records detail the arrival of ten ships with an aggregate of 453.5 tuns of "How to Pas" (Haut Pays) and "Byone" (Bayonne) wine.

Among the uses to which this wine was put was to pay what amounts to the 16th century equivalent of the "Councillors' Attendance Allowance". The Provosts of Glasgow generally did not reside in the burgh but would come up on special business or during emergencies. On such occasions, and more particularly when they provided some special service they were rewarded with presents, generally wine. In 1583 the records show that the Provost was awarded overnight expenses:

18th June – For wyne presentit to the proveist in time of trublis, being caused to abyde in this toune for pacifeing thairof.

One of Glasgow's early Provosts – Lord Boyd – benefited considerably from such largesse.

The Glasgow Council had a long tradition of raiding the burgh's treasury for the wherewithal to buy wine for diverse purposes. More often than not the magistrates would be among those present when the wine was being shared out so decisions to purchase wine generally went through on the nod. In fairness to them there were some occasions when they were unlikely to get even a sniff of the bouquet of the wine bought, nor, once or twice, did they have much choice but to vote money for such purposes. In 1714 for example during the period when the local MP in Westminster, Daniel Campbell of Shawfield, was assisting a bill renewing the town's right to 2d on the pint of ale he directed the magistrates to send wine up to him in London "for the use of some friends of the toun". To make matters worse he was not content with requesting some run of the mill growth but specifically requested two hogsheads of "Obryan" (Haut Brion). There was worse to come. Obryan could not be found in Glasgow and the magistrates were obliged to order the wine from Mathew Campbell in Edinburgh, and everyone knows how much Glaswegians love lining the pockets of their neighbours in the capital ... The total cost of the operation was enormous by 1714 standards:

Two hogsheads Chateau Haut Brion	£50. 0. 0
44 dozen and 8 bottles for bottling the wine	£ 3.15. 0
Four gross corks for bottling the wine	£ 10. 0
Duty	£14. 6. 4
Custom House Officers	£ 7. 6
Bill of Loading, and Shipping	£ 2. 3
Freight and duty at London	£ 3. 8. 6
Six casks for putting the bottles in	£ 1. 2. 0
Total	£73.11. 7

Why suitable claret could not be found for Campbell in Glasgow was never made clear. Certainly there were numerous wine merchants operating in the city at the turn of the 18th century who could have been contracted to supply wine, but it may have been that their interest lay in the lesser growths of Bordeaux and not in the *grands crus* which Edinburgh could supply.

There is firm evidence that at least 34 merchants in the city were dealing in wine in 1674. Their names are preserved on a document which relates to one of the more interesting examples of co-operation between retailers in the history of the Scottish wine trade. In an attempt to support the retail price of their goods these merchants formed a cartel to organise "ye importatioune of French wyne for this present cropt and vintage" in the firm belief that "the great increase of trad lyes in being erected in societies and companies for preventing of confusione and damage that may aryss throw clasing on against ane other".

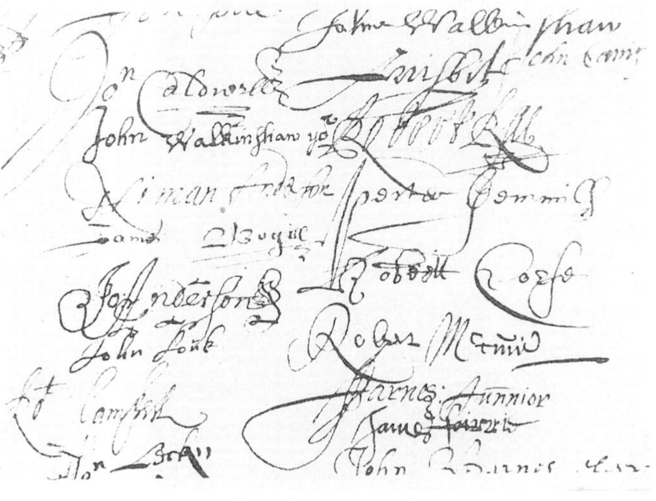

The Glasgow Cartel

This scheme was tantamount to a collective decision on the part of the signatories to monopolise the purchase and local sale of French wines of the 1674 vintage. One of its main proponents, John Cauldwell, was with five other merchants, Knox, Gemill, Nisbet, Anderson and Walkinshaw, appointed as director of the society and charged with the responsibility of ensuring that its objectives were achieved.

Little more is heard of this cartel, though records still exist for John Cauldwell's wine importing activities in the years thereafter. His agent in Bordeaux was Henry Lavie, a négociant who not only reported to Cauldwell on the quality and quantity of claret vintages, but also ensured that Cauldwell's orders were loaded, often on the *"Amitye"* from Glasgow, and safely dispatched. One such order was in 1675 for about 50 tuns of "Graves Claret", 15 tuns of white wine and one tun of what was described as "blacke" wine.

During the 18th century it was tobacco rather than wine which constituted the basis of Glasgow's commercial relations with France. By this time the single biggest market for tobacco in Europe was France and in the 1770s Glasgow supplied more than 50 per cent of her requirements. Tobacco exports to Bordeaux alone amounted to more than three million lbs. in 1775. The trading triangle which linked the American tobacco producers with Glasgow and Bordeaux was naturally dominated by tobacco shipments, but other commodities were exchanged. Claret figured significantly among the products exported to the Clyde on the return leg from the Gironde estuary and doubtless this inclusion on ships' manifests was vigorously welcomed by the local populace. But despite this solid link with Bordeaux the west of Scotland in general fared no better than anywhere else in securing supplies of the much requested claret particularly in the final decades of the 18th century when the Westminster conspiracy against the liquor finally began to bite north of the border.

Sherry was a popular alternative to claret in the Glasgow clubs and port was readily available and used ubiquitously in slaking the thirsts of her citizens. Port tended not to be the object of the Glaswegian wine-drinker's venom as it was elsewhere. On the contrary the contemporary historian Denholm wrote about the quality of the product used there: "The Port is excellent of its kind, not resembling the adulterated trash sold under that name in England."

For the continuing supply of wines of diverse types the west coast in general was indebted to the Ayr-based merchant Alex Oliphant and Co. With cellars also in Stranraer, Glasgow, Kilmarnock and Moffat, all operated by his agents, Oliphant appears to have cornered a substantial proportion of the west coast wine trade by the mid-18th century. His letter books of 1760-61 plot the nature of his commercial links with Scots shippers in Madeira, Cadiz, Oporto and Bordeaux, and with his clientele in the west and south-west. Oliphant was clearly nobody's fool and displayed an immense lack of tolerance for sub-standard products. In January 1767 his displeasure over the quality of wine supplied by James Duff of Cadiz prompted a strongly worded letter in which Oliphant described the sherry delivered as "good, but the Mountain was every-drop sour – so bad that we once thought of spilling it and redrawing the duty, the brandys very bad, particularly one cask which besides being 16 per cent under proofe is very sour tasted..."

On some occasions even the quality of the bottles supplied by the manufacturer Andrew Scott of Glasgow was the cause of irate correspondence:

> You'll send better bottles than the last. So many of them being cracked [the] flaws especially in the bottoms occasioned a great loss of wine in bottling...
>
> We must desire that they [the bottles ordered] are as good as possible and if you can get them made with smaller mouths, please get it done as our cooper complains that in the way the bottles are made at present, there is no way of getting corks large enough to stop them...

Some time later we find Oliphant looking for an alternative supply of bottles from a manufacturer in Bristol, Scott having definitely fallen into disfavour.

Throughout the 17th and 18th centuries Glasgow wines would not have been a disappointment to the connoisseurs. As early as 1618, French, Greek, Rhenish and

Spanish wines were all available in the town, and in 1660 Franck, an English traveller, could report that the people of Glasgow "generally excel in good French wine as they superabound with flesh and fowl". Her imports in 1775 list a range of wines from no fewer than 11 different continental ports. However there was little of the connoisseur about the rabble that frequented Glasgow clubs and taverns where a frightening amount of these wines were consumed. According to a 19th century chronicler "there was neither art nor science to restrain the levity of wit or check the profanity of conversation" in Glasgow clubs, and the bastions of civic society were in no small measure responsible.

Dr. Strang's descriptions of the clubs reveal that lawyers consulted there with the poor client footing the bill for liquor, generally sherry which was put away in incredible quantities. Helping the lawyers shift Glasgow's wine imports were the tobacco lords who after a morning's work generally repaired to the coffee house or taverns to read newspapers "in companies of four or five in separate rooms over a bottle of claret or a bowl of punch". At first the merchants would retire at a reasonable hour to return home for supper, but in time their resolve was weakened by

> an arch fellow from Dublin, a Mr. Cockaine, [who] came to be the master of the chief coffee house, and he seduced them gradually to stay for supper by placing a few nice cold things at first on the table, as relishes to the wine, till he gradually led them on to bespeak fine hot suppers, and to remain to midnight.

In the clubs and taverns where topers had gone far along the way to intoxication but not quite to stupefaction one of the favourite pastimes was to produce spades and shovels, and in turn the members of the company would try to raise each other on these. Once raised some way the trick was to throw the victim on the end of the implement as far as possible. As a precaution onlookers were charged with the task of breaking the fall of the projectile, but on occasions their intemperance had rendered them so incapable that the unfortunate was deposited squarely on a table, scattering glasses and bottles on the floor. This was considered as light relief in an evening of serious drinking. And how serious it was in Glasgow of the day! There is a story, probably apocryphal, of a long hard-drinking session which illustrates the determination with which imbibing was approached. Some time into this session one of the party ventured to ask: "What gars the Laird of Garscadden look sae gash?" The Laird of Kilmardinny, with an air of indifference, provided the answer: "De'il meane him! Garscadden's been wi' his Maker these twa hours; I saw him step awa', but I didna like to disturb gude company!"

Tay

Jam, Jute and Journalism was the standard school text-book description of Dundee's trades, but curiously mention was never made of another of the town's activities which though pre-dating the emergence of the three "Js" was nevertheless of considerable importance both locally and nationally. The wine trade made its mark in Dundee at an early date, her fairs being visited during the 13th century by King Alexander's henchmen on wine-buying missions. The Exchequer Rolls for Scotland detail Dundee's involvement in this trade from then till the 16th century. There were regular transactions between merchants of the town and the Royal households, even to the extent of shipping wine from Dundee through Blackness port on the Forth for the king's use at Linlithgow palace. The monks of St. Andrews, Arbroath and Restennet were also in receipt of their essential supplies of wine from Dundee, as were the residences of the Countess of Strathearn, the Earl of Strathmore and other local gentry.

Probably the town's earliest wine merchant was one Hugo de Leyis, brother of Thomas de Leyis, a merchant-burgess of Dundee, whose premises stood on the south side of the Fluckergait. He appears to have met with good fortune as a wine merchant for among other substantial contracts his was the task of supplying the garrison at Stirling Castle in 1361. Another of his coups was the acquisition in 1365 of a safe conduct pass from Edward III for himself and four companions, authorising travels through England on business. Some two centuries later Dundee could boast a veritable army of merchants who had some involvement in the wine trade. The Register of the Privy Council for 1607 lists a score of Dundonian merchants who had defaulted on payments due on wine to the aggregate tune of £1376.1.8d. Among the worst offenders were the merchants Gray (owing £250.7.0), Mudie (£199), Caird (£76) and Robert Jack (£47).

At any one time there were colossal quantities of wine cellared within the burgh. In 1559 when English troops were asked to help out against Mary of Guise and her French Forces, a total of 200 tuns was requisitioned in order to supply Scotland's temporary allies. By way of compensation the Dundee merchants received £34 Scots or £8.10 Sterling on every tun appropriated.

Dundee's early advances in the wine trade were largely a consequence of her strategic location on the Firth of Tay. The River Tay, its associated strath, together with Strathearn and Strathmore, made penetration of consignments of wine upstream and into the Highlands relatively easy. The river itself was navigable as far as Perth, and all the wine required by the "Fair City" could be landed at her quays.

There were occasions however, when navigation on the Tay was impossible, but this was not to frustrate the movements of wine upstream. The Chronicle of Perth records an intense frost in 1624 which iced over the river and suspended all traffic. Undaunted some Dundee merchants transferred their cargo of 21 puncheons of wine into 13 carts and made the journey to Perth over the ice.

Drinking in the Vault, Dundee circa 1850.

Beyond Perth wine was transported overland, most probably in skins slung between horses. To the west Breadalbane was supplied by way of Strathearn. Here Estate Books for 1536 itemise the arrival of claret and white wine brought from Dundee. The quantities delivered are described in terms of unusual measures – "Barrekins" and "Rubbours" – possibly ones which pertained to overland carriage in skins. Another curiosity in the Breadalbane records was the arrival of "Ulet" wines, thought to mean wine transported in flasks stopped by a layer of oil rather than rags or corks. Northwards to Blair Atholl wine would have been brought by way of Strathtay. Anything transported beyond Blair into Badenoch would have followed the precursor of the A9. This route was described in Gordon of Rothiemay's *Noates and Observations* made about 1650

> Ther is a way from the yate of Blair in Athoil to Ruffen in Badenoch maid by David Cumming, Earle of Athoil for carts to pass with wyne, and the way is called Rad-na-Pheny, or way of wine wheills. It is laid with calsay in sundrie parts ...

Rad-na-Pheny, or in its more correct form, *Rathad an Fhiona* (The Wine Road), built by David Comyn in the 13th century, adopted a route to the east of the present A9; through the Gaick Forest, issuing just to the south of Kingussie. This marked the northern-most extent of Dundee's sphere of influence in the early wine trade.

Wine was brought to Dundee in exchange for local produce. Wedderburne was prominent among the town's merchants at the beginning of the 17th century and his practice was to export cloth and other local goods from there, entrusting the master of the ship contracted to barter these for wine and other exotic produce. In 1597 a quantity of linen valued at £90 was dispatched by Wedderburne and in his instructions to the master of the ship, John Scrymgeour, he suggests that the cargo be exchanged for "gude Alagant Wyn or the fynest wynes in rubberis or fyn Muskedallis as ye think best, and lyk as ye by to yourself". From the city's shipping lists at the turn of the 17th century it is apparent that any shipment of wine for the port had already been earmarked for one merchant or another. When the *"Hope for Grace"* arrived from Bordeaux in March 1618 her cargo of 40 tuns of wine was to be divided among 19 merchants. Their share of the cargo was proportionate to the value of the goods they contributed to the outward cargo.

A list of Wedderburne's "vyvours" – food and drink for his family's use – includes an interesting range of liquors. Among the wines mentioned were Alicante, Muskedallis, Rouen, claret and white wine, but for the average Dundonian such variety of choice was exceptional. More often than not only two sorts of wine were available and both were shipped from Bordeaux. In the shipping lists they are described as "Town Wine" and "Land Wine", Dundonians making the distinction between "Vins de Ville" and "Haut-Pays" wines which the authorities in Bordeaux were at pains to maintain. They would have been delighted to learn that their policy of discrimination against the wines of the high country was having effect in the place of consumption also. But all was not as the Bordelais intended – according to the respective quantities of wine imported, Dundonians displayed a clear preference for "Haut Pays" growths.

Shipping on the Firth of Tay

The arrangements for importing wine into Dundee could operate smoothly provided there was no State interference. As it happens they were constantly being confused by the avarice of successive Scottish monarchs, to the intense fury of the merchants involved in the trade. Perhaps because the Town Council of Dundee had sent King David II a couple of bottles of vinegar on his deathbed, no doubt precipitating his demise, relations between Dundonians and Royalty, particularly over wine, were generally at a low ebb. Towards the close of the 16th century the latter had engineered a situation requiring that all wine arriving in the port should "remain within the ship onsellarit for four days" to allow His Majesty's taster or "symeler" (from the french *sommelier)* sufficient time to assess their quality and select ones which should be appropriated for the Royal Household. Queen Mary made frequent use of this right and by way of compensation to the merchants for their losses, she allowed them to sell the remaining wines in the cargo at prices higher than those fixed by the authorities. Not content with having the "pick" of the vintages, Mary on several occasions exhorted the Dundee council to provide for her household needs free of charge.

King James VI was also an exponent of this cunning technique. In 1579 he instructed his "symeler", Jeremy Bowie, to seek out suitable wines from ships newly arrived in the harbour from Bordeaux. To his credit George Spens, a Dundee merchant, refused Bowie access to his wines and was duly charged with contravening His Majesty's instructions. Charged with him were several others including James Fletcher, Peter Clahillis, John Finlayson, William Hendrie, all of whom refused to part with the wines Bowie tasted and approved, unless they could be assured of "present payment or obligatioun to schort dayis for greter prices then wynes are commounlie sauld for within the said burrow". In passing judgement on the offenders the King exercised leniency. Having procured all the wine he wished, he compensated the merchants for their losses to the tune of £50 Scots for Bordeaux wine and £46 Scots for "Hottopyis" (Haut Pays) wine. Some years later when the King's cellars were once again near to exhaustion a general instruction went out at the market crosses in Dundee, St. Andrews, Montrose, Aberdeen, Ayr, Irvine, Glasgow, Dumbarton, Edinburgh and the Port of Leith, that wines were not to be disposed of until they had been "sichted, taisted and wailled" by James Bowy, symeler. This time there was the threat of confiscation of entire cargoes, to encourage merchants to conform with the King's wishes.

Dundee's prominence in the wine trade declined and was totally eclipsed by her sister city on the Tay, Perth, partly because Perth was better able to exploit her location as "Gateway to the Highlands" once dependence on shipping waned as the railway network extended northwards. Also the "Fair City's" wealthy hinterland was graced by a more resilient wine-drinking tradition than in the industrialising city a little more than 20 miles downstream. It would be frivolous to suggest that Perth made her way as a centre for the trade because the convivial bug of the 17th and 18th century seems to have hit this area particularly badly, but it may have helped...? To prevent shirking and reluctance to drink, a rule obtained at dinners and social gatherings in the county that if a glass was not emptied the offending guest was compelled to drink the same toast a second time. This practice was called "Kelpies Mends" and perhaps it was a surfeit of these that did away with Henry Lord Ker, the second son of the Earl of Roxburgh, who died after "ane great drink" at Perth in 1643. There were some hosts in Perthshire during the 18th century who had the feet removed from glasses so that they could only be set down when empty. One of the characters of this period, William Maule, Earl of Panmure, was renowned for his habit of locking guests in, and passing around bottles carefully constructed so as to prevent them from standing, the result being that drinking was continuous. Dinners and social evenings were interminable and hosts were expected to maintain the flow of wine until guests were hopelessly inebriated. One such dinner at Foss which began after the service one Sunday, was so protracted that it was only with the sound of bells calling the faithful to the Kirk on the following

Sunday that the company dispersed.

The wine which inflamed these revelries and which was generally available at the beginning of the 18th century was claret. By the century's end the only claret in the city was rather expensive high-quality wine of the more famous growths, and much of this was imported via Scandinavian and the Low Country ports. In provincial burghs port wine was virtually unknown before the mid-1700s. It is significant that the magistrates of Stirling had never come across the liquor until it was provided for them at a collation in 1746 to which they were invited by the Prince of Isenberg, who commanded the Hessian troops in the garrison. On their first acquaintance with port they were not particularly impressed, their palates being more attuned to the smoother claret. In port's defence perhaps it should be mentioned that the circumstances under which it was tasted were not exactly conducive to revealing its best qualities. That night salt herring had been provided as a relisher! However three decades later the Perth merchant, John Bisset, could provide his clientele with little else but Portuguese and Spanish wine.

The two principal Perth merchants at the time were John Bisset and John Brodie, and in both firms wine was one of several commodities traded. Selling mainly Iberian wines, both were in regular correspondence with producers and shippers in the Peninsula, many of whose names are still familiar – Warre Bros, Sandeman, Duff Gordon and others. Despite their direct contact with the vineyards, their supplies of wine came through middlemen based mainly in Leith, and sometimes in Aberdeen. In the latter Brebner was still operating (though now his function was rather more that of wholesaler than retail merchant), and between 1780 and 1800 regularly supplied Bisset with port. In Leith, the firms of Cathcart & Co., Walker, Thompson & Co., Bell, Rannie & Co. were prominent among the shippers which broke down larger cargoes for delivery coastwise to their clients. The pattern was for ships such as the *"Peggy"* and the *"Hunter"* to freight wines from St. Lucar, Cadiz and Oporto to Leith, where they were transshipped to coasters and delivered to provincial merchants.

During the period in which Bisset and Brodie operated, the Scottish wine trade was entering a new era. Vestiges of the pattern which was to establish itself in the 19th century can be identified in the dealings of both merchants with their suppliers. No longer were the latter general traders, to a large extent they were now specialising in wine importing. Theirs was a rather better organised activity, with printed wine lists and vintage reports and strong commercial links with firms based at the ports for the vineyards. Cathcart and Co., for example, were agents for Messrs. Gordon & Co., in Jerez and Kopke in Oporto. There is also evidence that the reputation of the shippers of this new breed was almost as important as the origin of the wine in guaranteeing its quality. Illustrating this new departure was the delivery of a hogshead of "Teneriffe" wine from Andrew and Alex. Allan of Leith to James Brodie in March 1814. The wine when it arrived was accompanied by a note from Allan reassuring the purchaser as to its quality:

> We are incapable of serving you better, nor is there a superior of this kind in Leith. The importers are the same as the last hogshead you got and they declare the new wine is as good as the other. To our knowledge the first bottling houses have bought parcels of this sent to you, such as Cockburns, Bertrams, Cathcart and Co....

The interest of these houses in the Tenerife was Brodie's proof of its quality.

Within the context of the modern Scottish wine trade, Perth is an interesting anomaly. She is one of Scotland's smaller cities but despite this sustains a more healthy interest in wine commerce than in conurbations many times her size. Somehow the family wine-shipping businesses in the "Fair City" have withstood the pressures for concentration, specialisation and rationalisation to which most others in Scotland eventually succumbed.

There is little physical evidence in the modern life of the city to suggest that merchants such as Brodie and Bisset from the end of the 18th century were ever operating there. However two firms of a slightly younger age, Matthew Gloag and Peter Thomson, which date from the first half of the following century remain, and are still very much part of the economic life of the town. The exact establishment date of Matthew Gloag's is a little uncertain but it is thought that Gloag, at one time an employee at Scone Palace, began business in Perth's Atholl Street around 1800 or shortly thereafter. Initially Gloag was a general grocer; his interest and specialisation in liquor sales came at a later date. Being in the "Highland Gateway" Perth's licensed grocers were able to attract the custom of swarms of summer visitors from the south as they bought up what little of "civilisation" they could in Perth before disappearing into the Highland wastes for a month or two. The descendants of these 19th century patrons still place their wine orders with Matthew Gloag's for their annual forays northwards.

Gloag's are based in the significantly-named Bordeaux House in Kinnoull Street, where they moved from Atholl Street in 1907. True to the Scottish tradition clarets make up more than one third of the natural wines in their list, but the most celebrated of Gloag's wine is a sherry selling under the name "Pintail". This name evokes a Hispano-Scottish connection in itself. The pintail duck is a common visitor to the Scottish islands which over-winters in the Guadalquivir estuary in the vicinity of Jerez de la Frontera.

Thomson's history is more recent, though in many ways similar. Its origins are in the flitting of Alex Thomson from Grandtully to the town about 1850 to set up a grocery business. Two of his sons, Alex and Peter, continued in this trade but in 1904 parted company, the former to develop his interest in the retail sale of tea, the latter to buy over the wine grocers John Paton, originally established in 1832. This merger gave Thomson's liquor side of the business a new lease on life, and also marked the launch of one of the firm's longest standing wine brand names, "P.T. Port". Within a few years Thomson's client list extended over Scotland and as far south as Manchester.

R.B. Smith, now part of Griersons wine group, continued this tradition of selling throughout Scotland and the north of England. The firm was established in 1820 and until recently was bottling its own wine in the cellars at their former premises in Tay Street.

Perth's location contributes to her continuing success in the wine trade. Her strategic position was particularly important when for a time in the 19th century she was the Highland railhead. Perhaps the stability afforded by the whisky blending and selling dimensions to the firms have allowed for their unusual longevity in commercial circumstances which have tended to operate against locally-based family businesses. The very "Famous Grouse", "Beneagles" and other brand names are more readily associated with Perth in the minds of the clientele than perhaps are their wine *marques.* Whatever the reason there is no denying the special place Perth has had in the history of the Scottish wine trade. She provided the background for the development of some of the country's most celebrated firms and furthermore one of her sons, was a prime mover in the Port and Sherry trade, George Sandeman, born in Perth in 1765.

THE PENINSULAR CAMPAIGN 14

PORT & SHERRY

A great proportion of the wine consumed in this country is brought from Spain and Portugal: government has always discouraged the importation of French wines by heavy taxes. We are not sure how far such conduct is founded on good policy, as the French wines are confessedly the best and might be the cheapest. *(Encyclopaedia Britannica)*

Some 80 years after the Methuen Treaty and the Union had set in motion the inexorable process of replacing claret on Scottish tables by Iberian wines, Scotsmen were seemingly still aggrieved about what they considered the denial of a basic right to choose drink on a basis of preference and not because of the nation's ideological leanings. Even in the columns of the 1797 edition of the *Encyclopaedia Britannica* – granted an Edinburgh edition – the normal matter-of-fact tones are forsaken to cautiously reflect the Scots' continuing sense of outrage over the effect British international policy has had on the availability of their favourite beverage. But the writer conceded, "the advantages which Britain derives from the Portuguese trade are very great, and it would not be easy to secure them on any other terms".

The "terms" should be familiar to the reader. Since the Methuen Treaty of 1703 England and in later years the United Kingdom was bound to charge one-third more duties on French wine than on Portuguese and Spanish. The most galling thing for the Scot about these measures which discriminated against his "natural element" was that their existence had little to do with wine and even less to do with Scotland. The Treaty bound the English to this built-in bias in duties in order to secure unhindered access for English woollen goods in the Iberian markets in preference to those of other countries. Hume in his *Essay on the Balance of Trade* (1752) put it succinctly:

We lost the French market for our woollen manufactures and transferred the commerce of wine to Spain and Portugal where we buy much worse liquor at much higher prices.

While the Methuen Treaty and the Union four years later were, through time, to have a devastating effect on the complexion of the Scottish wine trade, their impact in England was much less marked. For the English imbiber the Union changed little other than closing a loophole through which claret could be imported more cheaply. The Methuen Treaty simply reinforced and formalised trends which began about half a century earlier. The ultra-protectionist policy of Colbert, one of Louis' ministers which was put into effect in 1667 curtailed English cloth imports into

France; with a policy of "tit for tat" prevailing, the English prohibited the import of French wine. About this time the quality and quantity of Italian wine exported through Florence was beginning to fall away and, starved of French imports, red wine on the English market became very scarce. The English colony at Viana, then centre of the Portuguese wine trade, seized this opportunity and bought up all the red wine for the home market, but the supply could not keep pace with demand. In an attempt to expand the production of Portuguese wine the English, in the words of John Croft in his *Treatise on the Wines of Portugal* (1727), began a programme of "teaching the Portugueze to cultivate vineyards on the heights or mountains bordering on the river Douro". Producing more wine in the Upper Douro valley engendered an increase in the volume of wine shipped downriver to Oporto, the town at the river's mouth, and gradually the centre of the industry in Portugal moved there from Viana. Before then the merchants of the English factory established there had little connection with the wine trade. Their mainstay was selling cloth and cotton goods in exchange for local produce.

Relations with France having got no better, there was a constantly high demand for wines from this area. Ability to cater for this demand was improving slowly and in such circumstances there were opportunities for all forms of adulterations to take place. In the vineyards where there was no tradition of production for export the port produced was thinnish and a touch raw, largely as a result of mixing both the red and white grapes in the pressing. One trick employed to endear port to its clientele was to rectify its light colour with liberal additions of the juice of elderberries. This was by no means the worst – a Victualler's Guide from the 19th century goes one step further – describing how to make more than 60 gallons of "port" using only 12 gallons of the wine as a basis. The other ingredients were 6 gallons of rectified spirit, 3 of cognac brandy, 42 of rough cider, elderberry or cogswood to be added for colour, powder of catechu added to each bottle to form a crust, and the ends of corks to be soaked in a strong mixture of Brazil wood and a little alum to give the appearance of age! It is little wonder then that Scots in general abhorred the taste of the new liquor being foisted upon them, and even the most robust Caledonian spirit would have wilted at being administered this form of "poison".

If Scots disliked the taste of port, they were even less impressed with what the wine symbolised politically. Throughout the greater part of the 18th century port drinking was tantamount to condoning the Union of 1707 and for that reason was avoided by huge sections of the Scottish populace. But not all Iberian wines were viewed so dimly. For over 150 years Scots had been enjoying the growths of Lisbon, Malaga, Jerez and Alicante and were quite happy to stock them in their cellars to

◄ *Oporto*

provide a change from the staple, claret. As a measure of their acceptability to Scots one needs to look no further than an alternative version of *"Auld Lang Syne"* which Burns discovered while collecting songs. In a letter to Mrs Dunlop in 1788 he sets out the verses:

Should auld acquaintance be forgot
And never thought upon
Let's hae a waught o' Malaga
For auld lang syne
For auld lang syne my dear
For auld lang syne
Let's hae a waught o' Malaga
For auld lang syne.

From the mid-1700s onwards at least a few Scots were beginning to view port in a new light and were not averse to cashing in on the wine's commercial potential. The essential conditions for the production of fine ports had been discovered and applied to Douro wines with such success that their popularity had risen immeasurably. The growing interest of Scots in the port trade at this time was particularly opportune since troubles in France were further reinforcing the advantage Iberian wines had in the British market. Already in 1766 a Scot called Marshall was operating in Oporto and selling port to Oliphant of Ayr amongst others. The main surge of Scottish involvement in the trade came in the three decades before and after the turn of the 19th century, and the success of Scottish enterprise in this period is testified in the plethora of Scots names which are still identified among modern port wine shippers – Cockburn, Gould, Campbell, Robertson, Tait, Dow, MacKenzie, Campbell and Menzies, Graham and Sandeman. Their names read like a modern port wine list.

Among the earliest of the Scottish port shippers was the house of Sandeman. The founder, George Sandeman, a member of an old Scottish family first recorded in 1594 in Alyth, left Perth for London in 1790. Like so many Scots then and since, his move south was an attempt to widen his commercial and social talents, an objective which he approached with characteristic determination and abundant confidence. On the 14 May 1790 he wrote his sister Jean, spelling out the ambitious task he had set himself:

> I can scarcely bring myself to think seriously of leaving London … when a person has left his native place for a long time he wishes to show some sort of splendour when he returns, therefore I shall remain where I am, till I shall have made a moderate fortune to retire with: which I expect will be in the course of nine years; which to be sure is a long time, but some lucky stroke may possibly reduce it to five or six.

He borrowed £300 from his father to finance the purchase of a modest wine vault in London and so the Sandeman business was born. For the first six years of his sojourn in London he was in partnership with his brother David, of whom Sir Walter Scott was later to note in his diary: "[He had] as intellectual a head as ever I witnessed". But the partnership was shortlived. David and George parted amicably in 1796, the latter preferring to devote his efforts to helping set up the Commercial Bank of Scotland. His connection with the wine trade was not severed however. In 1814 he was co-partner in a firm bearing his own name which was based in Perth and selling a variety of Iberian wines including those shipped by George.

George must also have had an exceptional head particularly for commerce, for within a few years of leaving for London he became established as one of the city's principal wine shippers. Sandeman had decided to specialise in port and sherries and by 1792 he was successfully representing in England the sherries of James Duff of Cadiz and in 1809 James Gooden, one of the firm's partners, took up residence in Cadiz to begin shipping sherries bearing the Sandeman name. In virtually his first year of business George was fortunate enough to secure quantities of the ports of the 1790 vintage, now considered to have been among the first port vintages ever. Only seven years after leaving he did return to the Fair City in "some sort of splendour" as he had hoped – in that year he was presented with the freedom of the city. By 1809 he was in Portugal and being referred to as "Mr. Sandeman, the head of a great Wine House in Oporto". There he was a frequent guest at the Duke of Wellington's table where they engaged in long discussions over the relative merits of port vintages.

The vintages the Duke and Sandeman compared would almost certainly have been drier and less powerful than those of later years. Vintage port as we know it belongs to the 19th century – until then it was rare to keep wine in bottles for any length of time. In Henderson's *History of Ancient and Modern Wines,* written in 1824, his description of how port was to be treated is closer to the modern practice:

> When it arrives in this country, it is of a dark purple or inky colour, in a full rough body, with an astringent bitter-sweet taste, and strong odour and flavour of Brandy. After it has remained some years longer in the wood, the sweetness, roughness and astringency of the flavour abate, but it is only after it has been kept ten to fifteen years in the bottle that the odour of the brandy is completely subdued, and the genuine aroma of the wine is developed.

It had been discovered by this time that the addition of brandy at a crucial point in port's fermentation was absolutely essential. Initially this practice was introduced to ensure the stability of the natural port wines during their journey northwards to the market. The brandy certainly provided stability but it also contributed a good deal to the quality and character of the wine. Sandeman was at the forefront of the early experiments with brandy and port, and some time later he gave an account of his trials with the 1815 vintage – the celebrated "Waterloo", which was as delightful in the Douro as it was in Bordeaux.

> I selected three pipes drawn from the same tonnel to one of which I put one-third the usual quantity of Brandy, to the second two-thirds, and to the last a full dose of Brandy. Recollect that this was one of the finest vintages I ever had to deal with, and the tonnel was one of the best of the year. I bottled all three pipes at the same time, and between one and two years afterwards, I found the first pipe becoming sour, and was obliged to start it again into a cask and dose it with Brandy. In three or four years I was obliged to do the same with the second, but the third was so much liked that I was offered a guinea a bottle for it. But I kept it to be drunk on the premises.

Baron Forrester's study of Douro fieldworkers.

There was a market for port in Scotland by this time, the events of the previous century being gradually forgotten as the qualities of the new, improved wine wooed the discriminating Scottish palates. Even the judges who had displayed so much loyalty to claret in the previous century, were finding port a pleasant beverage. So pleasant in fact that it made regular and frequent appearances on the benches of the Law Courts by way of refreshment for the legal fraternity, as Lord Cockburn recalls:

> At Edinburgh the old judges had a practice at which even their barbaric age used to shake its head. They had always wine and biscuits on the Bench when business was clearly to be protracted beyond the usual dinner hour. The modern judges – those I mean who were made after 1800 – never gave in to this, but with those of the preceding generation it was quite common. Black bottles of strong Port were set down beside them with glasses, caraffes of water, tumblers and biscuits, and this without the slightest attempt at concealment. The refreshment was generally allowed to stand untouched, and as if despised, for a short time during which their Lordships seemed to be intent only on their notes. But in a little while some water was poured into the tumbler, and sipped quietly as if merely to sustain nature. Then a few drops of Wine were ventured on, but only with the water; till at last patience could endure no longer, and a full bumper of the pure black element was tossed over, after which the thing went on regularly and there was a comfortable munching and quaffing to the great envy of parched throats in the gallery. The strong headed stood it tolerably well, but it told, plainly enough, upon the feeble. Not that the Ermine was absolutely intoxicated, but it was certainly sometimes affected.

The judges mentioned would have been in complete empathy with the terms and conditions laid out in a missive signed by Norman MacLeod of Glenelg dated 24th June 1799:

> I hereby bind me, secluding heirs & assignees, having at the time power of lith and limb, to attend the call of Mr. George Jeffrey of Lochcarron to the baptism of his first-born after this date, upon express condition that he perform his promise voluntarily given to come to my son's baptism on Wed first the 26th inst. Under a penalty of the party not performing to give to the party performing the best dinner Shealhouse can afford to not fewer than six and not more than twelve friends, when called upon, at which no less than two dozen port wine to be given by the party failing and to have beside a circle of three inches diameter shaved upon the crown of his head before dinner, after which he must drink a Constable holding no less than one half bottle of said wine … In witness whereof I have written & subscribed these presents place & date as above.

The purpose of the "constable" MacLeod refers to is explained in Jamieson's Scots Dictionary. Apparently it was "a large glass, the contents of which he is obliged to drink who has not drunk as much as the rest of the company, or who has transgressed its rules".

On the home market Sandeman's Ports had become a great success. They were aided, no doubt, by the efforts of the original partner in the firm, David Sandeman. His printed circulars of 1814 which were distributed to all his retail contacts reads:

> Our wine concerns will be principally in connection with my brother's house ... whose establishment at Oporto, Messrs Geo. Sandeman and Co., possess a stock of wines of the first description, their present shipping prices are as follows:
>
> Ports, Young Wine ...... £46)
> Old.................... £50)
> Superior Old...... £52)

George Sandeman was succeeded by his nephew George Glas Sandeman whose son Albert, born in 1833, was for a time manager in the Oporto House before succeeding his father in 1868 as senior partner in the firm of "George G. Sandeman". Albert took his three brothers into the business. One of them, Colonel John Glas Sandeman, saw service in the Crimean War and having survived that became one of Oporto's most respected shippers. Incongruous though it may seem, one of Colonel John's achievements was inventing the penny-in-the-slot machine!

Graham's, another port shipping house with strong Scottish ties, was originally a general trading company founded in Glasgow by William Graham Senior in 1784. A branch of the firm was opened in Lisbon by his son William Graham Junior, with the intention of selling cotton and cloth to the Portuguese. In 1820 his brother John established himself in Oporto and the two Portuguese branches merged to form the company of W. & J. Graham. Though trading in general merchandise they soon acquired a bad debt which was only recoverable in kind in the form of wine from the Upper Douro valley. This was sent back to the parent firm who by all accounts were none too pleased to receive port instead of cash. The port, however, found a ready market in Scotland and William and John were forgiven with the instruction to send more port.

From this unusual beginning the Grahams developed their port-shipping interests considerably. Not only did they become a leading Port House, but they also acquired a vineyard in the Upper Douro valley – the Quinta dos Malvedos, which was later to be described by the Viscount de Villa Maior: "The Quinta yields about sixty pipes of wine, considered to be of the very first quality among the best in the Douro". Today it is a showpiece estate with a magnificent dwelling-house, lovingly preserved by the Symington family. There, portraits of upright Presbyterians gaze earnestly at you in the cool shade of a house built in the Portuguese style, which dominates spectacularly one of the few straight furlongs of the river. Visiting Malvedos as guests of the Symingtons, it did not take too great a stretch of the

Douro valley

imagination to visualise the Glasgow merchants of a hundred years syne; sipping chilled tawnies on the balcony as high-prowed *Barcos Rabelos* glide across the still waters of an autumn evening, carrying pipes of their young wine down stream to the lodges of Vila Nova de Gaia.

Joining Oporto's growing colony of Scots in 1814 was Robert Cockburn, a young man descended from a notable Lothian family. Cockburn was the younger brother of the celebrated Lord Cockburn whose *Memorials* have provided so many valuable insights into wine-drinking in late 18th century Edinburgh. But Robert's achievements also deserve attention, for three of the most notable wine firms in the history of the trade stem from his involvement – Cockburn and Campbell, Cockburn and Co. (Leith), both established in Edinburgh and London, and Cockburn and Smithes, the internationally famous port wine shippers. Robert removed to Oporto in 1814 and with the aid of George Wauchope (of Messrs. Wauchope and Moodie, Leith) founded the firm of Cockburn and Wauchope. Later they teamed up with another Scot, William Greig, with whom they had become acquainted in Oporto, and in 1828 his name was added to the style of the firm.

During his stay in Oporto Cockburn found life pleasant but quiet, his social life being brightened periodically by dinners in the Factory House. His letters, now held in the British Association in Oporto, provide some insights into the lifestyle of a British port shipper in early 19th century Oporto.

> I can find very little to tell you of what is going on over here, as for some time past things have been rather quiet; reading a little; in the evening at Mr. Reepes twice or thrice a week, or at the Opera House when there is one, and every now and then a bachelor's party, and this round over and over, ad infinitum; luckily the round is a very pleasant one.

In fact Cockburn had been married in 1805 and his second son Archibald was with him in Oporto in 1828, presumably to learn the trade, for he mentions in a letter to his sister Ellen in Edinburgh: "I work a good deal at the Portuguese and think I shall get on well enough, and I taste wine most laboriously."

Despite the latter attraction Archibald found it difficult to settle in Oporto. In particular he hankered after the fishing on the Earn and Ruchill. The Douro, he complains in another letter "has not a fish worth the catching". The lack of news from Scotland irritated Archibald and in letters home his sister is continually being pumped for information.

> Are the Dundases and Davidsons as intimate with the Bonars as ever, and when is there to be a marriage, and who is it to be? What are David and Louise about? In short, tell me all the scandal?

There was not even the prospect of more formal news from Scotland "as no Scotch paper comes here, a parcel now and then...". As a diversion from the humdrum of Oporto life ethnic social evenings were organised. Archibald refers obliquely to these in his letter of 24 October 1826 to Ellen.

> I petitioned some time ago for a copy of the "Scottish Minstrel" ... A copy of that set of Russian Quadrilles would be a great favour and of any Scotch one you can get – they have one set of Scotch Quadrilles, but very poor.

If the social life in Oporto during the 1820s palled a little, there was plenty of excitement during the 1830s. In 1832 Dom Pedro, ex-Emperor of Brazil, landed at Mindelo to the north of Oporto with 7,500 men, his intention being to wrest the Portuguese crown from his brother Miguel, who had seized power in 1828. Dom Pedro's army was a hotch-potch of an International Brigade including many Scots mercenaries and possibly one or two idealists. They were led by Colonel Shaw whose appearance seems to fit the Scottish stereotype perfectly. He was wild, red-headed and thirsted for the blood of Tories, absolutists and reactionaries. On landing in Portugal he vowed not to shave until his band marched into Lisbon, and as the months wore on his flowing red beard could easily be picked out where the fighting was thickest. His men were no better turned out according to the descriptions provided by Colonel Badcock, an observer from the British Government:

> I never beheld such a motley crew as this corps ... and if there had not been something of the devil in their eyes I could not have supposed them my countrymen. They were mostly in rags and tatters, some without breaches; few with shoes and stockings.

The Pedronist commander, Marshal Solignac, affectionately termed them his "wolves". Once when reviewing the corps he ordered them to go through the motions of priming, loading and firing. It was at this juncture, with arms, guns and shot going in every direction but the correct one that Badcock came to the conclusion that either these gallant Scots were totally ignorant of their drills or were drunk. Their *pièce de résistance* occurred when Solignac ordered an advance with fixed bayonets:

> the men immediately charged, and put all the spectators to flight, who ran till the lines stopped them, the Marshal stepping out of his way as fast as he could.

The Scots inspired fear in their friends. One wonders how their enemy Dom Miguel, or as his Caledonian foe called him, "John MacDougall" viewed them.

After being in Oporto only eight months Archibald Cockburn had come to certain conclusions regarding the unfamiliar physical characteristics of the local population, as he explains in a letter to his acquaintance Thomas Tod:

> The contrast of national appearance is very striking, and in point of size, make and most particularly cleanliness was much in favour of the British: in point of the face the Portuguese seemed to have decidedly the best of it. Their faces have more expression, their eyes being almost invariably good and though dirty, their features are generally well formed. The British looked so white-haired too, and so beardless that indeed the Portuguese laugh as they call them 'rapazes que não têm barba' [boys without beards].

Shaw's band of eccentrics were yet to make their appearance in Oporto and clearly Cockburn should have reserved his judgement until they had been viewed. Similarly the Portuguese would have had to re-appraise the appropriateness of their cat-calls having seen this hirsute bunch.

Robert Cockburn and Wauchope retired in 1830, and the former's interests were passed to his sons Archibald and Alexander as the firm continued as Cockburn and Greig. Alexander's sloth and unreliability was a constant source of irritation to his brother, indeed it was this he blamed for the financial difficulties besetting the firm some years later, difficulties which resulted in the dissolution of the company in Oporto and London. Immediately Archibald formed a new partnership with Henry Smithes and his brother John Smithes, thus creating the firm of Cockburn Smithes and Co. Alexander was not included in this arrangement because of his lack of application, but Archibald at a later date did set him up in work, this time as an agent for Cockburn Smithes in Northern England and as their representative in Edinburgh. Scrutiny of the results of Alexander's efforts in these posts allow for some comparison of the relative success of the larger Scottish port-shipping Houses towards the close of the 19th century. Of 4,051 pipes the firm imported into

Barco Rabelo, Oporto

England in 1875 only 71 went north of the Humber into Alexander's stamping ground. Meanwhile Sandeman's were delivering 128 pipes to Newcastle and Hull. His poor showing had spread to Scotland. At one time Cockburn Smithes were second only to Sandeman in supplying the home country with port, but now of 2,664 pipes delivered in 1875 420 had been shipped by Graham's, 323 by Sandeman, 271 by Clode & Baker, 261 by Martinez Gassiot, 183 by Van Zellers and only 178 by Cockburn Smithes.

Throughout the 19th century, during the crucial period of the port trade's development, many colourful Scottish characters were in Oporto. Some stayed and prospered, others stayed and did not. More came and went, some to return. For instance there was the Shetlander Robert Halcrow, a man of amazing strength who was so esteemed by the Portuguese that he became one of the leading skippers, shipping goods to and from Oporto and Lisbon. He was also responsible for adulterating many of the port wines he carried – a practice for which he never admitted guilt. There was also Mr. "One-Percent" Robertson, so called because of his fastidious interest in the quality of the port he shipped. This tradition is continued by the firm bearing his name today. His claim was that only one per cent of total production of the Upper Douro would be fit to be exported through his firm. The list of Scottish associations is never-ending...

One of the more recent involvements by Scots in the trade is perhaps the most significant within the context of the modern port industry, in that it forms the bridge between past and present Scots shippers. Andrew James Symington was born in Scotland in 1863 and at the age of 19 left for Oporto to join a British cotton company. Soon he was attracted to the wine industry and within a matter of years he had built up a solid reputation as a port-shipper. Eight of his descendants are in the business today and their interests include some of Port's most famous names – Dow, Graham (which they bought in 1970), Warre, Smith & Woodhouse, Gould-Campbell and Quarles Harris. The founder of the most enterprising family firm in Oporto today, was himself a character. On his frequent fishing trips home to a Temperance Hotel on the Tweed, he had the decorum to label his accompanying magnum of port "A.J. Symington's Mixture.!" He would have appreciated the balance and contrast between the old and the new his descendants have achieved at the bustling lodges of Vila Nova and the Quinta de Bomfim at Pinhão in the heart of the Alto Douro. Sitting on the lawn of a bungalow built in the style of the Anglo-Indian tea planter, sipping white port or drinking tea, one could be excused for gazing over to the high terraced slopes above the Douro and romanticising port as the drink of the Empire on which the sun never set. But one would be ignoring the reality of the winery down by the river where the very latest Californian and French technology prevail. The family are aware of tradition, but it is their dynamic adaptation to the competitive world of the 1990's which has brought them and their superb wines considerable success and acclaim.

In contrast to the apparently sudden emergence of the Scots colony in Oporto and the rapid development of the home market for port in the closing years of the 18th century, Scottish acquaintance with Spanish wines dates from a much earlier period but has been rather more subdued in its development. The wine from Jerez de la Frontera – sherry – was particularly popular with Scots in the 16th and 17th centuries. At that time they would have known it as "seck" or "sack" – a name purportedly derived from the Spanish "seco" (dry), thought to describe its quality. This term was still in use in Scotland at the beginning of the 18th century. Glasgow's council, for example, gifted the Duke of Hamilton "ane butt of seck" in 1694 and mentions are made of it at later dates. There was at this time a gradual shift from the original appellation to ones which appear to be more familiar. Scots throughout the first half of the 18th century called for "Zerrie" or "Zerrey" when a pint or two of wine from Jerez took their fancy.

There is no lack of evidence testifying to our early interest in Spanish wine. In 1548 a Scottish vessel of 100 tuns making her way from Flanders to Leith was arrested by the "*Sakyer*", an English naval ship, off Inchcolm in the Firth of Forth. Part of the ship's cargo was requisitioned by Sir Andrew Dudley. His pickings included "a pype of secke, a but of mamsy, to hoxedes of whyt wyne". In February 1614 a ship laden with wine arrived in Dundee from Cadiz, one of the principal ports exporting sherry. Many such shipments were being organised at source by Scottish merchants. One of these was Andrew Fansyde who in 1593 was in Funchal, Madeira. In his letter from there to Archibald Douglas, the Ambassador in London, Fansyde complains that there were no wines or fruit worth purchasing on the island and consequently he was going to make for Spain to continue his search for the commodities required. A few years later in 1602 we hear of wine merchants newly arrived from Spain carrying back intelligence for the King regarding an impending invasion of England. On Spain's previous invasion attempt Scotsmen inadvertently benefited from unexpected supplies of Cadiz wine. The Armada was commanded by the Duke of Medina Sidonia, whose base was at Sanlucar de Barrameda, near Cadiz, and many of his men came from the sherry district. The wine the ships carried on their voyage until they were in some cases smashed against Scottish rocks were also from that area. Beachcombers of the day would have been delighted to see some of their favourite Spanish growths floating towards the shore.

Some of the Scottish merchants remained in Spain to marry into local families. One permanent wine-exile was a Kirkpatrick from Closeburn whose grand-daughter was the Comtessa de Montijo. Her daughter Eugenia was Napoleon III's bride.

Apart from being a source of supply Spain had another major significance for the Scottish wine trade – she could provide the merchants of Leith and other ports with the corks required for bottling wine. Edward Burd, the Leith wine merchant, went on a cork buying mission as a young man. Aboard the *"Christian"* he set sail in 1726 from Leith en route for Cadiz. A variety of misfortunes befell this particular voyage, and for one reason or another the *"Christian"* did not manage to load in Cadiz and would have returned empty had it not been for a speculative visit to Bordeaux where they managed to pick up a cargo of claret for the Scottish market.

Though Sandeman and Co. were pioneers among the Scots colony in Oporto, by the time they arrived in the sherry country there were a number of compatriots already set up in the wine-shipping business. One of the partners in the firm, James Gooden, took up residence in Cadiz during 1809 with a view to shipping sherry under the Sandeman label. James Duff and Co., for whom George Sandeman had operated as agents in London some years before, was then well established having been in business for some forty years. There are records of him supplying Oliphant of Ayr with sherry, malaga and brandy as early as 1767. Duff was an Ayrshire man who removed to Cadiz as a young man. There he subsequently became Pro-Consul in 1784 and then full Consul for the British Government in 1790. Though he held the latter position for 26 years his wine interests were not neglected. With his business network becoming increasingly complex he enlisted the help of his nephew William Gordon in 1805. Gordon set up an agency to deal with Duff's wines in London. This he did in partnership with two Irishmen – Murphy and Farrell, and the firm operated under the name of Gordon, Murphy and Co.

Two years before Sir James Duff's death in 1815 the Edinburgh firm of Jas. Cathcart and Co. were dealing in

> the Sherries which our friends Messrs Gordon and Co. of Xerez have shipt to this country, since the re-establishment of our intercourse with the said city, having given general satisfaction and knowing their determination to support the ancient characters of the Brand-Name (D.G.) by shipping wines only of the best quality … We subjoin the present shipping prices at Cadiz.
>
> Sherry, First quality .... £65 per butt
> Second quality........ £55 per butt
> Third quality.......... £45 per butt

The Napoleonic wars had interrupted trade with Cadiz for some time. English ports such as Bristol and London were more fortunate than Edinburgh since Sherry

The Sandeman Bodega, Jerez

shipments were being shipped through surreptitiously from Sanlucar, another of Jerez's ports.

Already Duff's Sherry was being sold under the name Duff Gordon (D.G.) and when the firm passed to Sir William Duff Gordon after Sir James Duff's death, the brand name continued. The Duff Gordons remained in control until 1857 and retained a financial interest in the firm until 1872. Thereafter the firm was in the hands of the Osborne house, but the brand name was retained for the markets in the English-speaking countries. When Osborne & Co. wished to develop their sherry sales in the Spanish-speaking nations, the name Duff-Gordon which is nigh impossible for Spaniards to pronounce, was dropped in favour of their own.

Shortly after William Gordon had opened his London agency he engaged a confidential clerk called John James Ruskin. Ruskin was born and brought up in Edinburgh, his mother coming from Glenluce in Wigtownshire. In due course Ruskin was to set up an agency of his own under the name of Ruskin, Telford and Domecq. They initially acted for Hauries Sherry and then for Domecqs, and as a result of good fortune and hard work Ruskin amassed considerable wealth. He was a very effective operator, for under his influence Hauries' trade in Britain developed considerably. Before his death in 1864 he described his success with the firm: "I went to every town in England, most in Scotland and some in Ireland, till I raised their exports of 20 butts to 3,000"! Ruskin's life was a success in the material sense – his only son John Ruskin, the famous author, achieved success in the arts, and to some extent his father's wealth financed the early travel which inspired so much of his work.

Sir James Duff and Sir William Gordon.

Another recipient of wealth generated by the sherry trade was the Royal Scots College, the Catholic seminary then situated in Valladolid, but recently removed to Salamanca. When the Cadiz-based merchant Arthur Gordon died in 1815 he bequested part of his estate to the College. Gordon, no relation of his namesake Sir William, was a Banffshire Catholic, the younger brother of the Laird of Beldorney in the Cabrach. He was already functioning as a merchant in the city by 1770. Letters written by Gordon in 1774 announce a change in his business orientation.

> Mr Dalrymple [William Dalrymple of North Berwick] and I have bought some wines in Xerez and are resolved to invest our money in that article as soon and as fast as it comes to hand.
>
> William Dalrymple and I are now turned bona fide wine merchants. We have purchased cellars of wine well stocked in Xerez and have no reason to complain hitherto.

> Our orders from England of late are pretty numerous and we expect to do better in this branch than any other.

After his death, he was succeeded in the business by his son Charles Peter Gordon. Under Charles' management their Jerez bodega was a haven for travellers from the home country and his hospitality was legend. After a visit to Jerez in 1809 Byron wrote:

> At Zeres, where the Sherry we drink is made, I met a great merchant – a Mr. Gordon of Scotland – who was extremely polite, and favoured me with the inspection of his vaults and cellars, so that I quaffed at the fountain head.

In 1850 his son, a namesake, became the Vice-Consul of Jerez. He was also a Catholic but took his religion rather seriously, to the extent that he refused British Protestants rooms where they might worship when itinerant clergymen visited. This stance eventually led to his dismissal in 1861. There then followed an amusing interlude in which Gordon refused to hand over the official seal and would not agree to remove the British arms from above his doorway. This debacle took some time to resolve.

Some years before Gordon accepted the office of Vice-Consul another wine-shipping firm with Scottish connections was establishing itself in Jerez. Kenneth MacKenzie arrived in the town in 1846, and for more than a century MacKenzie and Company ran a successful bodega. Latterly the firm was operated by two of the original MacKenzie's great-grand-nephews selling sherries under the names of Vintner's Choice, Pasa Doble, El Catador and others.

Paradoxically one of the most famous Sherry "marques" with Scottish connections belongs not to a shipper but to an import house – Findlater, Mackie Todd – whose origins lie with Alexander Findlater who in 1823 entered the wine trade as a merchant. Their most popular brand – Dry Fly – coined in the 1930s by an avid fisherman, is accompanied on the label by an illustration of a Sherry Spinner Fly.

The other growths from this Southern part of Spain – Hullock, Bastard, Tent, Alicante, Mountain and Malaga – whose sweetness appealed to the Scots in days gone by have all but disappeared from the wine lists of Northern Europe. Of these only Malaga is still available and though not consumed in the "waughts" of Burns' day it is worth seeking out for auld lang syne.

MADEIRA

The Scots did not exactly discover Madeira, but they as much as anyone transformed the island from a wooded one to a paradise of sumptuous wines, exquisite embroidery and grand old world hotels for tourists to enjoy its pleasures.

The place was christened Madeira, Portuguese for wood, by Zarco in 1418 when he came across the deeply forested islands in what was one of the first of countless voyages of discovery his countrymen were to make in this, the beginning of their Golden Age. Although never quick to establish colonies of their own, the Scots were never slow to exploit others' hard work. On board the first ship taking Portuguese settlers to Madeira in 1424 was one John Drummond of Stobhall, or João Escocio as he was known to the Portuguese. One of the thousands of Scots whom poverty at home despatched on the "wyld aventouris", João Escocio married a priest's sister, and the resulting family were among the first to put down roots in Madeira.

Madeira

By the end of the century sugar and vines were putting roots in the rich island soil, the latter yielding the sweet Malvasia grape brought there from Crete via the Peninsula. The Malvasia gives us the English Malmsey, still the most revered of the four styles of wine produced on Madeira today: Sercial, pale gold, dry but full flavoured; Verdelho, perfectly balanced fruitiness with a hint of sweetness; Bual, pungently scented and a nut brown sweetness; Malmsey, among the fattest, most opulently generous wines in the world.

Scots merchants or pirates, depending on which flag you flew, were undoubtedly cruising the waters of the Atlantic islands looking for wine, sugar and plunder in the 15th and 16th centuries. One wonders how Drummond's descendants felt when news of Barton of Leith's excesses came through to them! It was the marriage of Charles II with Catherine of Braganza in the late 17th century, however, that cemented Portugal's relationship with England. Although they shared the same king with the Scots by then, England jealously protected her trading rights, and actively worked against Scottish attempts either to trade with English colonies or, in the case of the Darien scheme, to found colonies herself. It is said that Paterson's ships en route for Darien called at Madeira and exchanged homespun clothes for wine. Madeira's position between Europe and the Americas was its making, for both Portuguese bound for Brazil and English sailing to the West Indies called there to load provisions and wine. To protect English shipping and manufactured goods, Charles II issued a law insisting that all European produce had to be shipped to the English colonies in English ships from English ports. The only commodities exempt from this ruling were "salt for the fisheries of New England and Newfoundland ... in the Madeiras and Azores, wines ... and in Scotland or Ireland ... servants, or horses, and all victuals". The victuals referred to would be plain oatmeal, for servant and horse.

As soon as the political Union between England and Scotland was completed, the Scots could not be left out of the colonial trade and suddenly the Empire was swarming with Sons of Caledonia, a clannish lot who tended to deal with their own kind where at all possible. Francis Newton, a Fifer from Leslie who founded a firm still thriving today, Cossart Gordon & Co., writes to his brother in Virginia of the trials endured by the Empire-building Scot:

> I agree as yet very well with the climate which is very pleasant and perhaps one of the most healthful of any in the world but that is balanced by the people ... the whole Portuguese nation seems completely pervaded with a sluggish spirit of inglorious indolence. They are a very sullen, proud, deceitful people, and in short there is no such thing as finding one to make a Companion of, very few of them having good education unless the Priest and Collegeans whose ceremonies are so many and conversation so very narrow, being Roman Catholics, that their company is very disagreeable. As for the English here, they are much worse!

Choosing the best of a bad bunch, Francis enters a Portuguese house and with all of two months experience behind him he can write to David Campbell in London with the unbounded optimism of the Lad o' Pairts on the make:

> I like my situation well, it is the only house in the Island where one has a liberty to trade for themselves and to learn the business, the English being very jealous of their clerks, and in a little time when I am master of the language I think I will have in my power to ship wines as good and cheap as any here, there not being such secrets ... as people imagine".

The latter part of that statement is refreshingly direct, and should be noted by those who would raise wine appreciation to the level of mystique, purely for the sake of their own social cachet and prestige. Wine primarily is to be enjoyed ... "there not being such secrets ... as people imagine".

The first mention of adding brandy to Madeira in order to fortify it comes in one of Newton's letters of 1753 – "I really impute the complaints I have had of wines to my not putting a bucket or two of brandy in each pipe as other houses do." The characteristic hint of a burnt flavour in Madeira comes from a process of heating the wine gently in chambers called *estufas.* These replaced the older island method of simply leaving the wine exposed to the hot sun which gave the charming sounding *vinho do sol* or sun wine. These two processes resulted in a powerful but subtly flavoured wine which could sustain a voyage to India and retain its fruit and acidity to slake the not inconsiderable thirst of the British army baking in the plains there. The popularity of the wine in India led to the final discovery which made Madeira the taste of the Empire; that the wine matured beautifully after a long voyage, and thus East India Madeira was the most sought after of them all. Writing to James Stewart and Michael Scott in Grenada in 1788, Newton confirms that "an India voyage will make up for every deficiency of age, we are fully persuaded the wine will be found excellent". That romantic practice has unfortunately gone, though the name East India Madeira remains on Rutherford's labels.

The extent of the Scottish Empire can be gleaned from the order books of Cossart Gordon & Co. which survive in excellent condition from Francis Newton arriving on the island in 1748 till the present day. In the year 1800 alone, Newton, now partnered by fellow Scots to form "Newton, Gordon, Murdoch and Co." received the following orders from Bombay:

500 pipes Law, Bruce & Co.
300 pipes David Scott & Co.
250 pipes Forbes Smith & Co.

The chances are that every one of the above were Fifers, as Newton had a habit of hustling all his early trade in the Americas and London from people he had known in Scotland. To Mr Patrick Couts on 8th April 1753: "An old schoolfellow Wattie Hunter traded here lately on his way to Jamaica". To Mr Waddell Cunningham on 30th April 1753: "I am glad to hear of your welfare and settlement in New York ... I shall always be glad of the opportunity of promoting your interests".

The Jacobite Rebellion in 1745 brought major social upheavals in its wake and a lot of emigration from Scotland. Many of the *emigrés* were not directly involved in the uprising, however, they simply felt that their world had changed, wounds were left open, and they preferred to take their chance abroad. Of the 20 million Scots scattered all over the world, a good percentage migrated because they wanted to, rather than through political necessity. The romance of the '45 is so strong however that everyone claims descent from Culloden. If American claimants alone had been at the battle, the Duke of Cumberland wouldn't have stood a chance. It is possible that Francis Newton was a Jacobite, but his remark to his brother in 1748 is simply the expression of someone contemplating how the upheaval effected his friends – "The great changes that have happened to our friends is surprising, before you left Scotland". Francis and his friend joined the Lifeguards in Flanders, then went their separate ways when the Regiment broke up – the friend to be a plantation overseer in St. Kitts, Newton to Madeira.

Other Scots established themselves in the Madeira trade during the 18th and early 19th centuries. An English pioneer of the wine, John Leacock, was apprenticed to "Murdoch & Cattennach & Co". In the letter book of Oliphants of Ayr in 1766 we find orders for three Madeira companies, all Scottish – Pringle & Cheape; Fergusson, Murdoch & Co; and James & Alexander Gordon & Co. William Grant from Nairn, "run away to sea", married the daughter of a wine shipper, Mary Innes, in Madeira and along with a fellow Scot, Rutherford, founded another firm which exists today. The Rutherfords also left Scotland after the '45 and settled in the American States. The reputation of Madeira in the Colonies and possibly contacts with fellow Scots on the island, was enough to draw them to Funchal in 1814.

The community was augmented with new arrivals from home, sent out by firms there dealing with the firms in Madeira. Some were lucky and found employment but as the 19th century wore on, the firms were able to fill positions from people already living on the island. A friend of Newton's sent out young Mr. Price with letters of introduction in 1819, "but business being slack here and every house being full of hands, he was unable to get a situation in any of them – but in consequence of his being from Kirkcudbright and a connection of yours we received him into ours and rendered him what services we could during his short stay". At the same time MacKenzie and Balfour of Leith sent out a boy, who, unable to find work on Madeira, carried on to the Canaries and then Brazil in search of fame and fortune.

Later in the 19th century Robert Donaldson and Russell Gordon had prime vineyards and shipped wine from the island. Russell Manners Gordon was the last of his clan to belong to the firm Cossart Gordon & Co., which until recently was still in the hands of the Cossarts, a family of Huguenot stock who came to Madeira in 1808. Russell was a descendant of William Gordon, 6th Viscount Lochinver who was executed as a Jacobite rebel on Tower Hill in 1716. He married the Portuguese Countess Torre Bella and accepted a title from the King of Portugal. All this was taking him away from business so his partner Peter Cossart asked him to resign. This he did and became a Portuguese subject, settling into the life of his adopted country. He still had enough sense of history however to name his first born James Murray Kenmure Gordon.

A Presbyterian Kirk existed, so there must have been a fair number of Scots to constitute a congregation. One of the ministers, the Rev. A. Drummond Paterson, was almost run off the island for preaching pacifism during the First World War. Not so lucky was a Scottish physician called Kalley whose lay preaching in public enraged the Catholic authorities so much that he had to escape from Madeira in a British warship in 1837.

The various firms in the wine trade eventually formed an association for mutual benefit, but in the early days rivalry was intense and vitriolic. Francis Newton, for example, despised firms which procured trade from passing Men o' War…

> soliciting them like tavern keepers for supplying them with Butcher's Meat and Cabbage, we have always left these practices and we will leave such practices to our great and magnificent rivals, Murdoch, Masterton & Co., and Scott & Co. who not infrequently wrangle much to the surprise and amusement of their customers but assuredly to the degredation and disgrace of themselves and all Madeira merchants about the preference of supplying a few arrobas of raw beef and two or three dozen of pumpkins.

The old Scots proverb, "Scartin an bitin is Scots folk's wooin", was never proved more true, for a few years after that letter was written Newton's firm rejoiced under the name, Newton, Gordon, Murdoch and Scott.

While sometimes despising meat and pumpkins, most of the old wine companies were not averse to dealing in any other commodity that would yield a profit. Like Graham's in Oporto, Newton dealt in clothing, though with little success. To his early partner Spence in London he writes in July 1753 "… as for the jackets, I cannot sell on acct. of their smallness". January 1754: "I am greatly surprised at your sending such quantities of flax and jackets when you are advised of the great glut here". And to Joseph Gray & Co. in March 1753: "We should have sent you by this opportunity Accounts and Sales of last year's cargo; the largeness of the Portuguese back sides is the only impediment for in short, the breeches are so very small that we cannot sell them at any price." Also while despising the courting of captains of Men o' War, Francis would have sought the custom of great and famous men such as Lord Nelson or Captain Cook, both of whom heaved to at Funchal to supply their ships with Malmsey. Napoleon en route for St. Helena also stopped at Madeira. Selkirk-born Henry Veitch was the British Consul at the time, and as the only civilian allowed to visit him, took Napoleon gifts of books, fruit and wine, the latter being the foundation of Veitch's later wealth in the firm "Scott Pringle and Veitch". As for Napoleon, the archives of Chateau Lafite also claim that the Emperor carried a few cases of that noble liquid into exile with him, so along with Old Verdelhos and Buals rounded by their St. Helena voyage, life still had its compensations!

Because of the importance of its tobacco trade, which demanded regular shipping to the Americas, Glasgow became the main dealer and customer for Madeira wine in Scotland. Carrying salt herring to Madeira, the ships replaced that cargo with the favourite wine of the Colonies. Clothing, cotton and sadly, slaves were also transported. Writing to a friend in the West Indies, Newton apologises:

> Since my arrival here I have been endeavouring to sell your negro wench but have not as yet sold her. When I do I shall render your acct. Sales, – however that you may not be disappointed have advanced you a hogshead New York Wine shipped on the Jamaica packett.

Throughout Cossart Gordon's archives there are frequent bills of lading for wine which would undertake a profitable West Indies voyage to mature it for the tables of the Glasgow merchant class; "for two pipes of the best Old Madeira and a half butt of the finest old Malmsey on board the Belleisle bound to Berbice and the Clyde"; "a pipe of the best old Madeira on board the Cecilia bound to the West Indies and the Clyde…" These entries for 1819 are around the time J.G. Lockhart had his hero of *Peter's Letters to his Kinsfolk* enjoy the hospitality of a Glasgow merchant coterie:

> The dinner was excellent ... capital salmon ... and trout almost as rich as salmon, from one of the lochs – prime mutton from Argyllshire, very small and sweet ... beef of the first order, some excellent fowls in curry, everything washed down by delicious old India Madeira, which went like elixir vitae into the recesses of my stomach ... a single bottle of hock, and another of white hermitage went round ... After dinner we had two or three bottles of port, which the landlord recommended as being "real stuff". Abundance of the same Madeira, but to my sorrow no claret, the only wine I ever care for more than half a dozen glasses.

Peter's claret wish comes true in Edinburgh, as we shall see, among the lawyers. Their sense of history kept the claret tradition going while Glasgow lawyers drank whisky at their formal dinners until very recently. When one discovers that the beverages listed above were just aperitifs before the classic Glasgow drink of the age, West Indies Rum and lime punch, one realises the drinking propensities of the Glaswegians – strong and fiery. Scots merchants settled all over the Americas and Newton sent Madeira to people like Muir and Boyd of Charleston, South Carolina which still boasts a beautiful Scots Kirk, Turnbull and Co. of Savannah, Georgia where the Madeira Club still thrives, Balfour & Co. of Jamaica, James Bruce of St. Vincent, James Hay of Grenada and Robert Lennox of New York. A Scot travelling in Virginia in the late 18th century wrote:

> I never go no part but I meet Scotch people; there's more of them here in this country than what I believe there is in Scotland ... indeed there is more Scotchmen excluding the negroes than buckskins.

The same man, Alexander Trotter, goes on to describe how he is regaled by long lost family friends with Madeira and claret. The Scots of course have a lot to answer for in the American South, where Confederate champions of States Rights and Slavery flew a St. Andrew's Cross into battle, though Mark Twain probably went too far when he suggested that the mythology created by the novels of Sir Walter Scott were responsible for the American Civil War!

The blame for having a mediocre palate nevertheless can be firmly laid on Scott; his biographer Lockhart states, "he could never tell Madeira from sherry ... and he sincerely preferred a tumbler of whisky toddy to the most precious 'liquid ruby' that ever flowed in the cup of a prince". This could explain the somewhat erratic references to wine in his work. The Cleikum Nabob in *St. Ronans Well* drinks "Mont Rachet," one of the earliest references to that superb Burgundy, but when it comes to the island wine, his method of serving it would have been more appropriate to the author's whisky punch – "heated madeira", surely not the best way of presenting a fine Sercial.

As with claret, Madeira tended to be the drink of the aristocratic or wealthy elements of society in the 19th century. Cossart Gordon sent wine to Lord Reay, Sir James Ferguson of Kilkerran, Lord Roseberry, the Earl of Stair, Sir Andrew Cathcart and in 1847, to Robert Dundas of Arniston, one of many of his class in this period to holiday on the island. Dundas' memories would be revived with the following wines shipped on board the *Comet*:

A Quarter Pipe of very superior Madeira wine of extra age.
A 1/2 quarter pipe of Sercial 15 years old.
A 1/2 quarter pipe of the finest rich old Malmsey.

When the vines which produced these fine wines were attacked by the disease Phylloxera in 1872, tourism and the embroidery promoted by it, helped the island ward off economic disaster until the vines could be replanted from America. Both the alternative industries were pioneered by Scots from the west of the country. Ayrshire embroidery or white work which had developed from the old skill of tambouring was introduced to the women of Madeira by a Miss Phelps. The importance of her contribution is recognised by the square bearing her name in Funchal. Another Ayrshire name is still on the island's, and one of the world's most famous hotels – "Reids Madeira", whose old world elegance and 5-star service makes it a mecca for the tourist who can afford to be pampered. William and Alfred Reid of Kilmarnock held almost a monopoly of hotels catering for Victorian tourists who came to take the "healthful" air mentioned by Newton a century before. "The Royal Edinburgh", the "Carmo" and the "Santa Clara" were the forerunners of Reids Madeira itself, built in 1890, the perfect place to sip vintage malmseys, gaze seaward and think … "Here's tae us, wha's like us!"

In relation to Madeira at least, the boast has some foundation, for in addition to the luxuries of wine, lace and hotels we even provided Funchal's water supply, channelled from the mountains by Charles Murray, the British Consul in 1778. The great Scots scientist Lord Kelvin had the idea of earthly paradise in mind when investigating the tides in Madeira, he fell in love with a daughter of the Blandy family, and married into one of the oldest English wine shippers on the island. Their "Duke of Clarence" Malmsey recalls that other Englishman who was the butt of Richard II's joke, drowning in a tide of the most luscious liquid known to man. The Caledonian connection with the major Madeira shippers has actually been strengthened in recent years. The family which now owns a majority share holding in the Madeira Wine Company and runs Blandy's, Leacock's, Miles and Cossart Gordon are the self same Symingtons whom we discussed earlier in relation to Port.

Scotland's contribution to Madeira, then, has been considerable, but in turn Madeira has given us superb wines to savour. That Madeira appreciation has declined in the country is a great shame, for few wines have a more giving nature. The Portuguese term for fortified wine, *vinho generoso,* aptly describes Madeira's properties for generally a glass or two of Sercial before dinner and a glass of Malmsey or Bual afterwards, will leave you replete and satisfied with the world.

For our 18th century forebears, of course, satisfaction came in surfeit. In Boswell's diary for August 7th, 1768, he writes: "We took a mutton chop at Whitburn, [ironically, close to the present-day oasis for Portuguese food and wine, the Madeira Mar restaurant in Armadale] and I pushed about Madeira wine until four of us drank five bottles". A few decades later the fashion for gargantuan drinking sessions among the professional classes waned, leaving an embattled conspiratorial minority determined to maintain their convivial ways. Newly arrived at an aristocrat's country house where genteel moderation was practised, Principal Robertson of Edinburgh University was taken aside by one of the guests, the Parish Minister. In tones of strict confidentiality, the Minister addressed him: "Doctor, I understand ye are a brother of my guid friend, Peter Robertson o' Edinburgh, therefore I'll gie ye a piece of advice – bend weel to the Madeira at dinner, for here ye'll get little o't after". Times change, but the rich wines of Madeira do not, and believe me, they are still worth drinking hard, or as the minister said, "bending weel".

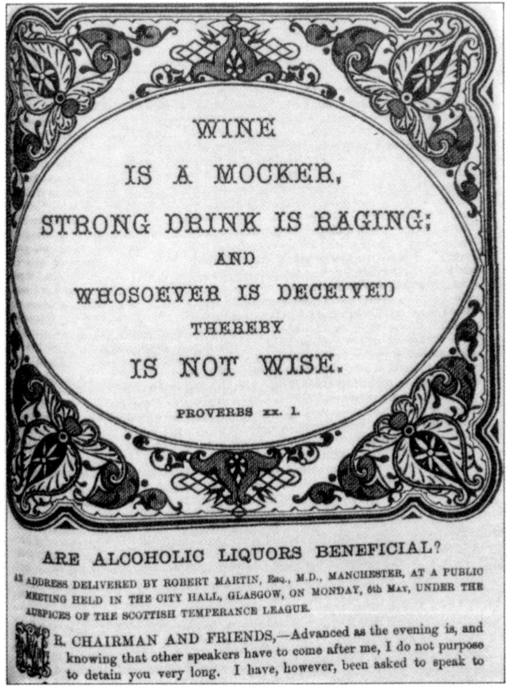

WINE
IS A MOCKER,
STRONG DRINK IS RAGING;
AND
WHOSOEVER IS DECEIVED
THEREBY
IS NOT WISE.

PROVERBS xx. 1.

ARE ALCOHOLIC LIQUORS BENEFICIAL?

AN ADDRESS DELIVERED BY ROBERT MARTIN, Esq., M.D., MANCHESTER, AT A PUBLIC MEETING HELD IN THE CITY HALL, GLASGOW, ON MONDAY, 6th MAY, UNDER THE AUSPICES OF THE SCOTTISH TEMPERANCE LEAGUE.

MR. CHAIRMAN AND FRIENDS,—Advanced as the evening is, and knowing that other speakers have to come after me, I do not purpose to detain you very long. I have, however, been asked to speak to

Temperance Tract

THE GOOD CREATURE WINE 15

> A happy change in the manners of the times fortunately renders such abuse of the good creature wine much less frequent and less fashionable than it was in my days ... Drinking is not now the vice of the times, whatever vices and follies they may have adopted in its stead.
>
> (Sir Walter Scott, 1825)

> So much has spirit drinking become associated with customs and practices in Scotland, that there is scarcely an event in life, scarcely a circumstance that occurs, not a transaction can be done, or a change can be effected, with which spirit drinking is not associated: it is associated with our births, and with our deaths, with our marriages and baptisms; it is associated with a man's entry on any employment, with his apprenticeship, with his change of employment in the same work; it is the symbol of hospitality where friends meet, and forms the complimentary usage of life among middling and lower orders; it is employed in making bargains, at the payment of accounts, at fairs and roups and every possible circumstance of life. And that is the greatest difficulty we have to contend with: ...... that to tear up the spirit drinking practices is like tearing up the whole social system of society.
>
> (William Collins, Temperance Pioneer, 1834.).

Two very different Scotlands are represented in these statements, but both reveal ways of looking at the role played by drink in Scottish Society. Behaviour regarded as jovial conviviality in the 18th century was now the vile drunkenness of the 19th century. Both terms were invented by the middle and upper classes, whose enlightened tastes led to reason, decorum and propriety rather than the old debauchery. Now that such behaviour belonged mainly to the whisky-sodden masses, terms to condemn it rather than glory in it came to the fore. Scott's world was that of the Edinburgh Literati and Border gentry. Collins' the degradation, through poverty and drink, of the teeming industrial population in Glasgow and the West. Throughout the next hundred and fifty years wine moved further up the social scale, till by the present age no knowledge of ever having drunk it remained with the people. Whisky became the national drink, and in its early days, the nation was certainly under its thrall. In 1822 the duty on spirits was reduced from 7/- to 2/10d per gallon. Whisky consumption more than doubled within a few years of the change and by 1829 over 5,777,000 gallons of the raw, fiery liquor were being downed. Seen from the vantage point of recently reformed middle-class respectability, drink was now a huge, working-class problem. The giant Temperance

Movement founded in Scotland tried to combat the trend, and although it confused drunken escapism as a reason for poverty rather than a symptom of it, its influence was a balancing and beneficial one. Scotland may have been more "whisky injured" without it.

Among the professional and upper classes the change was one of degree. The "5 bottle" ministers of the previous century, were now liable to run Band of Hope meetings by day and have a "wee" fly glass of Madeira, port or claret by night. The sobriety of the time was infectious but not entirely in keeping with the character of the people. H.W. Thompson cites an example from the early part of the century:

> In this country, wine seems necessary to inspire conversation after dinner. When Sir James Stewart the author of *Political Economy,* returned from abroad he invited a select party of friends to dine with him to welcome his arrival. After dinner he said: 'Nobody seems inclined to drink and I have been accustomed to confining my drinking chiefly to the time of dinner. Suppose we order away these bottles and glasses, and sit socially around the fire. The plan was unanimously agreed to; but Sir James soon found the conversation to flag and some of the company were almost asleep. 'I see gentlemen,' said he, 'this won't do in Scotland. We must have back the bottles and glasses and with their inspiration our conversation will be revived.' That was accordingly done and had the effect which he had predicted.

Temperance spirit was there but the flesh and genes were weak and conditioned to another philosophy!

Edinburgh was still an intellectual forging house with Scott presiding over a court every bit as influential and prestigious as Goethe's Weimar. Through *Blackwood's Magazine* the Tory faction expressed their romantic cultural nationalism and railed against Jeffrey's *Edinburgh Review,* with its Post Humean scepticism and enlightened philosophy the organ of the Whig hegemony. The flyting of the two parties gave bite to an already stimulating cultural milieu.

Perhaps predictably, the Tory faction with their awareness of national history, were the group who continued the wine-drinking and convivial tradition longest. Scott, Lockhart, Wilson, and Hogg, whether in the *Waverley Novels, Noctes Ambrosianae* or *Peter's Letters to his Kinsfolk,* expressed convivial continuation with the past. The latter work is a glorification of the Tory *côterie* in Edinburgh, written by Scott's son-in-law and biographer J.G. Lockhart. Peter, a young Welshman who befriends a Scot at Cambridge, comes North to visit William Wastle in Edinburgh and convey his impression South by letter. Peter's first Edinburgh repast is washed down by a "glass of rare sherry, as ancient as Falstaff, or Johannisberg, which my friend had imported himself from the very cellars of Metternich … and just before the cloth was drawn, I tasted, for the first time, a liqueur, which I prefer vastly to all the Marasquin – ay, to all the Curacoa in existence – the genuine *Usquebaugh* of Lochaber. Our Chateau-la-fitte and olives went down after this repast like very nectar and ambrosia."

For the Tory connoisseurs the whisky was not the rot gut driving the masses to distraction, but pure malt from Glenlivet or Brae Lochaber; similarly in 1819, the well-to-do were not drinking plain claret, but named growths from the Medoc, usually of the first order. "I declare the wine here is superb. I think some of Jeffrey's Chateau Margout [Margaux] beats the lot you bought at Colonel Johne's all to nothing." Of course a few of the old characters of the convivial age survived. Here, Peter visits Henry MacKenzie. His description of the Edinburgh of his youth makes Peter wish he had been alive then.

> He gave us an excellent bottle of Muscat-de-Rives-Altes during dinner, and I must say I am inclined very much to approve of that old-fashioned delicacy. We had no lack of Chateau-la-Rose afterwards … at that time, the only liquor was claret, and this they sent for just as they wanted it – huge pewter jugs, or, as they called them, stoups of claret, being just as commonly to be seen travelling the streets of Edinburgh in all directions then, as the mugs of Mieux and Barclay are in those of London now. Of course I made allowance for the privilege of age, but I have no doubt there was abundance of good wit, and, what is better, good humour among them, no less than of good claret. If I were to take the evening I spent in listening to its history, as a fair specimen of the 'Auld Time', (and after all, why should I not?) I should almost be inclined to reverse the words of the Laureate, and to say
>
> *of all places, and all times of earth,*
> *Did fate grant choice of time and place to men,*
> *Wise choice might be their SCOTLAND, and their THEN.*

Claret appreciation was not solely confined to the Tory side, as Peter's visit to the Constables, publishers of the *Edinburgh Review* reveals:

> This old gentlemen and his son are distinguished by their classical taste, in regard to other things besides books – and, among the rest, in regard to wines – a subject touching which it is fully more easy for them to excite the sympathy of the knowing ones of Edinburgh. They give an annual dinner to Wastle, and he carried me with him the other day to one of these anniversaries. I have seldom seen a more luxurious display. We had claret of the most exquisite La-Fitte flavour, which foamed in the glass like the cream of strawberries, and went down as cool as the nectar of Olympus.

Chateau Lafite appears to have been the most popular of the first growth clarets available, and even by then it had established a legendary reputation. In the mid-18th century, Lafite and the other wines of the region were promoted by the Duke of Richelieu who was Governor of Guienne and Gascony in the reign of Louis XV.

Richelieu took Lafite as a tonic which was so effective that in his 60th year, the King remarked that he looked twenty-five years younger. The Duke accepted the compliment, bowed and smiled, "I must tell your Majesty that I have discovered the secret of eternal youth, the wine of Chateau Lafite." The good Duke continued drinking Lafite and consummated his third marriage at the age of 84, finally dying happy at 92. With his knowledge of French history, Sir Walter Scott probably knew this story so Ballantyne's gift to him, purchased from Cockburns would be all the more welcome:

> 14 February 1823
> To 12 dozens Claret Laffite 1815, selected by Captain Mackenzie
> for Sir W. Scott Bart.,
> (& 109/6 being Hogshead price.) £65.14.0

Scott felt that the gift was over generous: "I feel all the kindness of your nature in the matter of the drinkables ... I sincerely pray you to think of me no further in this way than as far as a few seegars or Bramah pens may be concerned, which I will be happy to accept in the way of kindness." That said, Scott savoured the joy of such an excellent supplement to his already considerable cellar – the 1815 then was on the way to becoming like the '82 now, fast disappearing and expensive. The wine went with Scott to Abbotsford where "at the Sunday dinner he circulated the Champagne briskly and considered a pint of claret each man's share afterwards".

By the 1820's the taverns and howffs of the Auld Toun were deserted by men of fashion, the area sinking into the squalor that was its lot until the renovative zeal of recent years. The era of the great houses came in and Jeffrey's Craigcrook or Scott's Abbotsford became centres of intellectual exchange. The creator of the historical novel, Scott exerted tremendous influence over European and American literature, and his house became a place of pilgrimage. The man charged with the responsibility of slaking the pilgrim's thirst was William Dalgleish, Dall for short, Scott's butler. He has left us with a phonetically spelt account of the removal of Scott's cellar, 386 cases, from Castle Street to Abbotsford in 1822.

> At the time we was removing the wine oute of the sellar in the town hous to be sent to Abbotsford Sir Watter cumes down to see how I was getting on.
>
> "Well have you aney notion what quantety of wine there will be?"
>
> "I cannot answer your quasten just now Sir Watter but I am keeping a correct account of the dozens as I pack them up."
>
> "Verry good but you must not tast our (over) often or then you will be apt to forget."
>
> "Well Sir Watter I have packet up a good maney dozens already and I have not tasted yet but as you are here if you have no objections we shall have a tasting."

> "No no I have no objectens."
>
> "So drawing a bottle of white wine and offering him the furst of it he just put it to his lips and said it would be a verrey poor seller if it could not afford a little to support you when you was working so hard. I packet up three hundred and fifty dozens of wine and thirty six dozens of spirits and never tasted until we was putting it past into Abbotsford sellers.
>
> When Sir Watter came down I told him that I had been unfortinat at last for I had broken a bottle of port. "Oh niver mind that you will have wett the seller then. Well, Dall, I have heard say that a dry sellar is the worst of all sellars."
>
> "Yes Sir Watter when there is nothing in them."
>
> As Thomas Purdie was helping to carry in the wine to the paker, "God bliss me Sir Watter, Dall shurely dos intend us to carrey all the wine in or ever he asks us if we have a mouth."
>
> "Have you not had a tasting yet?"
>
> "Deed no, Sir Watter."
>
> "Oh but you must tast." So Sir Watter ordered Thomas to go and bring a glass and a cork screw. Poor Thomas not being verrey well acquainted with wine glasses he brought a tumbler.
>
> "Well Thom your wine glass will just give you a tasting if you take the full of it."
>
> "There is so maney glasses yonder I just took the first that I came to."
>
> Sir Watter just put it to his lips.
>
> "Sir Watter you show a verrey poor example," says Thom
>
> "Oh Thom you must not mind me."
>
> This Thomas Purdy was Sir Watter's game keeper and bottle holder. We gote all the wine and spirits poot past and onely one brock so Sir Watter ordered me to make sume toddy, and give all the servants a treet and make ourselves happy.

Scott lived out his cultural dream of a happy feudal society with himself as the benevolent Laird, giving out paternal largesse to the people. Astonishingly, his benign but outdated philosophy still exists among other land-owning Tories in the Borders today.

Scott's predilection for Champagne led to the increasing popularity of that wine in Scotland during the 19th century; a popularity which rendered the wine drier and drier till by 1900 the *Brut* taste valued today had been achieved. In Scott's time it was still sweet, but made by the *méthode champenoise.* He ordered his wine from Robert Cockburn: "I shall beg you at the same time to send 2 doz. of White Champagne and 1 of red, both sparkling, I am not dandy enough to take the still kind." Scott's novels were all the rage in France, so it is perhaps not surprising that letters from wine growers were among his fan mail. Alan Bell in an article for *Blackwood's Magazine* titled *"Scott and his Wine Merchant"*, takes up the story:

The literati of the Blackwoods group with Scott at Abbotsford

Early in 1823 he received an effusive letter from a Monsieur L.N. Petizon, of Elbeuf, near Rouen:

"...Je suis propriétaire d'excellent Champagne: serai je assez heureux pour vous faire agréer un échange de ce vin contre une édition complète de vos oeuvres?" Scott forwarded this letter from a "funny Frenchman" to his publisher Constable, and suggested that if Petizon thought the works were "worth a dozen Flaskes of Champagne", they could be sent to a London agent. Constable (who was promised "a sup" for his trouble) sent off volumes on 18th February – "the number of vols will I flatter myself astonish his library. They amount to 58, and I hope a proportionate reduction of the quantity of champagne in his cellar will be the consequence," Petizon visited Scotland in 1824 and met Constable in Edinburgh. He wrote ecstatically to Scott, urging him to visit France again: "Si votre coeur Anglais [sic] retient quelques préventions contre la France, puisse le vin de Rheims les noyer toutes!"

With Scott's *coeur Ecossais* and his French wife, he was in no need of Champagne to drown any reservations about the French; but we are sure he drank it with pleasure. A curious throwback to the Auld Alliance occurred towards the end of Scott's life when the exiled French King Charles X, his family and retinue settled in Edinburgh in the street where the present French consul has his residence, Regent Terrace. The Dauphine, descended from the Kirkpatrick's of Closeburn, a family long established in the Malaga wine trade, like most French people today had little idea of the historic precedents of French royalty coming to Scotland. At the height of the French Revolution the links had been strong with ironically the Comte d'Artois finding shelter at Holyrood in 1798 while the radical Scots leader, Thomas Muir, joined the Revolutionaries in Paris, trying to plan an invasion of Scotland from there. Holyrood's role in the decline of the House of Stewart and Bourbon are brought together in a poem by Victor Hugo.

O ruine
Qu'une auguste auréole a jamais t'illumine!
Devant tes noirs créneaux, pieux nous nous courbons;
Car le vieux roi de France a trouvé sous ton ombre
Cette hospitalité mélancolique et sombre
Qu'on recoit et qu'on rend de Stuarts à Bourbons.

The gloom of the exiled court was lifted by several invitations to Abbotsford, where Champagne and claret flowed so much that one of the courtiers remarked on its effect on Scott's command of the French tongue! It is doubtful whether the exiled Bourbon ever enjoyed the hospitality of the Edinburgh clubs that survived, but their meetings in the plush hotels of Princes Street or St. Andrews Square would not have been so different from his soirées in Regent Terrace either in setting or in deportment.

An 18th century club that deserted the Old for the New Town and sobered up its proceedings was the Wagering Club. Founded in 1775, the Wagerers had an annual dinner the *raison d'être* of which is stated in their regulations: "5th. The great object being to keep up acquaintance and promote mirth and good-fellowship, the Bets laid shall not exceed the value of one bottle of wine or half a mutchkin of punch for each person wagering." As the 19th century wore on the stakes were changed and sums of money replaced wine. The subjects the diners bet on could be petty or political, local or international –

1834 That Francis Jeffrey shall be Lord Advocate at the date of the next meeting. – He was.

1835 That a ship will be direct from China to Leith before the next meeting – There was not.

1839 Will Miss Burdett-Coutts be married before the next meeting – She was not.

When the Fors and Againsts were examined a year later, the losers paid their wine or money into the Club's funds.

The Friday Club too thrived in the 19th century but adapted itself to the new morality, as Lord Cockburn recalls:

> Unlike some old convivial clubs, the members of the Friday cannot be accused of excessive drinking judging from the bills that have been preserved. Eight bottles of claret, six of Port and four of Sherry seems almost frugal for a dinner of 16 members in June 1804 ... When the suppers were exchanged for dinners, claret became the standard. It was interspersed with other and more delicate production of the grape, but at first this was done timidly. Indeed in these days there was a paltry prejudice against rarer French and German wines, which besides were very dear, so that their cost and novelty made foolish people stare when they were rashly produced. The Friday had always a contempt of this and an innate propensity towards good taste, which from the very first was evinced by a generous extravagance. But I don't think it was till after the Peace of 1814 that the continent being opened, we soared above prejudice and ate and drank everything that was rare and dear.

The desire for quality and variety rather than quantity was endemic to all the clubs. The Gowks, the Scots word for cuckoos and idiots, met every April Fools' day "with Folly's flag unfurled to scout the wisdom of the world". The Gowks' Laureate was Henry Mackenzie, by now an octogenarian. His daft rhymes suggest that the Club members vied with each other to produce the rarest and most valued bottle at dinner:-

Their Chairman for himself propine
his last year's travelled German wine
fresh from the vintage of the Rhine
the brothers Bell the prize to gain
of tasteful trial, choice Champagne
or the long treasured wine of Spain...

...Your April day, if right I quote
Could boast of some old friends of note;
Erasmus, though her greatest foe,
Spoke all her praises long ago,
And show'd the learned and the wise,
that Folly's wisdom is disguise,
And yet his lauded state of folly
Was not like yours so gay and jolly

Did not from long neck'd bottles drain
High-flavoured Hock or rich Champagne;
Or if your brother's cellar spare it,
Delicious Vintage Fifteen Claret....

Written eleven years after the great 1815 vintage, the last verse suggests that the Gowks were hardly foolish when it came to claret, and their policy of laying down was standing the test of time and temptation.

While the Friday, the Wagering Club and the Gowks disappeared into cloud cuckoo land, the dining clubs with strong legal associations still thrive on fine wine today. The New Club still has its Wine Committee, though it is doubtful whether their resources could run to the quantities bought by their predecessors. In 1820, the Wine Committee comprising Alex Campbell, Sir John Hope, Sir James Fergusson, Mr. Earl, and Hon. Colonel Hamilton decided with due gravity to lay down a greater stock of the "extraordinary vintage of 1815". When stock was taken in 1822, "...upon making a trial of the 1815 claret and some other wines it appeared to be for the advantage of the club to refrain from drinking them for some time". When one looks at the list, one has to admire the Committee's self-denial.

8 Hogsheads	9	doz.	11	bottles	Claret 1815
2 Pipes	33	"	11	"	Port
1 Butt	51	"	10	"	Sherry
	14	"	2	"	Madeira
	2	"			Burgundy
	5	"	3	"	Champagne
	10	"	4	"	Sauternes
	2	"	7	"	Moselle

Throughout their history the Writers to the Signet have continued the imbibing tradition of their legal forebears. Organising themselves into clubs named after the year of formation, the 1790, 1808, 1850 and 1977, the Signet Club dinners are graced by the rarest wines, the fruit of judicious selection. The 1850 Club had among its rules for the year 1890 that "riddles of claret" were to be levied to help keep the club supplies well-stocked. It is uncertain what quantity of wine comprises a Riddle, but most members had to contribute at one point of their life or another:

> 1892, The practice was adopted whereby the Riddle was presented as a marriage tax by Bachelor members of the Club ... 1906, As all bachelors had contributed a Riddle there was a suggestion that grandfathers should present the Riddle as a grandfathers' tax.

The canniness of the lawyer meant that stock were never short. In 1982 the secretary of one of the clubs stated:

> Our current stocks are approximately sixteen cases of claret, four cases of Burgundy, two of Rioja, and seven and a half cases of port. When I pointed out to the members at our dinner last year that the then stock represented (at the current rate of consumption)

nineteen years stocks of red wine and fifteen years stocks of port, the only constructive suggestion I got was that the rate of consumption ought to be doubled.

Not content with the annual W.S. dinners, at least one Edinburgh firm of solicitors formed its own Wine Club in 1964. If ever proof was needed of the survival of claret appreciation in the Scottish capital, one has only to drool over the vintage clarets selected for the Club's dinners over the years.

Year		*Wine.*
1971	Chateau	Cheval Blanc 1955
1972	"	Lafite 1959
1974	"	Latour 1955
1976	"	Margaux 1959
1977	"	Lafite 1959
1979	"	Mouton Rothschild 1961.
	"	Haut Brion 1961
1981	"	Lafite 1959,
	"	Gruaud-Larose 1961

Even outwith their clubs, the rising price of first growth claret often made lawyers form cartels to supply their households with their Bordeaux. In the early 19th century, Saintsbury was told "it was customary for knots of four frequenters of the Parliament House, when a vintage promised well to lay down as many hogsheads of the best reputed first or second growths dividing the produce in bottles among themselves (a hogshead of claret makes 23 dozen so the subscribers would have that quantity apiece of the vintage, divided into lots between 5 and 6 dozen of each growth.)". The aristocracy too appear to have done the same, the Earl of Dalhousie importing his claret direct from Bordeaux to Leith and sharing the bill and the wine with the Duke of Buccleuch, Lord Cassilis, Lord Scott and the Duke of York. In 1825 the Earl had 41 cases of claret in Dalhousie Castle's cellars, half of it first growth – 10 Chateau Margaux, 8 Haut Brion, and 4 Chateau Lafite. Like the rest of the Scots aristocracy the Earl had been strongly influenced by English taste by this time and port, sherry and Madeira are all stored in greater quantities than claret. The Napoleonic wars where Scot and Englishman fought on the same side for the first time, galvanised British patriotism north of the Border.

In this increasingly North British age, it is perhaps not surprising that *"Ye Mariners of England"* and other patriotic anthems were composed by Thomas Campbell of Glasgow who along with the earlier composer of *"Rule Britannia"*, James Thomson, belong more properly with English rather than Scottish letters. Campbell however could recall a very Scottish phenomenon in his childhood, playing at his grandfather's house, a man who "fenced in garden, field and paddock in Claret Staves".

Despite the anti-French feeling, the lawyers remained true to claret, even when it was at its rarest. Lord Cockburn described a circuit dinner at Perth where Lord Eskgrove presents one bottle of the elixir then "dours out" the guests with the intention of keeping them to the plentiful port, and leaving him with the claret. Only one person dared defy the Justice's dour stare, the irrepressible Henry Brougham – "the Harangue":

> Many an eye, civil and military, was turning enviously to the untouched bottle, but nobody had the courage to meddle with it except the Evil [Brougham] who at every round stretched forth his long arm and filled his glass to the brim and replaced the bottle until the next time.
>
> The Justice whose alarm was not diminished by the enormous delight to his spectators, regularly tried to warn him off by exclaiming "Maister Broom or Brough-ham. That's the claret!" To which the Harangue, filling away regularly, answered with respectful impudence, "Yes My Lord, This is the Claret."

Supplying North Britain and the far flung outposts of Empire were firms who made Leith-bottled claret, sherry, port and eventually Leith-bottled whisky, synonymous with excellence; Cockburn's of Leith, Cockburn and Campbell and J.G. Thomson & Co. Ltd., until the early '80's owners of the Vaults in Leith. As with Shairp of Houston and the Sandilands in the 19th century, the Cockburns exhibited the Scottish trait of younger sons of noble houses entering trade. As dealing in wine meant intimate relationships with one's fellow aristocracy or legal luminaries, naturally wine was the most prestigious branch of trade for these lads to enter. Evelyn Waugh, a descendant of Lord Cockburn, wrote, "One does not share a pair of socks with one's wine merchant, so that … it was among wine merchants that the custom first grew of selling to customers by the agency of their social equals or, in some cases, superiors."

Lord Cockburn's younger brother Robert Cockburn started dealing in wine in 1796 and along with his brother John founded R. & J. Cockburn in 1805 which still exists in Edinburgh today as Cockburn & Co. (Leith) Ltd. Robert also began Cockburn's long Oporto connection while, after dissolving the partnership, brother John founded Cockburn, Campbell and Co. which again remained in existence until the early 1980's. With Robert's father Sheriff Depute of the County of Edinburgh, his mother a Rannie related to Prince Charles Edward Stewart's wine firm of Bell Rannie & Co., and his family name famed throughout the country as the Lairds o' Cockpen, Robert was ideally placed to build on Leith's already considerable reputation for fine wines. A thorough professional who reflected the increasing specialisation in society, Robert looked askance at amateurs handling the liquid ruby. The Duke of Buccleuch received a thoroughly disapproving letter in 1810, requesting the return of claret badly bottled in the cellars at Dalkeith Palace. Determined to establish his wine in a connoisseurs' market Robert is anxious to recover a wine which "would have done us some credit" but which had been so damaged in the handling that

> our character as Wine Merchants must have suffered considerably by it ... If your Grace would have the goodness in future to leave the management of your wine both with respect to choice and bottling to me, I would then be completely responsible for it, and would be able to do myself some credit by it, and your Grace might depend on having better wine than you have had for some years past.

The division between customer and friend was a narrow one among people bound through family ties and Tory politics. Walter Scott was a close friend of Cockburn and a dinner with Scott, Lord Melville and family, Sir John and Lady Hope, Lord and Lady Kerr, was typical of Cockburn's social life. After a meal in which Scott drank of his host's and therefore Edinburgh's best, the writer stumbled and fell his whole length in the mud of the building site that was Atholl Place. Sneaking home to Castle Street, Scott recorded the incident in his journal: "Luckily Lady Scott had retired when I came home; so I enjoyed my tub of water without either remonstrance or condolences. Cockburn's hospitality will get the benefit and renown of my downfall, and yet he has no claim to it."

The first bestselling novelist in history, Scott repaid his friend's hospitality by giving "plugs" to his wines in his novels. In *St. Ronan's Well* Mr Touchwood asks Meg Dods to "get the old Hock I had sent me from Cockburn and a bottle of the particular Indian Sherry". In the introduction to *The Fortunes of Nigel,* Captain Clutterbuck proposes a dinner "with a quiet bottle of Robert Cockburn's choicest 'black', nay, perhaps of his best 'blue', to quicken one's talk of old books". The colours refer to the wax sealing on Cockburn's different styles of claret or port, but the important thing is that Cockburn's fame spread throughout the Empire. Even after both Cockburn firms opened offices in London, much of the wine for that market had to come from the Leith cellars, to compete with other Edinburgh merchants selling to England. As the historian of J.G. Thomson put it, "Leith-bottled claret held in its day a cachet comparable to that which one now associates with Château bottled wines." This claim is supported by the evidence of the various firms' London *clientèle.* In 1832 alone Cockburn and Campbell received an order from Earl Grey the Prime Minister for 22 dozen 1825 claret and 50 dozen East

Lunch on the Moors by Charles Lees.

India Sherry to be sent to Downing Street. A few weeks later and probably after he had tasted the Prime Minister's consignment, a letter came from Sir Robert Peel ordering 6 dozen of the 1825 claret and 1 butt (52 dozen) of Sherry "corresponding with the sample bottle which had the Yellow Seal" to be sent to Drayton Manor. After thinking matters over a few days and probably tasting some more of the Yellow Seal, he wrote again ordering "two Butts instead of one of the Sherry and 10 dozen of Superior Port – not too long in the bottle."

Although dealing with England in huge quantities of Port and Sherry as well as wines which are no longer popular, such as Tenerife, Malaga, Lisbon, Bucelas, Carcavelos, Marsala and Frontignac, the Edinburgh firms were very jealous of the reputation of their clarets in their native city. An amusing letter from John Cockburn to Cunliffe, Garratt et Co., in Bordeaux, refers to the 1828 Medoc vintage and its suitability in Edinburgh.

> We regret for your sake and our own that we must report unfavourably on the Mouton and Lafite. There is a poverty about them which we did not anticipate ... Your opinion of them being so much higher than ours we hope you will have no objection to our sending you what remains which we cannot doubt your easily disposing of in London.

Edinburgh's golden age of claret drinking paralleled curiously her role as a European literary centre and from the death of Scott in 1832 till the early decades of the present century an already exclusive market diminished to a rarified one, composed almost entirely of traditionalist lawyers and gentry. Professor Saintsbury, the original doyen of wine writers stated, "before I left Edinburgh, the headquarters at one time of claret-drinkers, it was practically useless to open a magnum of claret for a dinner party of twelve or fourteen people, unless you selected your guests on purpose." The reasons for the decline are many: the high duty until Gladstone's Budget of 1860; the vast improvements in port and whisky developing truly noble liquids out of what originally were raw mixtures for mass consumption; and most importantly the question mark against the quality of claret itself whose vines were devastated by the diseases of Oidium in the 1850's, then Phylloxera in the late 1870's and 1880's. Claret drinking was an expensive gamble and thousands of customers turned to other beverages to sustain them. Sadly, it was after Saintsbury's time in Edinburgh that the *cognoscenti* returned to their original love. In 1914 he wrote:

> the folk here have deserted their Claret and love washy, woody Port like the Londoners. But there is a remnant and when old Lord Kincairney, one of the Judges (who is a quaint little man of Pictish build, but a stout Tory and full of letters and fun) was dining here the other night I gave him a magnum of that '78 Léoville and he and I and Prothero did fair justice to it.

The "remnant" he speaks of were a canny lot who gobbled up Saintsbury's cellar at bargain prices in 1915 when the Professor left Edinburgh University, "[the prices] were not *all* bad, but one wretch got magnums of '76 Léoville still in perfect condition, at 4 bob a piece."

If the faithful remnant was small the direct links between Bordeaux and Scotland continued well into this century. The Auld Alliance was maintained through personal contacts. The correspondence of Francisque Michel, the Frenchman who chronicled the Scots' contribution to his country, and David Laing the Signet Librarian lasted from the 1830's till the 1870's and was typical of the spirit of *la vieille alliance.* With the vogue in France for things Scottish, Michel has tartan sent from Edinburgh, in return for which he sends Laing "pour 5 ou 6 francs la bouteille d'excellent vins de Château Larose ou de Margaux. Nous avons a chaque instant des départs pour Leith."

As we have seen, more and more wines came on the Scottish scene during the 19th century as claret yielded a considerable part of its market to wines from all over the world. When Robert Louis Stevenson wrote his chapter on the Napa Wine of

California in the early 1880's, Phylloxera was at its height and the wines of France appeared doomed.

> I was interested in Californian wine. Indeed, I am interested in all wines, and have been all my life, from the raisin-wine that a school-fellow kept secreted in his play-box up to my last discovery, those notable Valtellines, that once shone upon the board of Caesar.
>
> Some of us, kind old Pagans, watch with dread the shadows falling on the age: how the unconquerable worm invades the sunny terraces of France, and Bordeaux is no more, and the Rhône a mere Arabia Petraea. Chateau Neuf is dead, and I have never tasted it; Hermitage – a hermitage indeed from all life's sorrows – lies expiring by the river. And in the place of these imperial elixirs, beautiful to every sense, gem-hued, flower-scented, dream-compellers: – behold upon the quays at Cette the chemicals arrayed; behold the analyst at Marseilles, raising hands in obsecration, attesting god Lyaeus, and the vats staved in, and the dishonest wines poured forth among the sea. It is not Pan only; Bacchus, too, is dead.

Cellar-workers and Champagne, the Vaults, Leith. Circa 1900

A true son of Edinburgh, Stevenson enjoyed his wine and with the demise of the ancient vineyards, he could but "look timidly forward to where the new lands, already weary of producing gold, begin to green with vineyards. A nice point in human history falls to be decided by Californian and Australian wines." Stevenson was not to know that in fact Californian root stock, resistant to Phylloxera, would be grafted with French vines for the salvation of Europe's wine industry. But both

Californian and Australian wines are now challenging French wines on merit alone, and in that sense Stevenson's prophecy was correct.

In both countries, Stevenson's countrymen played their part. The first commercial vineyard in Australia was established at Camden Park near Sydney in 1796 by Captain John MacArthur, while James Busby, the founder of the Australian wine trade, did so much to establish the Hunter River vineyard in 1824 on his Kirkton lands. Busby blended his love of wine with his Scots love of science and in 1836 he toured Europe, collecting 2,000 cuttings of 365 varieties of vine from France, Germany, Spain and Portugal. It is from these cuttings that nearly all the vineyards in Australia derive. In a country hoatching with Scottish immigrants, it comes as no surprise to find scores of wines with Scots names and winemakers of Scots descent. When the wine merchant chieftain of Clan Donnachaidh, Sandy Irvine Robertson organised a wine tasting to celebrate the centenary of the clan association, his Australian wines included the Thistle Hill Chardonnay made by Dave Robertson, and a McWilliam's Crooked Creek Semillon Chardonnay. The McWilliam family have been winemakers in New South Wales for more than a century. The rest of the New World was represented at the tasting; Colombards and Sauvignon Blancs from the Robertson Co-operative in the town of Robertson, South Africa; a Judd Chardonnay from Mutua Valley near Auckland, made by Mark Robertson, a fifth generation New Zealander whose ancestors came from Weem in Perthshire; and a Hell's Canyon Winery Chardonnay made by Steve Robertson at Caldwell, Idaho. Now that a precedent has been set, and knowing the clan rivalry that exists, it would not surprise me to hear of Malmsey-making Macdonalds, Syrah-making Setons, and Bastardo-making Buchans being discovered in remote vineyards very soon!

That was the situation, after all, when R.L.S. discovered one Mr. McEachran, pioneer from the Tail o' the Bank, in what was then the virgin vineyard of Napa Valley. In *The Silverado Squatters*, Stevenson wrote: "A California Vineyard, one of man's outposts in the wilderness, has features of its own. There is nothing here to remind you of the Rhine or Rhône or the low Côte d'Or, or the infamous and scabby deserts of Champagne; but all is green, solitary, covert." Of the two vineyards Stevenson comes across, one inevitably is owned by a Scot; the other by Jacob Schram. In the cool of the latter's cellar, the author tasted wine:

> To Mr. Schram this was a solemn office; his serious gusto warmed my heart; prosperity had not yet wholly banished a certain neophyte and girlish trepidation, and he followed every sip and read my face with proud anxiety. I tasted all. I tasted every variety and shade of Schramberger, red and white Schramberger, Burgundy Schramberger, Schramberger Hock, Schramberger Golden Chasselas, the latter with a notable bouquet, and I fear to think how many more.

As a man committed to, and haunted by Scotland, no matter the distance from the country he found himself, Stevenson experienced a different kind of pleasure meeting up with his countryman.

> Mr. M'Eckron's is a bachelor establishment; a little bit of a wooden house, a small cellar hard by in the hillside, and a patch of vines planted and tended single-handed by himself. He had but recently begun; his vines were young, his business young also; but I thought he had the look of a man who succeeds. He hailed from Greenock: he remembered his father putting him inside Mons Meg, and that touched me home: and we exchanged a word or two of Scots, which pleased me more than you would fancy.

Today, both vineyards belong to Schramsberg, the producer of the finest *méthode champenoise* wines of the Americas, but you still wind up a narrow mountain track where tangled woodland and parcels of manicured vines intermingle... "concealed from all but the clouds and the mountain birds". I visited a few years ago. McEachran's hut is still standing, and further up the hill Jacob Schram's wooden frame house and cellars have been lovingly restored. There, the Blanc de Noirs I tasted was particularly elegant and delicious, a refreshing antidote to the hot California noonday sun. Unfortunately, having a car to drive, I could not partake as deeply as my fellow countryman back then, but I distinctly remember feeling quite at one with the world when I left. Stevenson left with a similar glow. Afterwards, in his own cabin by the slopes of Mount St. Helena, he contemplates the visit and on examining his feelings for his homeland, and his countrymen abroad, comes to an objective conclusion: "The happiest lot on earth is to be born a Scotsman." Few Scots, similarly surrounded by vineyards would disagree.

The morning after, by Hill and Adamson

THE OLD WORLD AND THE NEW

16

"La Vieille Alliance, the love affair between Scotland and Bordeaux has been going for years. It is still there, it is very strong and it always will be"
Sandy Irvine Robertson, Wine Merchant

A wine revolution has taken place in Scotland in the past twenty years. So common has wine drinking become across all grades of society, that it is difficult for younger people to imagine how different things were a few short decades ago, and from there back to the turn of the century. The very word wine had a dramatically different meaning at the two extremes of society. To the well-to-do, it still frequently meant claret, the old national drink, enjoyed only by those fortunate enough to afford its delights; to the lumpen proletariat it was Eldorado, Four Crown, Lanliq, Red Biddy, Electric Soup, Jungle Juice – cheap, nasty and fortified for immediate oblivion. Outwith these groups wine hardly existed at all.

Just as high taxes on claret forced the majority of Scots to desert wine in favour of cheap whisky at the turn of the 19th century, so it was the government's increasingly severe taxation of whisky this century which forced the lower end of the market to look for a potent alternative. "South Africa Sherry" and "British Sherry" marked the labels of this powerful concoction. As its consumers tended to flaunt their drunkenness in public places, wine drinking became associated with the down and outs of society. The word *wino* was coined to stigmatise such people. The respectable working class abhorred the behaviour and the drink and until as recently as the early 1970's the word wine was reduced to this association among a great many people. I can still recall the expression of horror on the landlady's face when an American friend innocently asked for a glass of wine in a douce Ayrshire pub at this time. *The Scottish National Dictionary* confirms the polarisation of meaning:

wine, n. As in English, but in Glasgow and other urban areas often specifically cheap fortified red wine or sherry.

wine shop a public house which serves cheap wine.

Wine shops were dives where the Electric Soup was served with a chaser of beer, the drinker entering a "doolallie" state quickly afterwards. Respectable pub hosts scorned such places and because of the stigma, resisted selling table wines in their establishments long after wine's tarnished reputation had been re-established.

In the days that drink could be taken to football matches the confraternity of Lannie drinkers came into their own. On our way to Hampden for a Scotland v. Norway match in the European Nations Cup once, my cronies were surprised when the usual decision to buy a carry out of whisky was queried by Bobby, from East Lothian, "Whit about the LD.?" he said reproachfully. "The what?" we chorused. "The El-do-ra-do," he replied. "Oh come on, Bobby, ye don't take that stuff, dae ye?" said the respectable working class in disbelief. "Are you trying tae deprive me o' my heritage?" was Bobby's closing riposte before buying his wine. Ironically, with the whisky long gone, not a few of the respectable working class joined the confraternity that night in the tension of the last five minutes as Scotland came from 2-1 down to crush the mighty Norwegians 3-2 … from scenes like these auld Scotia's grandeur springs!

This branch of wine drinking is celebrated in a number of West of Scotland urban folk songs of a humorous nature. Typical is Adam MacNaughton's brilliant burlesque of the florid style loved by the Irish hedge poets of the past. Having compared Sadie from Tradeston with Greek Goddesses and getting absolutely nowhere with her, the poet concludes:

> … for maids residing by the shores of Clyde
> Will not be won by a honeyed line
> the only art to win their heart
> Is a bottle o' Lannie, and a Chicken Chow Mein

At the other extreme of the market claret remained king, returning to its traditional supremacy in the 1920's and staying there until the present day. But even at the upper end of the market the effect of the Total Abstinence movement was felt though scarcely heeded. The late Henry Metcalfe, a former Director of Cockburn's of Leith, recalled:

> I came up to Edinburgh after the war and I noticed an enormous difference between the trade in London and the trade in Edinburgh. For example, there was considerable embarrassment at people to be seen ordering wine particularly frequently and we had a van, an open van and we delivered all our wine in the old-fashioned laundry basket. It's just as easy to store bottles in that as laundry. There was no name on the van, except on the running board, a tiny little, legally required notice – and this was one way that the citizens of Edinburgh concealed from the – pulling the curtain back, looking through neighbours – what was going on and how frequently they ordered their wines.
>
> There is a mistaken belief that Frenchmen have the expertise on – well apart from the obvious thing – on wine. This is not so. The best judges of wine – fine wines and I'm speaking now of claret and burgundies – champagnes – are the British people and Scots principally. I think some of the finest cellars in the world are to be found in Scotland.

Kirk ministers were particularly vulnerable and went to unholy lengths to conceal their habits. The story is told of a rural minister who ordered stocks from his wine merchant in Edinburgh while attending the General Assembly, then eagerly awaited the bottles arriving by train a few days later. Out walking one afternoon, he was accosted by a Kirk Elder: "I've been up to the station, sir, and I see there's a wooden box lying there addressed to yourself." "Quite so, Tammas, quite so. Just a few books I was buying when I was in Edinburgh." "Aye, Imphm. Ah, weel, sir, I wadna be ower lang. They're leakin'."

Leith-bottled claret.

The landed gentry in their country residences had no such problems of concealment or conscience and continued to stock their cellars with the best. The auctions of cellars by Christies of London have yielded fabulous prices in Scotland. Lord Rosebery's and Glamis Castle both contained pre-Phylloxera first growth claret, fitting testimony to the fine wine tradition. Sandy Irvine Robertson acts as a wine consultant for Christies Scotland, and is aware of the great cellars which still exist. He has been known to call Michael Broadbent from a secret treasure trove somewhere on the West Coast and describe in loving detail the great vintages of Petrus, Cheval Blanc, and Lafite he has before his very eyes. Inevitably, the question comes, "Sandy, where is it?". The keeper of this national secret stays mum. "I still haven't told him and he still doesn't know where it is!". No nation worth the name sells off all its national treasures, after all. The great cellar in Glamis Castle was "explored" by wine consultant Freddie Stimpson, who did sterling work promoting knowledge and appreciation of wine through the sadly defunct Wine Development Board. Freddie, whose very house is called Montclaret, is proud of the continued links between Scotland and Bordeaux, although on at least one occasion the Scots have astonished French guests when their love of wine superseded their appreciation of gastronomy:

> [There was] an incredible friendship that developed between a great many of the Bordeaux big houses and people over here in Edinburgh. Once when I was in France, I do

> recall someone producing a photostat of the old passport of Mary Queen of Scots time, where we had joint nationality, and that, to my mind, is something they wouldn't have shown if they weren't still proud of the possibility. But I can remember quite vividly, a wonderful man, Édouard Cruse of the old House of Cruse, and he came over, as his father had done before him. And they were very highly regarded in the trade and they always drank very fine claret at the Château Pontet-Canet and in Bordeaux and therefore it was not unnatural the trade tried to reciprocate. But there is one very reputed Edinburgh House, and I'm certainly not going to mention names, who, on a day when we had given prior notice of calling, duly said that they would lay on a luncheon in the Boardroom and they did just that. And we were absolutely delighted when we got down to find some superb claret decanted on the side table – all First Growth and all '55. The astonishment on Édouard Cruse's face when he saw the main dish which was fish and chips from a nearby little cafe was something that I shall remember for the rest of my life!

Freddie gives the Scots the benefit of the doubt, and ends that story with the words "something must have gone very wrong in the kitchen for that to have happened".

The recognition of the claret tradition and the realisation of its sales potential drew many established English firms to Scotland this century, especially after the Second World War. Peter Sichel of Chateau d'Angludet in Margaux followed the pioneering footsteps of the previous generation of his family:

> Well, when I started in the trade in the early 1950's, my father, uncle and grandfather had travelled to Scotland before me and I think perhaps that a good part of our success in Scotland is due to the fact that they were some of the first London wine shippers to go up above the Border and sell wine in Scotland – in spite of the historic connections – through the 20's and 30's. But perhaps the most clear-cut difference as far as I was concerned starting in those days was that soon after the war like that, there was very little market for fine Bordeaux wine in England and it was quite a different feeling in Scotland – right through the fifties we were selling even our top wines like Chateau Palmer, in barrels to some of those Edinburgh wine merchants … [also] there must have been four or five first class licensed grocers, like Young and Saunders, Dymock, and Howden bottling very fine claret indeed.

Not only did London firms begin to supply outlets in Scotland increasingly after the war when Leith's direct links with Bordeaux closed, but also old English wine firms such as Justerini & Brooks established themselves in Edinburgh and competed successfully for a share of the market enjoyed by the older Scots firms.

Some of the older firms such as Cockburn's of Leith are still in existence, indeed the tradition of the old established licensed grocer with a specialist knowledge of fine wines exists in pockets as well. Aitken's of Dundee immediately comes to mind. But the '80's and '90's have seen a speeding up of the rationalisation of the industry

Billy Kay in the robes of the Commanderie du Bontemps, Medoc, 1982.

which has been happening over three decades. The fact that the number of independent wine merchants in Scotland has dropped dramatically in this period tells its own story. Whighams of Ayr, however has guaranteed its continued existence through a judicious alliance with the equally prestigious London firm, Corney and Barrow, the royal warrant holders. Other names survived but became part of international brewing or distilling companies who were perhaps more concerned with profit margins rather than providing the personal service which had existed in the trade in the past. The old order changed too in the types of wine drunk and the people drinking them. The post-war period was the turning point. Ordinary Scots whose taste for food and drink had been narrowed by the poverty of the early 20th century, came back from the war with a taste for the cuisine and wine of the places they had visited. Valvona & Crolla Ltd., an Edinburgh institution which dispenses huge quantities of Italian wine to its legions of customers, noticed the change in business. Dominic Crolla says:

> It wasn't a very successful business in these days [1930's] because people didn't know anything about spaghetti, wine or olive oil. It only dealt with Italian customers and with Italians who had small shops ... But after the war it was a huge success because British soldiers who had been in Italy and tasted the spaghetti ... some had been in France and Germany. When they all came back they wanted a change in their kitchen, hence the prosperity, the slow prosperity of Valvona & Crolla Ltd. We were the only ones in Edinburgh at that time from whom they could purchase all these nice goods.

By the 1960's high employment and increasing affluence sent hundreds of thousands of Scots holidaying regularly abroad for the first time in their history. Fish teas in Rothesay no more, it was now cheap package holidays for maw, paw an the bairns, and whether it was Chianti in Cattolica or Rioja in Alicante, a taste for the grape was developed and a revolution in the nation's drinking habits was instigated. The majority believed this was a totally new phenomenon, but those with a sense of history realised we were simply getting back to our roots. Exotic words like Liebfraumilch, Mateus (often pronounced Matoose!) and Lambrusco entered the vocabulary as wine was chosen for home consumption as often as the home produced beverages. Wine connoisseurs may turn up their noses at the people's early choice of wines, but everyone starts somewhere, and eventually the palate demands finer wines. As the only Galston man in history to have lunched twice at Chateau Lafite, the Lowland author of this work has to confess that at the age of 16 he and a friend hitch hiked to Italy and survived with one meal per day which, requested in broken Italian, translated thus: "Two pizza Margherita and a bottle of your cheapest, sweetest wine please." The year before at a penfriend's home in Normandy, he found Muscadet wersht and refused to eat what he thought were dods of chalk set down at table. It was his first sight of Brie and Camembert. I cite these examples, to illustrate how personal tastes change, and how dramatically the Scottish approach to food has changed in our lifetime. Beyond cafés selling fish and chips, ordinary folk did not go to restaurants until around the 1970's. There again, they drank wine, and gradually grew to appreciate the subtle range of tastes it offered. When we wrote the first edition of this book in the early 1980's the wine revolution was still on-going, and the popular taste was towards white wines with a touch of sweetness. The basic Rhine and Moselle wines supplied the demand perfectly. By the mid 1990's, the revolution is over. Wine drinking is integrated into our society in a way which would have been inconceivable even twenty years ago. As we cannot produce our own wine, cost may determine that it never becomes a part of every one's daily dining routine, the way it is in countries where the vine flourishes, but there is no doubt that it has become a regular part of Scottish life. What was the revolution is now the status quo.

The wines drunk now show the growing maturity of the clientele. White wines may still hold sway over the reds, but chardonnays and sauvignons are as likely to be preferred as their sweeter cousins. Another factor in the increasing sophistication of wine drinkers is the great range of competitively priced wines available in supermarkets. Some people may have been intimidated by the pukka atmosphere of the traditional wine merchant in the past, but in the classless world of the supermarket they are happy to experiment with cabernet sauvignons from Oz, Chile, Bulgaria or Bordeaux. Ian Cumming of Whighams for example, feels the business he does is complementary to the supermarkets, recognising their contribution in introducing more and more people to wine.

The other change on the Main Street has been the arrival of specialist chains of wine shops. Oddbins is a very successful example of a young, new approach to selling wine. Their staff always appear enthusiastic and try to pass that on to the customer. They have filled an important niche between the impersonality of the supermarket and the more formal world of the traditional merchant. They are also knowledgeable. When we had to organise wines for a charity claret tasting in Aberdeen, the wines supplied were exactly right. Everyone present can still recall the flavour and bouquet of a memorable second wine from Chateau Latour savoured on that evening. Not surprisingly, this confident new arrival promoted aggressively-marketed challengers to claret's supremacy from the New World, particularly California and Australia. The up-front, forward, concentrated and intense fruit flavours of Australian Syrahs and Cabernet Sauvignons have, I feel, brought a lot of people back into the red wine fold. Since 1985, sales of Australian wine in Britain have increased over thirty times. Their immediately approachable style has made people appreciate the warmth and richness, and appropriateness to our climate of big, generous wines made from noble grape varieties. Once in that fold, the palate can tire of varietal wines, and it is natural to turn to an old friend. Jeffrey Kelly owns and runs Kelly's Restaurant in Edinburgh.

> People are more enterprising these days. They will certainly try the New World wines, they are excellent wines and good value for money. The younger people who maybe have learned via the New World wines then graduate onto the clarets and the more complex flavours that are intrinsic in these wines.

> Ian Cumming
> Particularly in recent years the Australian wines have brought a lot of new people into the market. The Australians produce a very good middle of the road product, but then people realise that claret has got that extra something and a lot of people are moving up. I think it has been challenged by the New World wines but I think that has started to die as the New World wines have become more expensive. There has been a great democratisation of claret, it's not the rich man's wine any more. More and more people are discovering claret. We have in fact doubled the number of customers over recent years who buy claret and there is great interest. We actually have seminars and wine tastings to help people learn about it. This has always been the Scottish tradition, it suits our climate too. It is warm soft wine with a bit of tannin, which people like. I think it is still the most popular drink in Scotland.

One of the strengths of the relationship between Bordeaux and Scotland throughout the centuries has been the personal contacts which have been maintained. That still goes on. My co-author Cailean Maclean studied the rise of the Bordeaux vineyard as a geographer. His research took him to several chateaux, and he is still friendly with the Vialard family of Chateau Cissac. As a result of that, he and I both are still enjoying Cissac's fine '82 vintage, of which he purchased five barriques *en primeur!* His justification: "It gets cold in Skye in the winter." Through contacts made making the radio and television features which accompanied this book, I was given the honour of being asked to act as *parain* or Godfather at the christening of William, the son of Jean-Marie and Isabelle Johnston at the Episcopal Church in Bordeaux. Although the wine trade is big business, personal contact and trust still counts for a lot. I asked Ian Cumming if this was helped by the Bordelais being aware of the Auld Alliance.

> Oh yes, very much so. They like the idea they are dealing with Scotland … and they are very aware that Scotland is a country in its own right. We go out there twice a year … and we source all our wines direct – at the producer level. And I think this is very important to maintain quality. They see us face to face, we can explain what we want, in certain cases with chateaux that we've been dealing with for many years, we've actually had a hand in getting them to produce the type of wine that we find is most suitable to our customers.

The first time Freddie Stimpson met Baron Philippe de Rothschild at a visit to Chateau Mouton Rothschild he was delighted to see at the entrance a splendid ram's head snuff mull from his old regiment the Royal Scots Fusiliers. Freddie presumed it was there simply because it tied in with the Mouton name. Baron Philippe, however, explained that he had been a liaison officer with the Fusiliers' sister regiment, the Royal Scots, so the snuff mull was a cherished personal memento of fond memories of working with the Scots. While the peoples of the two countries are bound together through common history and a love of wine, Esme Johnstone is aware of another factor which cements the relationship.

> Bordeaux is the centre of French rugby and they are terrific enthusiasts, and every time the Scots play the English, the French are 100% on the side of the Scots and in deep depression if England ever win … and similarly when England play France the entire Scots community in Bordeaux naturally turns out to support France. I think the affinity between the Bordelais and the Scots is extremely strong, and is a lot stronger than any affinity between the French and the English. If ever I have to negotiate the prices for bottles or corks, if they know I am Scots, I normally get a discount … I'm sure if they thought I was English there would be a bit of a premium on the price somewhere.

Making wine at Chateau de Sours, in the area west of Bordeaux, Esme is reviving a family tradition. Most of the old north European families still in the business today, act purely as negociants, but at one time many were *négociants-éleveur* who not only sold wine but made it themselves in their own chateaux. A cousin of the Bordeaux and Pauillac Johnstons, Esme's family left Dumfriesshire fifty years ago, and became involved in the wine trade in the English Midlands. In 1990 he moved his family to

France attracted by the challenge of producing fine wine with the historic Borders family crest on the label.

> I think we are probably the oldest Scottish or French family still involved in the wine trade in Bordeaux. I mean the only two places in the world I would like to live would be either in Dumfriesshire or Bordeaux and luckily my business takes me to Bordeaux and we sell our wine to Dumfriesshire, so it all works out very well. It's a fabulous life. There's a bit of art involved, there's a bit of commerce, there's a bit of selling, and one's making a product which people enjoy, which is a wonderful thing to do.

A Scot, living out his countrymen's dream in a vineyard in the land of sweet Bordeaux. While few may achieve that level of nirvana, we have the consolation of knowing that there are gey few vineyards in the world which have not been touched by our presence. So, while sipping, one's imagination can range the terraced slopes and gravel soils of the old world and the new and recall ... Robert Louis Stevenson tasting sparkling Schramsbergs in the Napa Valley; the Monks of St. Anthony rolling hogsheads into the Vaults at Leith and thinking of the sun of their native Rhône; Lauder of Fountainhall marvelling at the rare Eiswein of the Rhine; James Busby experimenting with hundreds of vines in Australia's Hunter River; Cockburn and Graham at harvest time in the remote quintas of the Upper Douro; Dunbar tempting James IV to court with the rich growths of Angers and Orléans in the Loire; Newton preferring the company of Malmsey and Sercial to English and Portuguese in Madeira; the Scots Italians from Tuscany and the Abruzzi selling their regional wines in city delicatessens; Duff, Gordon and Sandeman nosing salty Manzanillas at Sanlucar on the Guadalquivir; and finally the shippers of Dumbarton and Leith, Dundee and Aberdeen, entering the Gironde and saluting the Guard at Blaye en route to the vineyards of the Sénéchaussée of Bordeaux and her fresche fragrant clairettis. After seven hundred years, the enduring appeal of the Auld Alliance and the wine which was its bloodstream is still given passionate and eloquent testimony today.

> Sandy Irvine Robertson.
> Bordeaux is there and always will be in Scotland, I'm not awfully worried what happens in England and Ireland or Wales. I remember one wonderful Bordelais saying to me, "Sandy, France and Scotland – great amis. The only good thing about England, it is near France and Scotland." I said, "Michel, you are right."

> Esme Johnstone
> Bordeaux is the greatest wine producing area in the world and it always will be. It's on the top of the pyramid and people always knock it, but in a hundred years time, the best wine in the world will always still come from Bordeaux.

Freddie Stimpson
I believe that there is such a volume of fine wine made in Bordeaux – and by that I do not mean the classed growths, I do not even mean the Cru Bourgeois, – I merely mean the rather beautifully made Bordeaux ordinaires which are so even tempered in their normal tasting. It is the most natural wine of them all, the most easily consumed, the most readily assimilated of all the fine red wine. It is perhaps accused of being more intellectual – it is merely more complex because it is a blend of several grapes. Those who drink claret in reasonable quantity with civilised food, to my mind are civilising life.

Moray MacLaren
I know of no wine which is more subtly yet completely satisfying. It does not assault the senses but delicately and insidiously pervades them. It does not befuddle the mind nor weigh the liver down. At the end of a bottle of good claret however one's whole being is suffused with intelligent benevolence. Claret moreover is a great aid to wit. Without the exuberance of Champagne or the boisterousness of Burgundy, it is, I suggest, the happiest of wines.

So whether your taste is for the rich opulence of Pomerol or the classical austerity of St. Estèphe, the magnificence of Mouton and Lafite or the honest simplicity of Bordeaux Supérieur, claret deserves its place on the Scots table on merit and in the Scots heart for its ancient, noble and delightful historic associations. After all, we have been drinking it so long, it is in our blood.

Vive la France! Vive l'Ecosse! Vive la Vieille Alliance!

GLOSSARY

Barrique – a cask containing 225 litres, equivalent to hogshead.

Bordelais – pertaining to Bordeaux; the people of Bordeaux.

Les Caves – the cellars.

Clairette – the word from which "claret" comes, meaning originally a light, pale-coloured red wine.

Cru – a growth.

Cru Classé – a classed growth.

Cuisses – the "legs" of glycerol which form on the inside of wine glasses.

Haut-Pays – the high country. For the bordelais this meant the upper reaches of the Dordogne and Garonne valleys.

Hectare – 2·471 acres.

Hectolitre – 100 litres.

Hock – White wine from the Rhine. Derived from the place-name Hochheim.

La Mise en bouteille – the bottling process.

Mise en Bouteille à – bottled in…

Le Maître de chai – cellar master responsible for making the wine.

Le Négociant – the shipper or dealer.

Nouveau – new. When describing wine it refers to very soon after the vendanges have been completed, often before the New Year. Beaujolais Nouveau is the most celebrated example in modern times.

Sénéchaussée – Seneschalcy. The ancient administrative district which for Bordeaux was roughly coincidental with the modern Gironde département.

Le Sommelier – Symeler (Scots), Wine-butler, Cellarman, wine waiter (English).

Le régisseur – the vineyard and winery manager.

Le Tonneau – a tun. Equivalent to four hogsheads, i.e. 900 litres.

La Vendange – the wine harvest.

Le Vigneron – the wine-grower, or vineyard worker.

Vin – Wyne (Scots), Fion (Gaelic), Wine (English).

Vins de Garde – wines to be laid down.

Vins Noirs – black wines, generally associated with the deep red wines from Cahors.

MEASURES

Mutchkin – a liquid measure equal to two-thirds of an Imperial Pint.

Chopin – une chopine (French), equal to two mutchkins.

Scots Pint – two mutchkins or three Imperial Pints.

Hogshead – *Togsaid* (Gaelic) *Barrique* (French) a cask of 225 litres.

Tun – Tonneau (French) Four hogsheads or 900 litres.

Pipe – the usual container for Port wine.

Butt – the container for Sherry.

INTERNATIONAL GLOSSARY OF LABEL TERMS

GERMANY

Tafelwein – ordinary table wine.

Qualitätswein – superior table wine (subject to certain controls).

Qualitätswein mit Prädikat – strictly controlled wine, bearing one of the grades of extra quality.

Kabinett – the basic grade of above.

Spätlese – wine made from late-gathered and therefore riper grapes. Generally better than Kabinett.

Auslese – Spätlese from which all unripe grapes have been rejected.

Beerenauslese – made from only the ripest individual grapes.

Trockenbeerenauslese – made from grapes which have been shrivelled either from very late gathering or "noble-rot".

Weisswein – white wine.

Rotwein – Red wine.

Sekt – sparkling wine.

Eiswein – wine made of grapes which were frozen during the harvest and pressing. Rare and usually very sweet.

Trocken – dry.

Eigene Abfüllung – bottled by the producer.

Weinkellerei – wine production establishment.

ITALY

Vendemmia – vintage

Denominazione di Origine Controllata e Garantita – Italy's "appellation contrôlée".

Riserva – Better quality wine.

Classico – from the heartland of the wine-growing region.

Imbottigliato nel'origine – Estate bottled.

Fiasco – Flask (typical of the Chianti region, in wicker work).

Vino da Tavola – table wine.

Bianco – White.

Chiaretto – Light red.

Rosso – Red.

Nero – Very dark red.

Rosato – pink.

Secco – dry.

Amaro – bitter or very dry.

Amabile – medium sweet.

Dolce – sweet.

Spumante – sparkling.

Vino liquoroso – very sweet wine.

PORTUGAL

Quinta – estate.

Denominacão de origem – Portugal's "appellation contrôlée".

Colheita – vintage.

Reserva – Quality wine.

Garrafeira – (i.e. private cellar) Top quality.

Vinho de mesa – table wine.

Vinho verde – green or young wine.

Maduro – old or matured.

engarrafado na origem – bottled on the estate.

Branco – white.

Tinto – red.

Rosado – rosé.

Clarete – light coloured.

Doce – sweet.

Seco – dry.

Vinho generoso – fortified wine e.g. Madeira, Carcavelos.

SPAIN

Bodega – maturing warehouse.

Vino de mesa – table wine.

Reserva – the best.

Embotellado de origen – estate bottled.

Denominacíon de origen – Spain's "appellation contrôlée".

Cepa – vine type.

Viña/viñedo – vineyard.

cosecha – vintage (i.e. the year).

Vendimia – vintage (i.e. the harvest).

2 Años – bottled when two years old.

Blanco – white.

Tinto – red.

Seco – dry.

Dulce – sweet.

Espumoso – sparkling.

Fino – good, very dry Sherry.

Oloroso – a full sherry with more aged wine, sweet in the U.K. (All *olorosos* drunk in Jerez are dry).

Manzanilla – a Fino from San Lucar de Barrameda with a taste of the sea.

Amontillado – a dry but full flavoured Sherry.

Solera – a pile of Sherry butts of differing ages from which the shipper creates his blend.

BIBLIOGRAPHY AND FURTHER READING

Barrow, G.W.S., *Robert the Bruce,* Edinburgh University Press, 1976.
Fenwick, Hubert, *The Auld Alliance,* Roundwood Press, 1971.
Michel, Francisque, *Les Ecossais en France, Les Francais en Ecosse.*
MacKenzie, W. Mackay, *The Poems of William Dunbar,* 1932.
Aitken, A.J. ed. *The Dictionary of the Older Scottish Tongue,* Aberdeen University Press.
Accounts of the Lord High Treasurer of Scotland.
Irons, J. Campbell, *Leith and its Antiquities,* Morrison and Gibb, 1897.
Marshall, James S., *Old Leith at Leisure,* Edina Press, 1976.
Russell, John, *The Story of Leith,* London, 1952.
Lythe, S.G.E. and Butt, J., *An Economic History of Scotland,* Blackie, Glasgow, 1975.
Scottish History Society Publications – *The Letter Books of Baillie John Stewart; Wedderburne of Dundee's Compt-book 1587-1630; The Household Book of Lady Grisell Baillie.*
Ramsay, Dean, *Reminiscences of Scottish Life and Character,* Edmonson and Douglas, 1874.
Marshall, Rosalind K., *The Days of Duchess Anne,* Collins, Glasgow, 1973.
Graham, H. Grey, *Scottish Men of Letters of the 18th Century,* London, 1901.
Carlyle, Alexander, *Autobiography,* Edinburgh, 1860.
Cockburn, Lord, *Memorials of His Time,* Scottish Classics No.1, Edinburgh, 1946.
Lochhead, Marion, *The Scots Household in the 18th Century,* Edinburgh, 1948.
Lockhart, J.G., *Peter's Letters to his Kinsfolk,* ed., W. Ruddick, Scottish Academic Press, 1977.
Gray, W. Forbes, *Some Old Scots Judges,* Constable & Co.
Topham, Edward, *Letters from Edinburgh,* James Thin, Edinburgh, 1971.
Bell, Alan, *Scott and His Wine Merchant,* Blackwood's Magazine, August, 1971.
Burt's Letters From the North of Scotland, vols 1 & 2, John Donald, Edinburgh, 1974.
McNeill, F. Marian, *The Scots Cellar,* Paterson, Edinburgh, 1956.
McNeill, F. Marian, *The Scots Kitchen,* Mayflower, St. Albans, 1974.
Stuart, M.M.W., *Old Edinburgh Taverns,* London, 1952.
Boswell, James and Johnson, Samuel, *A Tour of the Hebrides,* London, 1795.
The Culloden Papers.
Maclean, Alasdair, *A Macdonald for the Prince,* Acair, Stornoway, 1981.
Strang, Dr. J., *Glasgow and its Clubs,* Glasgow, 1864.
Robertson, Joseph, *The Book of Bon-Accord,* Aberdeen, 1839.
MacLeod, Canon R.C., *The Book of Dunvegan,* Spalding Club, Aberdeen, 1938.
Nicolson, Alexander, *The History of Skye,* Maclean Press, 1994.
Burton, John Hill, *The Lives of Simon Lord Lovat and Duncan Forbes of Culloden,* London, 1847.
Martin, Martin, *A Description of the Western Isles of Scotland,* Stirling, 1934.
Journal of the Episcopal Visitations of Reverend Forbes.
Various works by Messrs. Roudié, Pijassou, Enjalbert, Institut de Géographie, Université de Bordeaux III, Bordeaux.
Johnson, Hugh, *The World Atlas of Wine,* Mitchell Beazley, London, 1971.
Francis, A.D., *The Wine Trade,* Adam and Charles Black, Newton Abbot, 1972.
Penning-Rowsell, Edmund, *The Wines of Bordeaux,* Penguin, 1979.
Saintsbury, George, *Notes on a Cellar Book,* London, 1963.
Cooke, Rupert Croft, *Madeira,* London, 1961.
Kay, Billy, ed., *Odyssey – The Second Collection,* Polygon, Edinburgh, 1982.

ACKNOWLEDGEMENTS

We should like to acknowledge the help given to us in the completion of the first and second editions of this book. Their assistance contributed greatly to the success of the books. Others have helped in the preparation of this, the third edition of Knee Deep in Claret:-

Freddie Stimpson; Sandy Irvine Robertson; Esme Johnstone; Ian G. Cumming; Jeffrey Kelly; Andrew Leslie; João Kay; Shona Maclean; Alasdair Maclean; the late Pascal Vialard; Paul D. Symington, Miguel Carr Potes, Edite Cunha, Symington Port and Madeira Shippers.

Dave Herbert and Oliver Perritt of the Duncan of Jordanstone College of Art, Dundee; Roy Adlard of Adlard Print; Jean-Claude Richard, Consul General of France, Edinburgh.

Michael Shaw, co-producer of Fresche Fragrant Clairettis, winner of the Wine Guild of the United Kingdom's 1994 Houghton Award.

INDEX